Drawing Mentor

Volume 1

Drawing Materials

Volume 2

Lines and Shapes

Volume 3

Perspective and 3-D Shapes

And

A Brief History of the Pencil and the People Who Shaped it

By Sarah Bowles

ISBN-13: 978-1475106381

ISBN-10: 1475106386

Preface

The *Drawing Mentor* series of books is intended to help beginning to intermediate drawers learn and improve their drawing skills. Each book is written as a stand-alone lesson which can be used on its own, this gives the reader the ability to pick and choose the lessons and skills they would like to learn to the exclusion of all else.

The earlier lessons in the series are very foundational, designed to improve the reader's technical ability and understanding before going on to later lessons which are more project-based and written assuming technical skills have already been developed. If you're an absolute beginner it's recommended that you proceed from Volume 1 as that will ensure your understanding of how to use the techniques employed in later lessons as occasionally these lessons will refer to principles and skills taught in previous volumes.

This book includes Volumes 1, 2 and 3 which are beginning and intermediate lessons which teach the most basic drawing fundamentals from the ground up. If you're new to drawing or want to improve your basic skills this is the book for you. Volume 1 is an introduction to basic drawing materials and explains some of the pros and cons of each. Volume 2 covers lines and shapes and how to apply them to create very basic drawings. Volume 3 is an in-depth lesson covering perspective, tone shading and highlights to create objects that look three dimensional. Each concept is explained thoroughly and examples given, opportunities to practice are also included to help you master the skill taught in each section. These lessons should be completed before moving on to the more advanced lessons in later volumes.

The intent of the *Drawing Mentor* series is to periodically add new lessons over time to help you continue to improve your skills. If there is a particular skill or lesson you would like covered please feel free to send an email to drawingmentor@gmail.com. Your feedback suggestions and reviews are very much appreciated and will be used to help create lessons that will benefit you the most.

Thanks for choosing *Drawing Mentor*. Here's to your success.

Sincerely,

Sarah Bowles

Help support someone in need.
10% of all profits are donated to organizations
giving humanitarian assistance.

Contents

Materials   1

Pencils   1
Paper   4
Erasers   9
Sharpeners   13
Other   17

Basic Pencil Marks   19

Pencil Grips   20
Pencil Pressure   22
Drawing Lines   24
Curved Lines   26
Drawing Shapes   28
Using Shapes to Draw Objects   33
Conclusion   38

Perspective, 3-D Shapes and Shading   39

Perspective   39
     One Point Perspective   39
     Two Point Perspective   53
     Three Point Perspective   66
     Zero Point   79
Tone & Shading   80
     Adding Tone   81
     Smudging   81
     Hatching   82
     Adding Shadow   84
     Constructing a Shadow   87

Penumbra 97

Highlighting 99

Conclusion 101

A Brief History of the Pencil and the People Who Shaped it 103

Just the Facts 109

Materials

There are only two things you need in order to draw; something to draw with, and something to draw on. Sounds pretty simple when it's put that way but there are thousands of different combinations of pencils and paper. Each combination produces a different look. Some combinations will work better than others to give you the result you want. What you decide to draw, and your location, can be big factors in determining the materials you use.

All the examples and practice exercises in this series of lessons were done using a No. 2 pencil and regular white 8 ½" X 11" paper. These items are relatively inexpensive and most people already have them. It's definitely good to experiment with different materials, it will help you learn faster, you're more than welcome to use whatever you want for each practice exercise, but if a No. 2 pencil and plain white paper is all you have that will be good enough to follow any of the examples in these books.

This lesson gives a quick overview of some of the most common materials used in drawing, highlighting their strengths and weaknesses.

There are also many items which aren't necessary for drawing but can be useful to have. This lesson will also discuss some of the extra items you may want to eventually get if you don't already have them.

Pencils

There are many types of pencils; big, small, rectangular, round, mechanical, wood, plastic, the list could go on. Only the most common drawing pencils are discussed below.

1H - 9H

Hard pencils, the "H" stands for hard. 1H is two grades harder than a No. 2, or HB pencil, 9H is the hardest. Remember, the higher the number the harder the pencil (The pencil one grade harder than No. 2 is the F pencil, "F" stands for fine point).

Pros:

Keeps a point or an edge for a long time without needing to re-sharpen

Draws clean lines that don't smudge easily

Good for quick sketches in sketchbooks and drawing fine details

Cons:

Writing core can damage the paper surface

Difficult to make dark lines and shadows

Difficult to fully develop a drawing

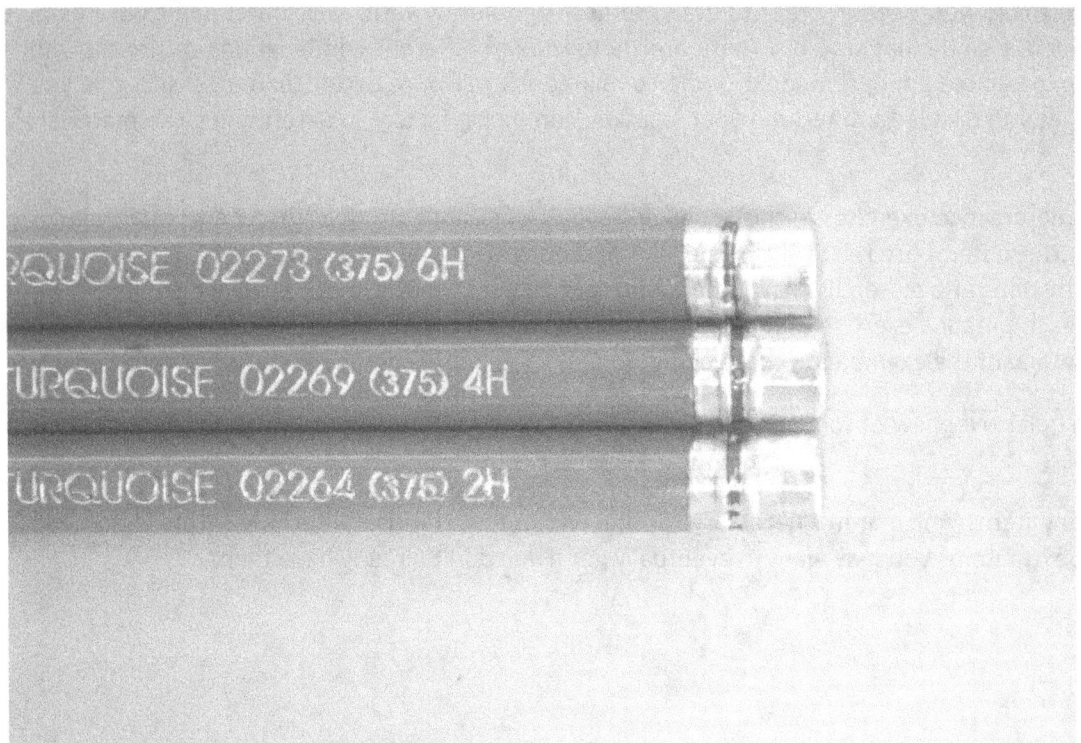

Figure 1-1. Common H pencils

1B - 9B

Soft pencils, the "B" stands for blackness. 1B is one grade softer than the No. 2, or HB pencil. 9B is the softest; the higher the number the softer the pencil. 7B – 9B do not come in the same form as a regular pencil. Because they're so soft, they usually come as a very thick graphite core without a wood casing.

Pros:

Versatile, can develop light lines and shades as well as dark lines and shades

Can make a fully developed drawing with a single pencil

Good for exploring dark shades and sketches with a lot of contrast

Cons:

Lead is soft and smudges easily

May have to sharpen often

Creating light lines can be challenging

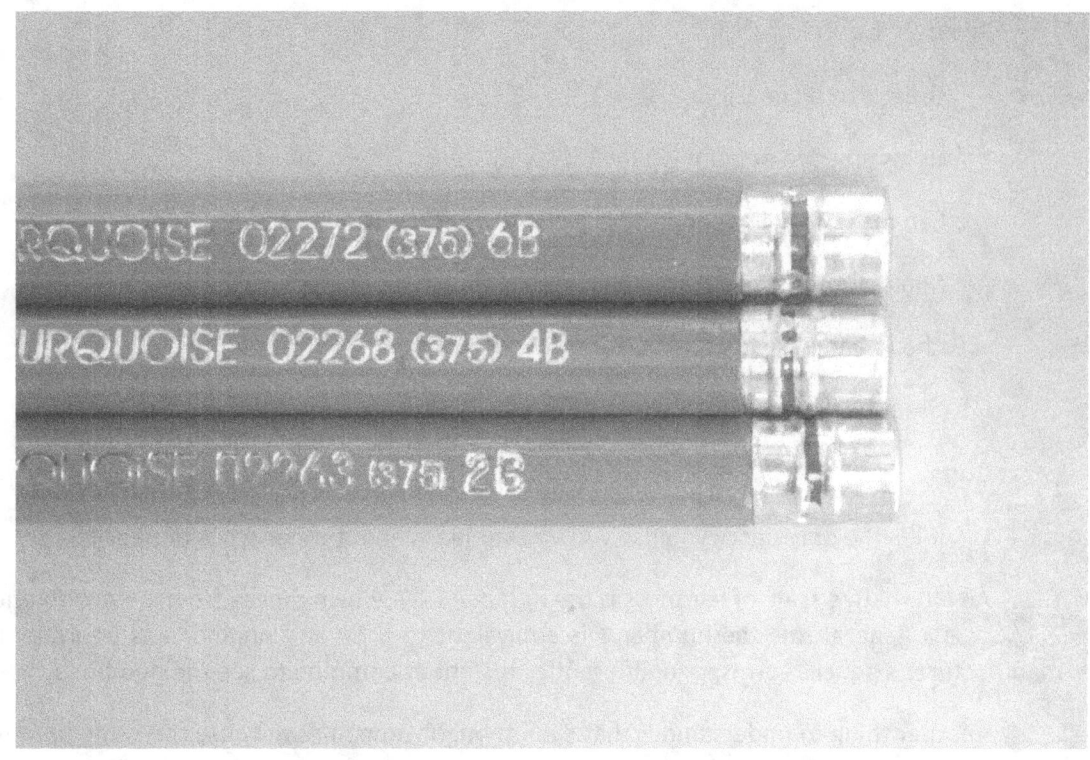

Figure 1-2. Common B pencils

No. 2 or HB Pencil

The No. 2 or HB pencil is right in the middle of the B to H hardness range. The reason so many of these pencils are made is because they're very versatile.

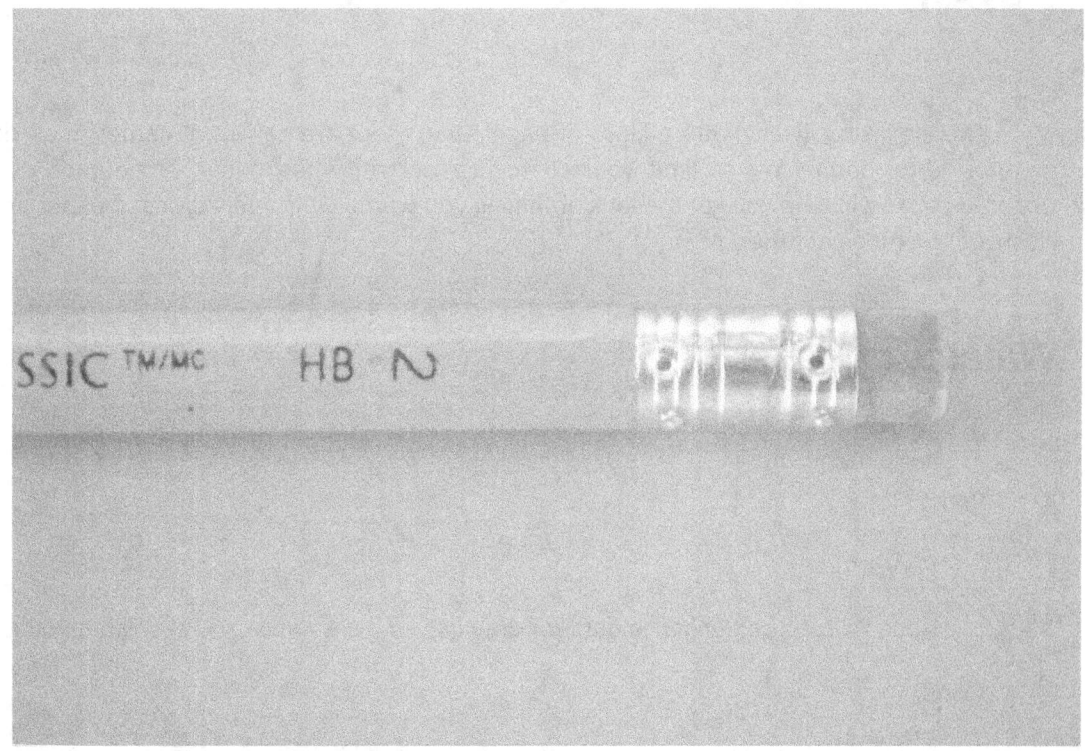

Figure 1-3. No. 2 or HB Pencil

Pros:

Great overall pencil

Holds an edge or point well

Can make dark lines and shades as well as light lines and shades

Minimal smudging

Cheap and easy to get

Great beginner pencil

Cons:

If it's the only pencil you use you'll never learn about other types of pencils

An alternative scale of hardness is the number scale which ranges from 1 – 4 with one of the pencils being a 2 1/2. As a general rule the number 1 is equivalent to a 1B and number 4 is equivalent to 2H however some manufacturer's pencils correspond differently. It's not as common to see the number system in the artist's world.

Another thing to understand is that even though companies may use the same number system, their pencils aren't necessarily the same; a 3B pencil from one company may be as soft as a 5B pencil from another company. It's a good idea to get a set of pencils from the same company so you can be consistent.

Paper

There's probably even more kinds of paper than there are pencils; it comes in all shapes, sizes, colors and textures. You don't have to limit yourself to just normal white paper, sometimes using a colored paper or textured paper will help you get the look or feeling you want. Only a few types of paper are listed below simply to illustrate the range of differences.

Watercolor Paper

Very thick and strong, it's made to be able to get wet and not rip or become weak.

Pros:

Very strong

Good texture, can enhance outdoor drawings of trees, fields and even some buildings

Cons:

Paper surface and texture can be damaged by hard pencils

Not good for small details

Erasing marks is difficult and can damage the surface

Figure 1-4. Watercolor paper

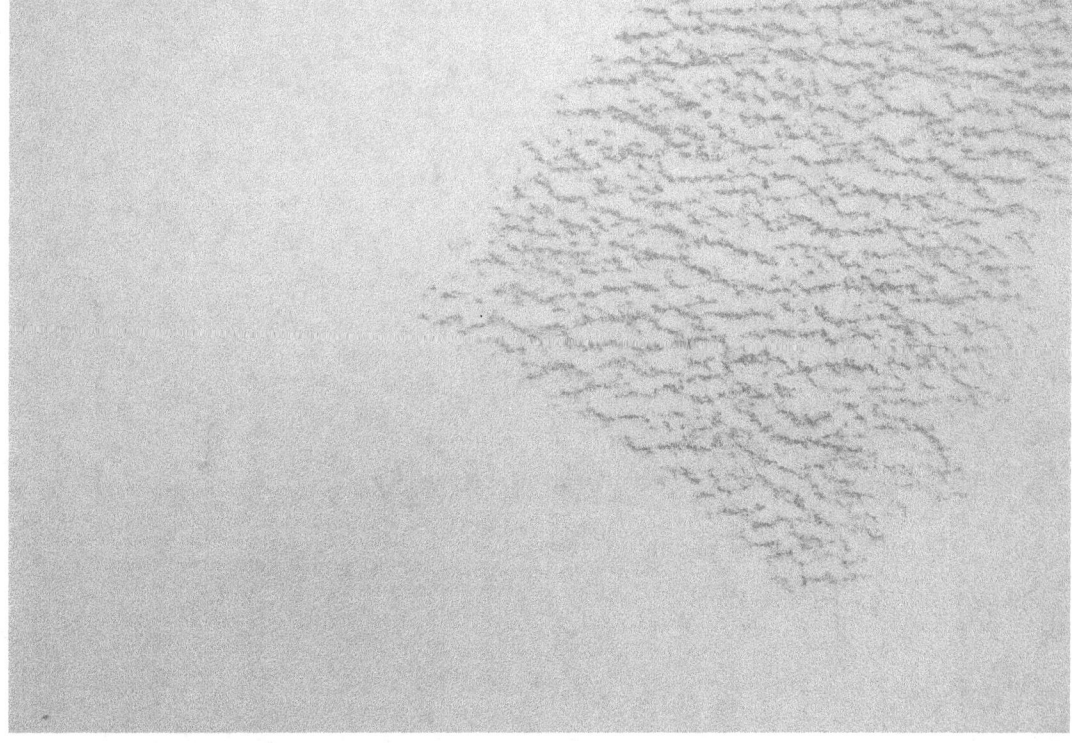

Figure 1-5. Watercolor paper close-up

Tracing Paper

Very thin paper, the surface underneath the paper will be visible.

Pros:

Can be used to trace and practice pencil motion

Can give your drawing an old faded or light feel

Very smooth, it can be used to capture small details if you're careful

Cons:

Tears easily

So thin that texture of the surface underneath will affect the drawing

Smudges are easily seen and the paper will look dirty

Difficult to erase marks without wrinkling or tearing paper

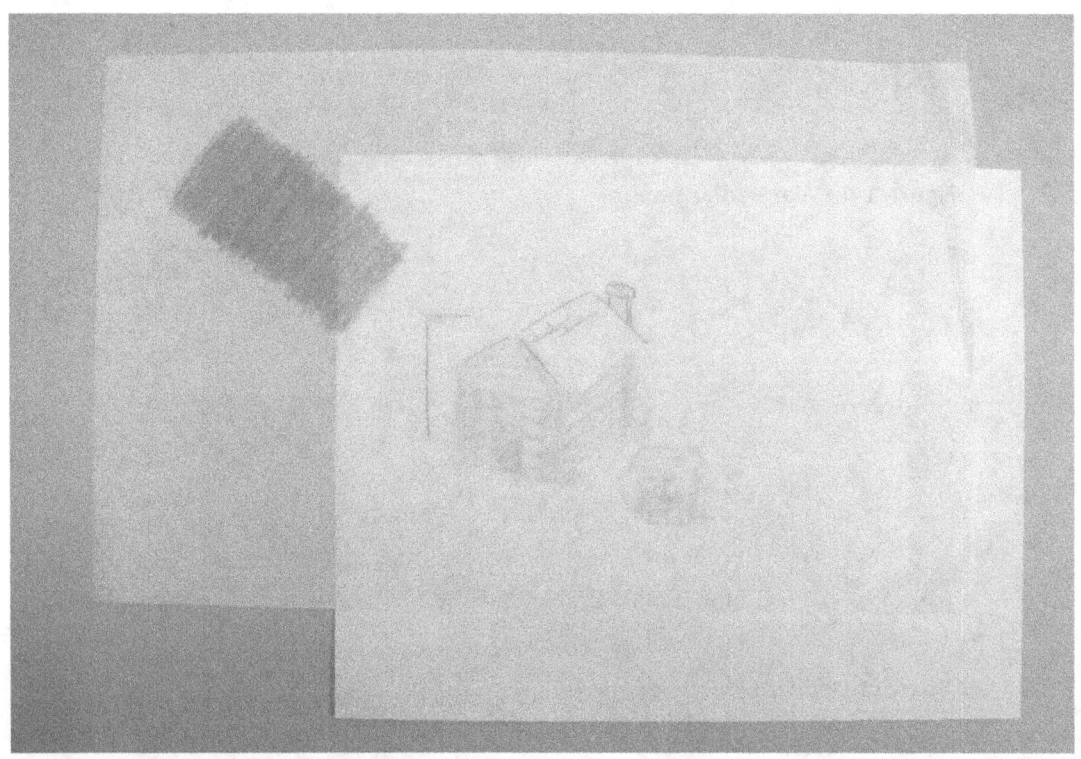

Figure 1-6. Tracing paper

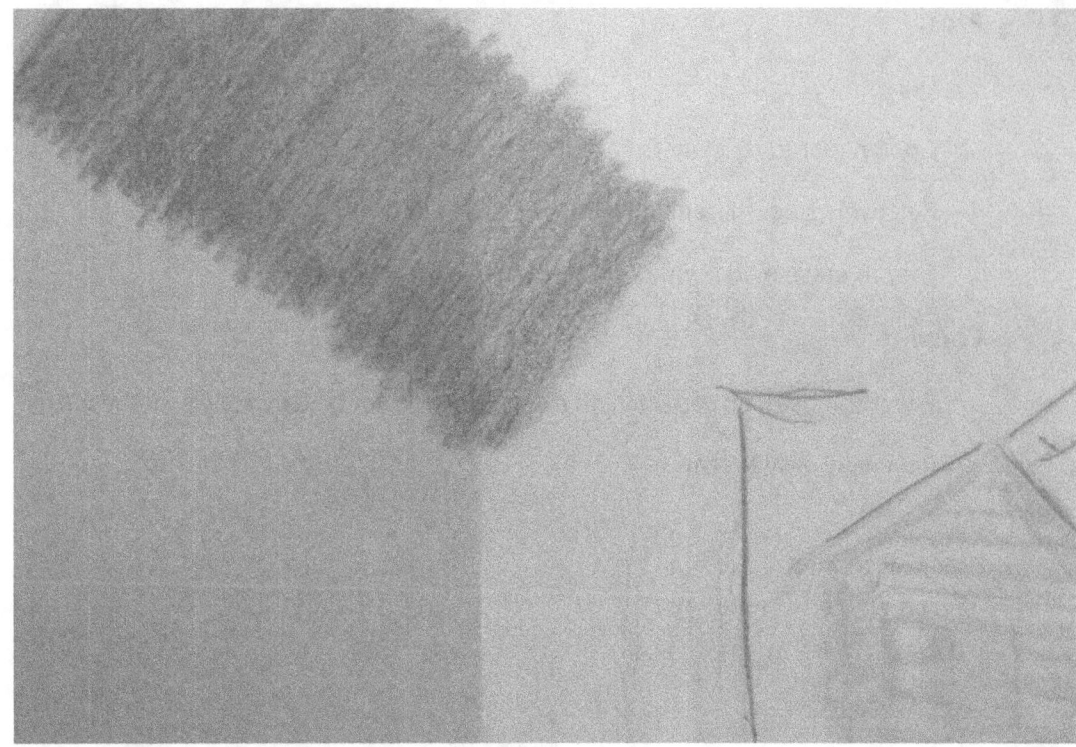

Figure 1-7. Tracing paper close-up

White Lineless Printer Paper

Yes the paper that comes in packages of 500 sheets that you put in your printer.

Figure 1-8. White printer paper

Pros:

Durable yet light

Good paper for beginners because it's inexpensive

Relatively smooth, can make bright clean lines

Easy to erase marks without too much impact to the paper

Cons:

Paper is loose, can easily fall off drawing surface or be blown away in the wind

Relatively easy to tear

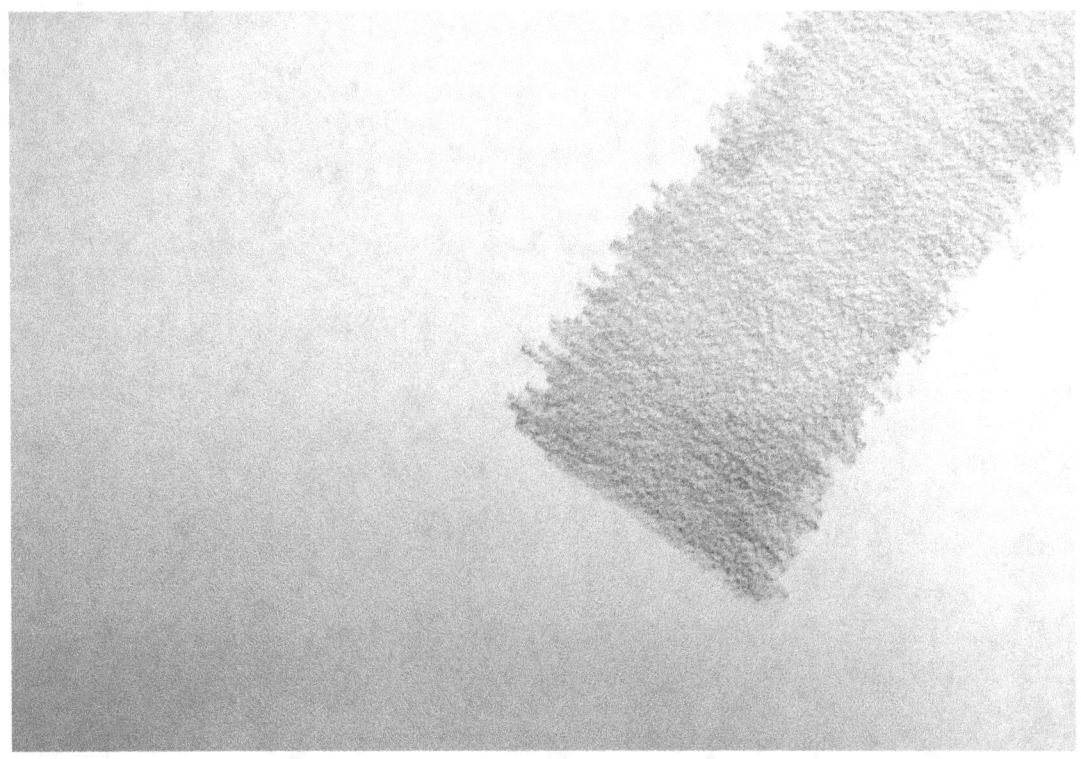

Figure 1-9. White printer paper close-up

Sketchbooks

Sketchbooks have many of the same pros the white lineless printer paper does but they don't have the same cons.

Sketchbook paper is usually thicker than normal printer paper and some can even get wet without being damaged. The only real cons to sketchbooks are that they can be relatively expensive and the bindings can get in the way of your hand when drawing.

Initially it can be difficult drawing in a sketchbook you're holding in your hand or on your lap but the more you do it the easier it gets. If you're going to use a sketchbook I recommend placing it on a table at first, as time goes on it'll become easier to use a sketchbook without a table. An added pro to sketchbooks is that you'll have a record of your skill development over time.

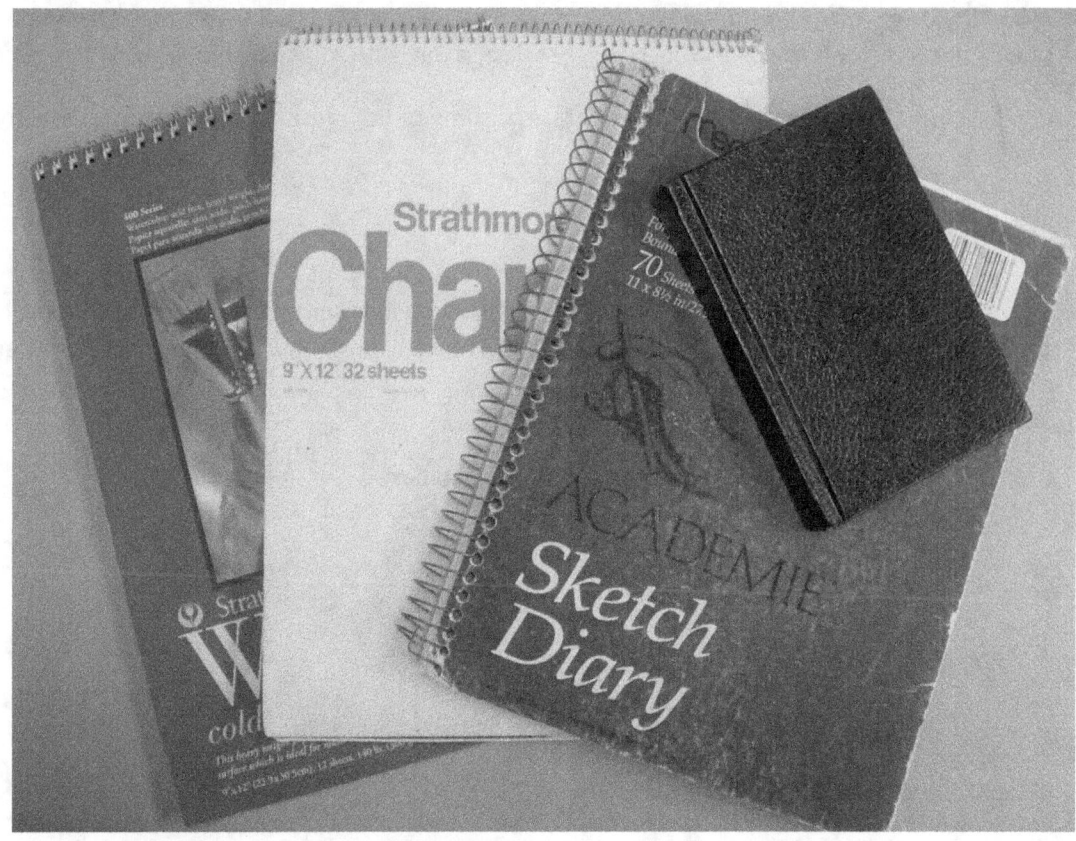

Figure 1-10. Various sketchbooks

Other Paper

There's a wide range of papers that haven't been mentioned. As you become more skilled you may want to experiment with some of these other papers.

Papers you may want to consider experimenting with include newsprint, construction paper, charcoal paper, and wallpaper. These papers will actually change what your drawing looks like; it will give them a quality you won't be able to achieve using plain white paper. You may like the look, you may not, you must experiment to find what you like best.

Erasers

Erasers can be a valuable tool. They can be used to enhance a drawing but be careful not to rely on them. Erasing a mark changes the surface of the paper which may have a negative effect on the drawing.

Another thing to be careful of is wiping away the eraser residue, it's easy to smudge the drawing in the process. Blowing residue off can be damaging as well because no matter how careful you are you will sometimes blow tiny drops of spit onto the paper. These drops will leave small water marks behind. A soft bristled brush is one of the best tools to use to wipe eraser residue away with minimal smudging.

There are a few different types of erasers; some of the most common are discussed below.

Kneaded Eraser

Soft and malleable, they lift the graphite off the paper without the need of rubbing hard. They can be used for a long time by pulling and folding it over and over to expose new eraser surface. They are typically gray.

Pros:

Absorb pencil marks without rubbing the paper

Long life

No residue on the paper

Cons:

Difficult to create a precise point or erase a small specific detail

Difficult to fully erase very dark marks

Figure 1-11. Kneaded eraser

Rubber Eraser

These are the typical pink erasers on the end of a No. 2 pencil. They're typically bendy and can come in many colors. The colors usually represent different grades of roughness although some of the colors are just for fun. They're made from vulcanized rubber mixed with pumice to increase the roughness.

Pros:

Can create a sharp edge to erase specific lines and areas

Can erase very dark marks

Can be used to erase more than just pencil marks but we don't really care about that now do we

Cons:

Wear down over time

Leaves residue on the paper that must be wiped off

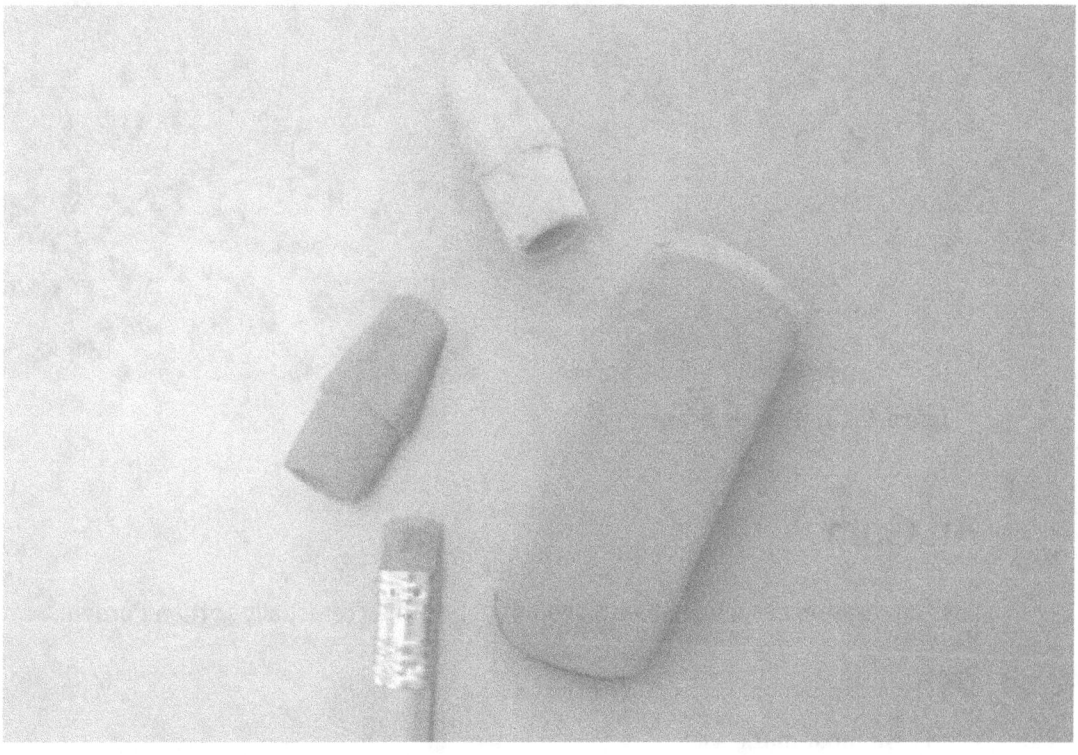

Figure 1-12. Rubber erasers

Plastic Eraser

These are synthetic erasers and are rather bendy. A good example of one is the white Mars Eraser. They are typically made of vinyl which is a durable flexible plastic.

Pros:

Can erase dark marks well

Can create a sharp edge to erase specific lines and areas

Can be used to erase more than just pencil marks

Cons:

Can damage the paper surface

Wear down quickly and leaves residue on the paper which must be wiped off

Figure 1-13. Plastic eraser

Art Gum

Art gum erasers are made of soft, coarse rubber; they're usually soft and brown.

Pros:

Erase most marks well

Soft, so lower chance of damaging the paper surface

Cons:

Wear down very quickly

Leaves a lot of residue on the paper

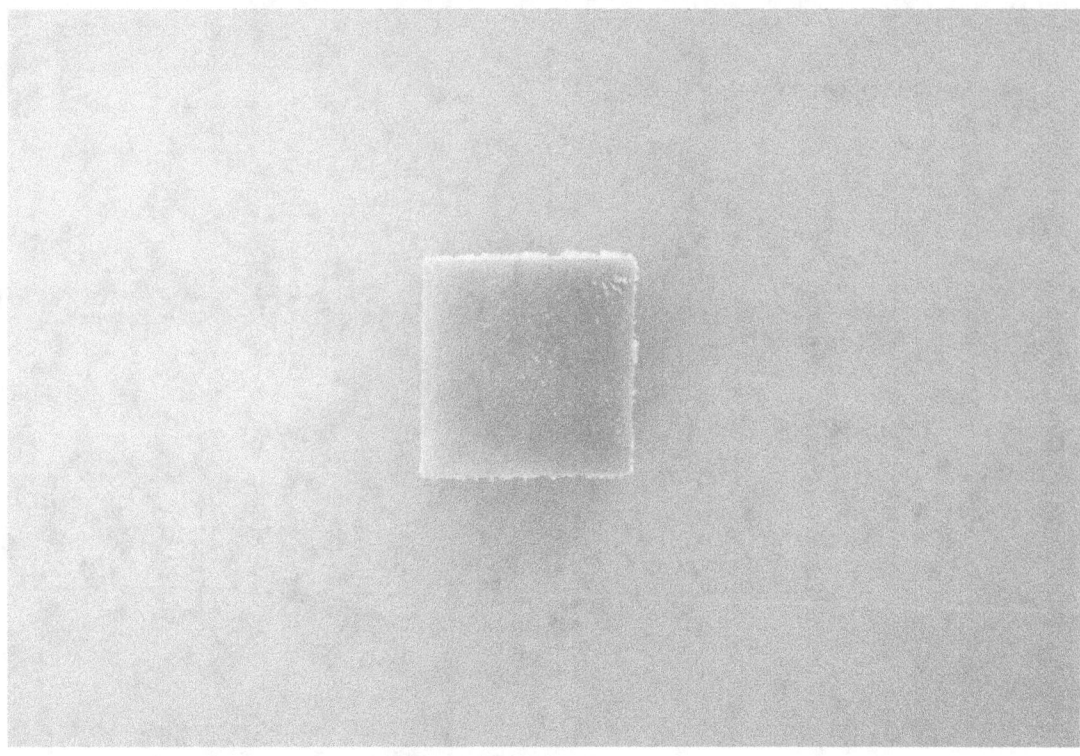

Figure 1-14. Art gum eraser

Sharpeners

If you've ever owned a pencil you've probably had to sharpen it. There are a few ways to sharpen a pencil and it's a matter of preference.

Electric Pencil Sharpeners / Crank Pencil Sharpeners

Electric pencil sharpeners use electricity to spin a spool of small blades around a shaft to sharpen pencils. Crank pencil sharpeners are basically the same except you spin the spool of blades by turning a crank. If you don't own an electric or crank pencil sharpener that's fine, there's really no advantage to using one. If you have one, go ahead and use it but it won't enhance your drawing ability.

Pros:

Creates a very sharp point

Quick and consistent

Cons:

Expensive

Non portable

Loud

Can only make a round point

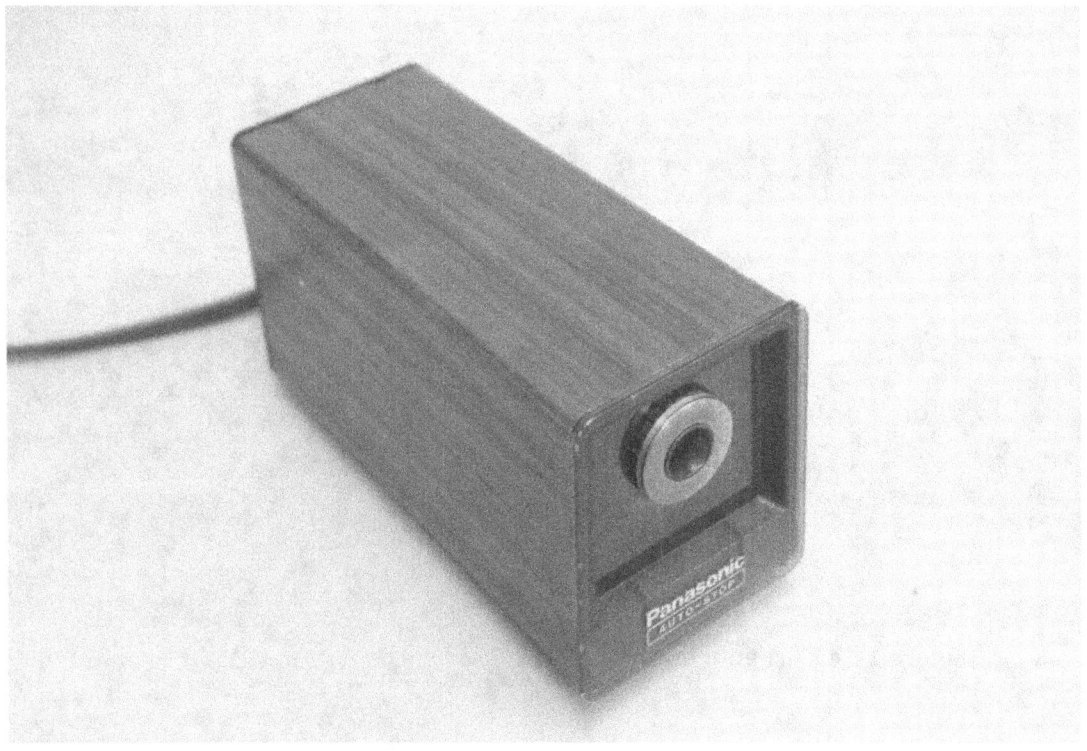

Figure 1-15. Electric pencil sharpener

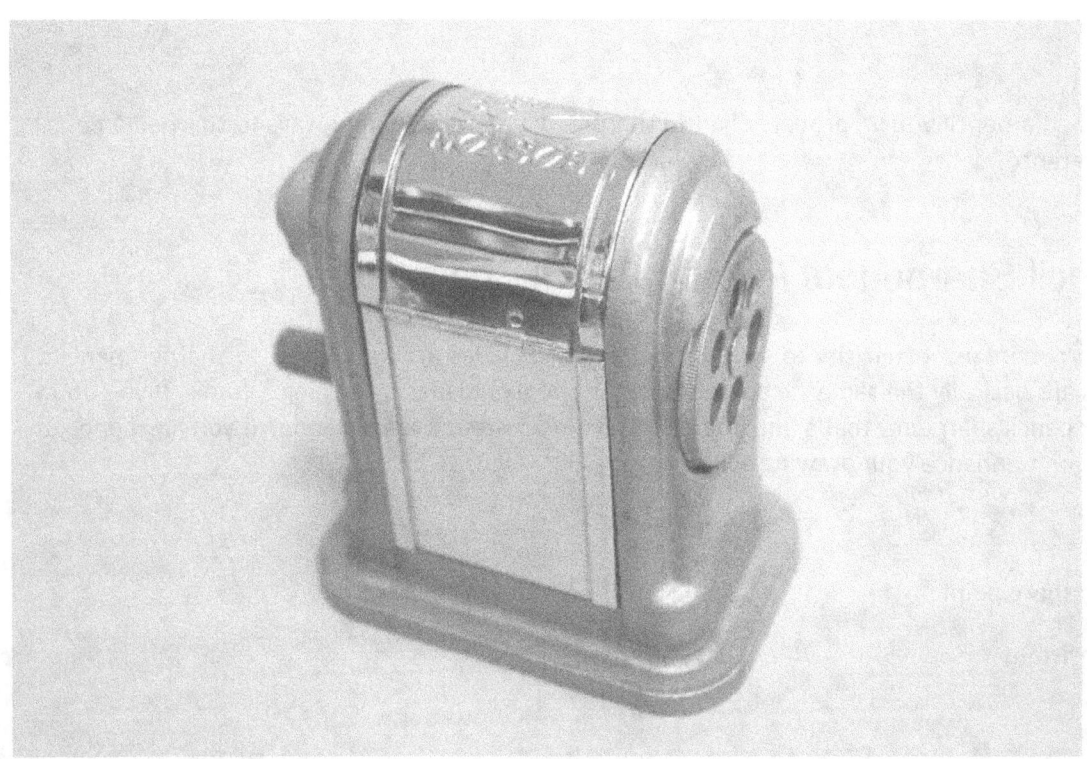

Figure 1-16. Hand crank pencil sharpener

Hand Held Pencil Sharpener

A hand held pencil sharpener is a great alternative as a beginner and even as an advanced artist. They have many advantages over other types of sharpeners.

Pros:

Light, small, and portable

Inexpensive

Makes a good point

Many many many styles to choose from

Cons:

Can only make a point

Can be messy

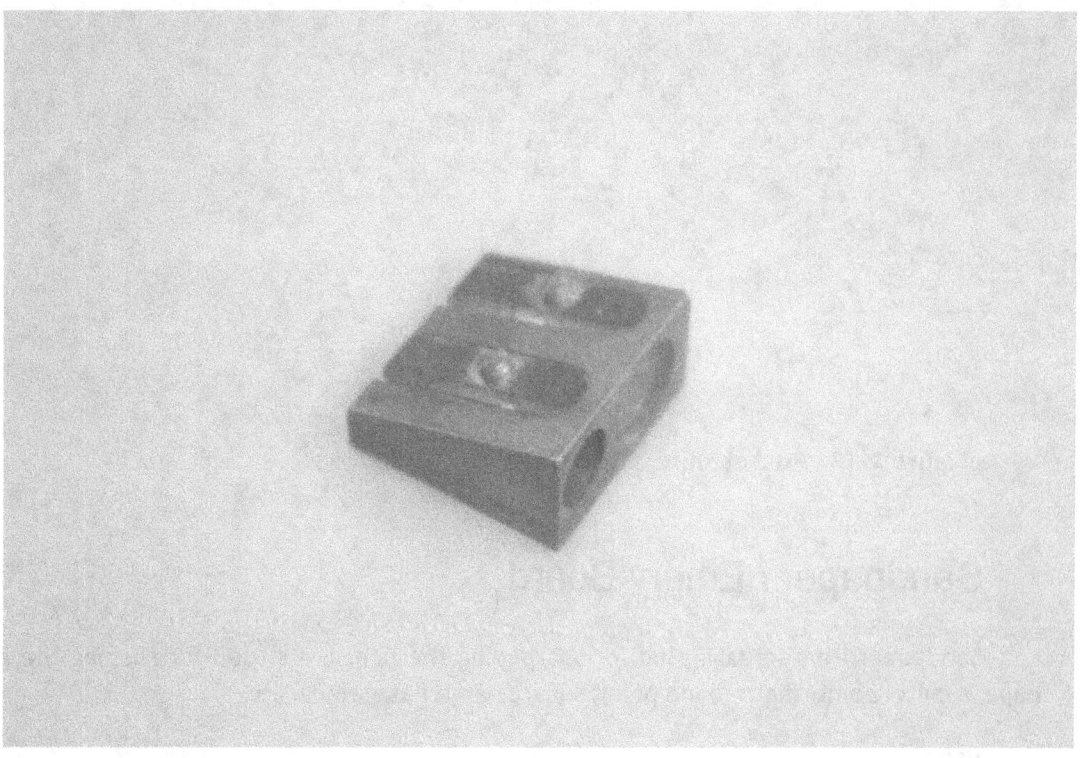

Figure 1-17. Hand held pencil sharpener

Pocket Knife

A knife is a very versatile sharpener but if you're not use to using a knife it can be difficult at first, it takes practice to get good at using it. Don't use a knife unless you already know how to use one or someone is there to help teach you, it can be dangerous.

Pros:

Can form the pencil lead into many shapes and lengths

Cons:

Difficult to use

Dangerous, you could possibly injure yourself

Messy

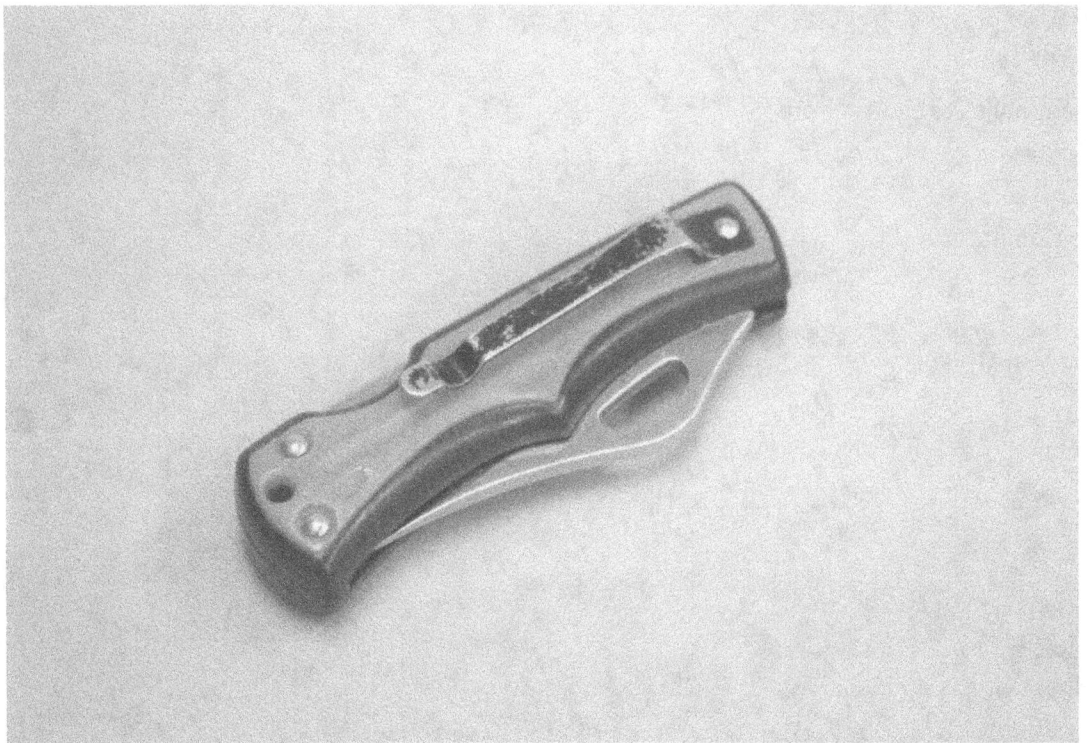

Figure 1-18. Pocket knife

Sandpaper / Emery Board

Sandpaper isn't actually used for sharpening the pencil, it's used for shaping the pencil core to a desired shape, a chisel point, sharp round point, square, large flat surface, etc.

Pros:

Inexpensive

Adds versatility to the pencil and other sharpening methods

Cons:

Creates a lot of graphite powder which is messy

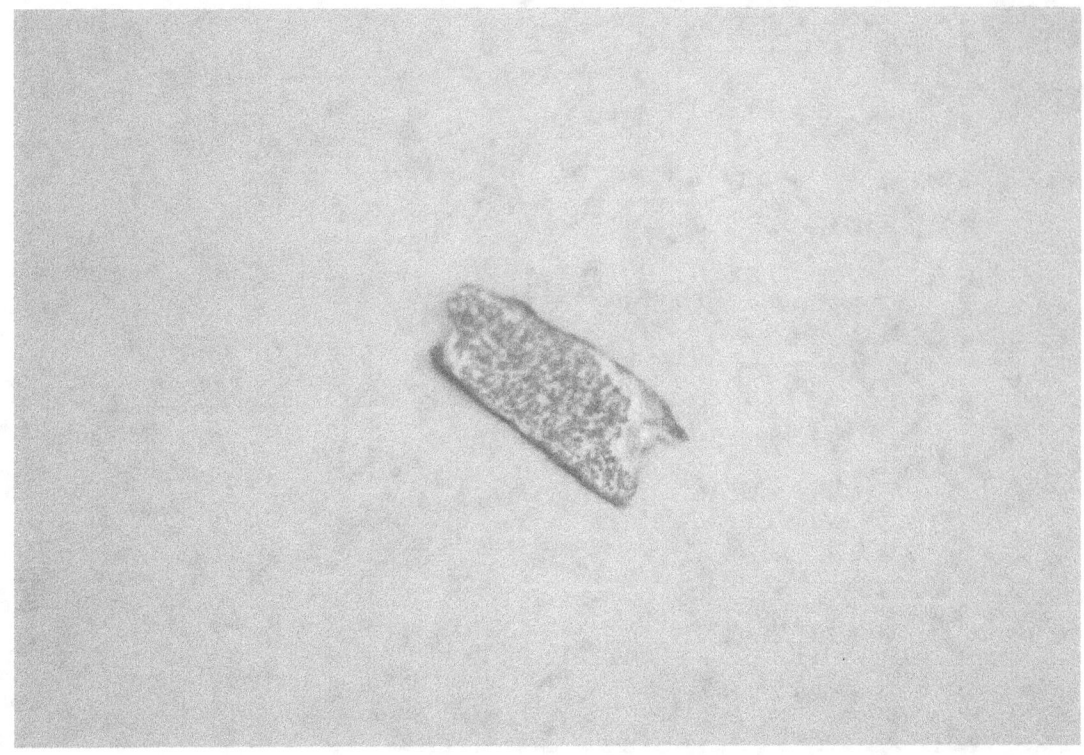

Figure 1-19. Sandpaper

Other

Everyone eventually collects other things to assist them in drawing. Some of the things that I have and use from time to time include a camel's hair drafting brush, a straightedge ruler, a small tackle box type carrying case and masking tape.

You'll find as you draw more that you will collect odds and ends that aren't essential but helpful to you; that is part of creating your own style.

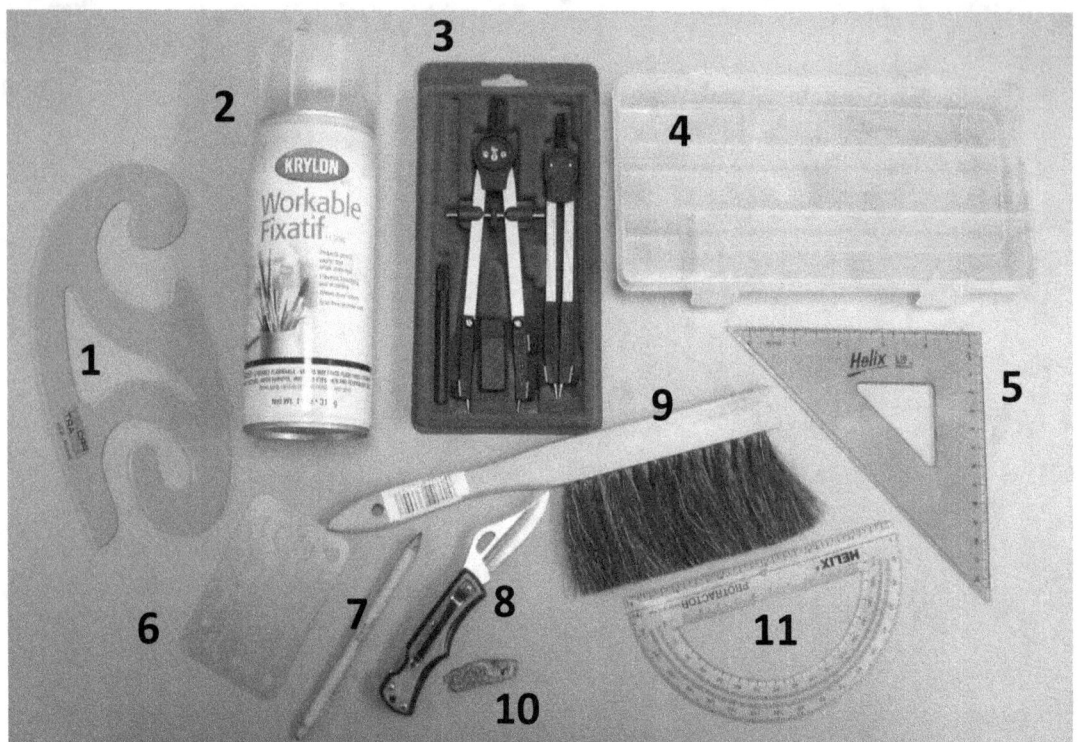

Figure 1-20. Various items used for drawing: 1. French curve, 2. Fixative, 3. Compass set, 4. Pencil box, 5. 90° Triangle, 6. Eraser shield, 7. Tortillon, 8. Pocket knife, 9. Soft brush, 10. Sandpaper, 11. Protractor

Basic pencil marks

Welcome to Volume 2 where we will discuss the most basic pencil marks.

There are three basic types of pencil marks, they are: dots, lines, and tone. This lesson will discuss dots and lines, how to make them, and how to use them (for a comprehensive lesson on tone see Volume 3). As dots are fairly simple they will just be discussed briefly, most of this lesson will focus on the skill of drawing lines.

Dots

A dot is made by touching a pencil to paper, then lifting the pencil without moving it across the paper. You can make dots darker and larger by rotating the pencil while it's touching the paper. Dots are mainly used for detail or texture. It's possible to make a drawing using only dots but it takes a lot of patience. The technique of using dots to create a picture is called pointillism.

To draw a picture using pointillism you simply place dots closer together for dark shaded areas, and farther apart for light areas, no lines are ever drawn. When seen from a distance the dots blend together and a picture is seen. It takes patience and persistence to do a pointillism drawing and few people really do a lot of it. And while there are no examples of pointillism in this lesson it is something you should try at least once just for the experience.

Lines

Lines come in all shapes, sizes and thicknesses but really there are only two types of lines; straight lines and curved lines. Any drawing can be done with straight lines, curved lines or a combination of both. The majority of this lesson focuses on learning to draw good lines, but before we begin let's discuss pencil grip and pencil pressure.

Pencil grip refers to the way you hold the pencil in your hand. How you hold the pencil will affect how you draw lines and what kind of lines are comfortable to draw. Pencil pressure is how hard you press the pencil down against the paper; it affects how dark the line is.

Pencil Grips

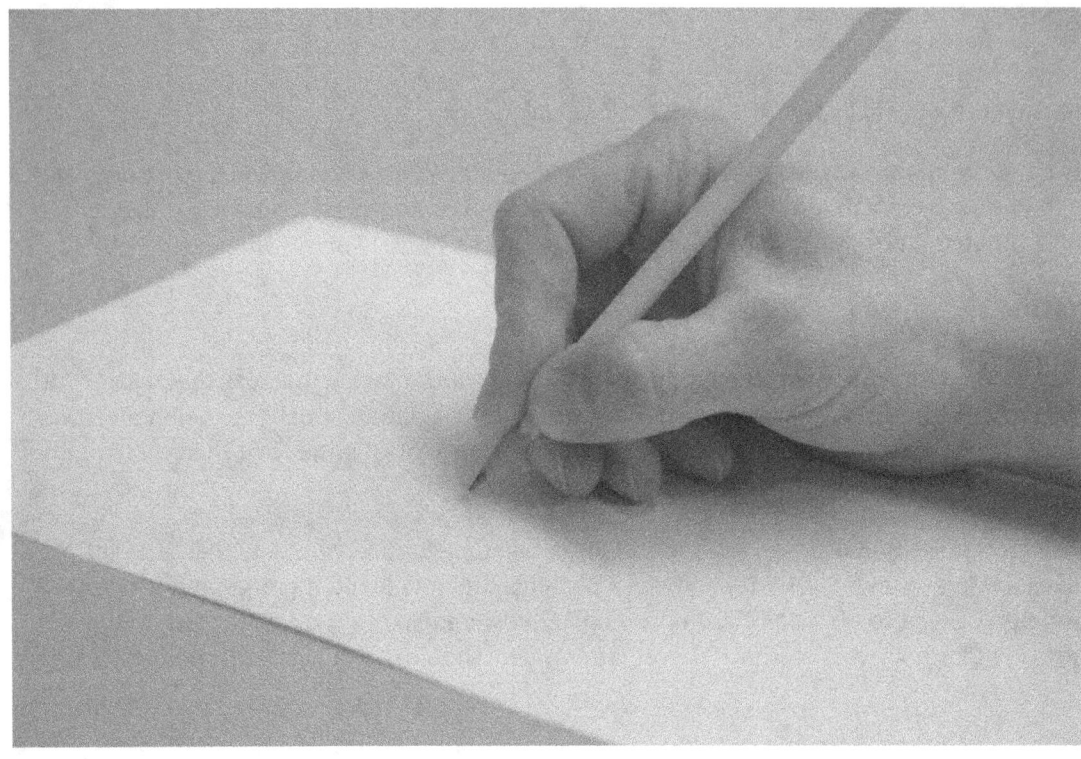

Figure 2-1. Tight grip

Three general pencil grips are commonly used.

Tight

The tight grip is very familiar and comfortable for most people because it's the grip typically used for writing. Most of the movement comes from the fingers and wrist. This grip will give you the most accuracy and control. This is a good grip to use when adding fine detail, for making very dark marks, or when you're drawing something small. The range of movement is not great so lines will be shorter and drawing speed a little slower compared to the other grips.

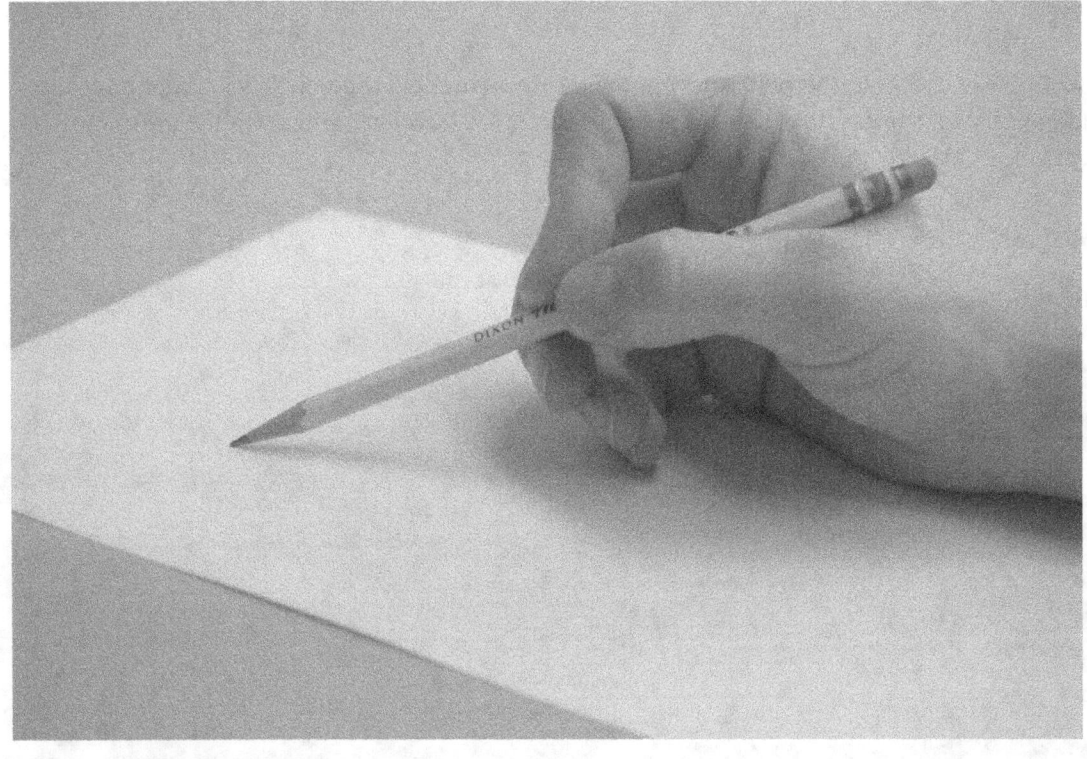

Figure 2-2. Loose grip

Loose

The loose grip is versatile. It's similar to the tight grip except you hold the pencil so that the tip extends a few inches past your fingers.

In this position your fingers and wrist can make large sweeping motions across the paper. You'll still be able to draw details in this position but not quite as accurately as when using the tight grip.

Drawing with a pencil held this way feels much more fluid than a pencil held with the tight grip and you may find that you start to move your whole arm as you draw. For example, resting your elbow on the table and rotating around it you can make large sweeping movements, or, taking your elbow off the table it's easy to use your whole arm from the shoulder through the elbow and wrist to make very large motions in any direction. This grip is a good starting point if you're sketching, drawing fast, or drawing across a large surface.

Overhand

The overhand grip is mainly used for large motions or very quick inaccurate work and general shading. It feels natural to hold the pencil this way when you're working with a large piece of paper, making long lines from your shoulder or shading a large area. Drawing fine detail with this grip is more difficult because you don't have the fine muscle coordination of your fingers to help move the pencil.

You'll rarely use the loose grip or overhand grip while drawing on 8 ½" x 11" paper, there just isn't that much room. A tight grip or a grip in between tight and loose will usually work very well for paper that size. The other grips are better suited for larger areas.

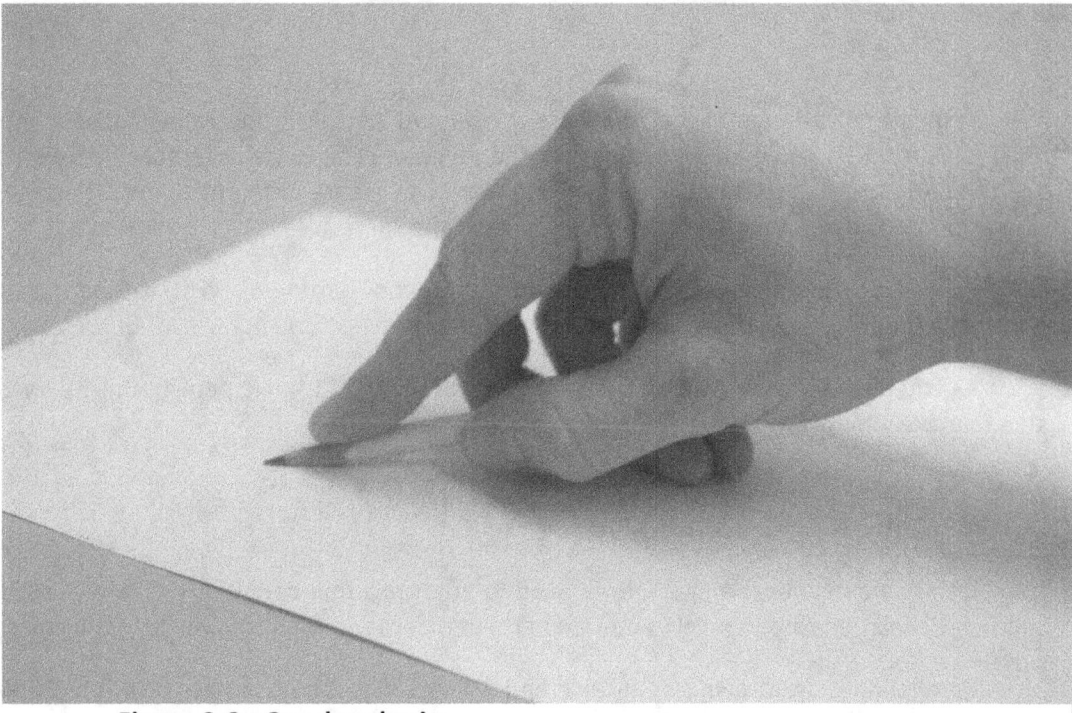

Figure 2-3. Overhand grip

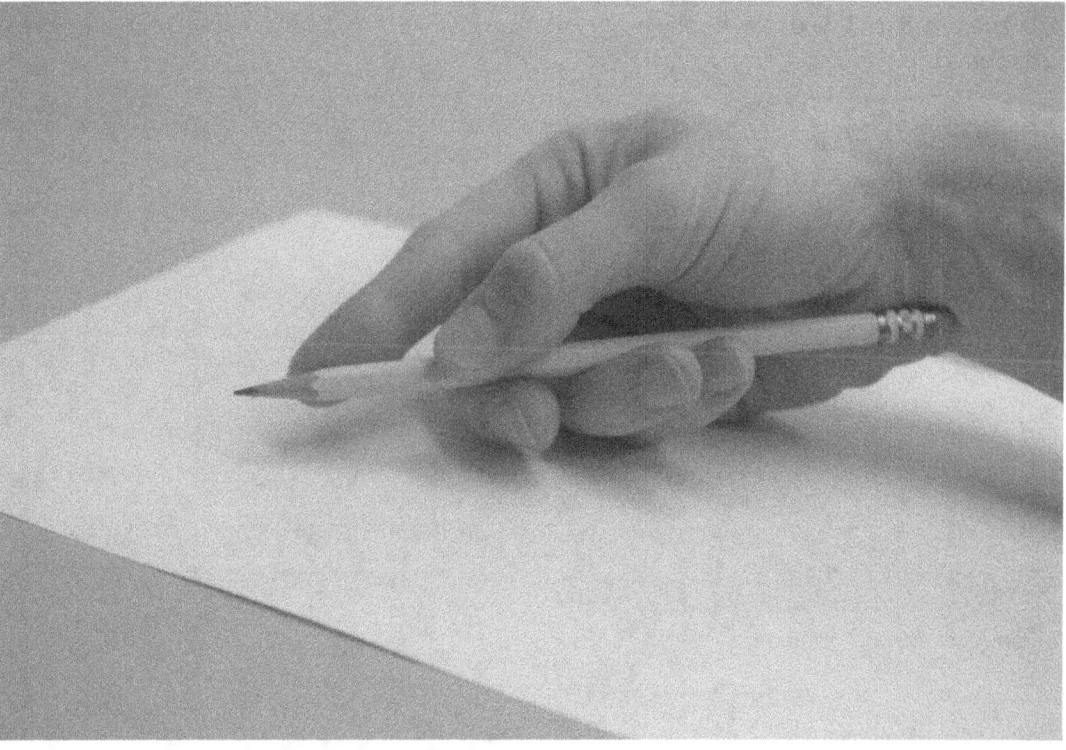

Figure 2-4. Overhand grip from below

Pencil Pressure

You can get a larger range of **tone** out of a soft pencil. Tone refers to how light or dark a mark is. It represents a color by using a shade of gray. The range of tone is the difference between a drawing's lightest area and the darkest area. Using only one pencil, the way to create different tones is to change the pressure you put on the pencil or the amount of times you draw over the same area.

As was mentioned in Volume 1 there are many pencil hardness'. With soft pencils, making thick dark lines is easy while harder pencils make lighter thinner lines even when you apply a lot of pressure.

As you learn to control pencil pressure you will see that a single pencil can be very versatile, you will also be able to make your drawings look more realistic.

Parallel and Perpendicular

Before we begin drawing lines we need to go over a few definitions of how lines can relate to each other. Some basic relations are parallel vs. non-parallel, and perpendicular vs. non-perpendicular.

Parallel lines are drawn side by side and will never touch no matter how far you extend the lines in either direction. If you can extend two lines and they eventually touch, they are not parallel.

If two lines are drawn so that they touch and there is ninety degrees of rotation between them, they are **perpendicular**. If lines are at any other rotation besides ninety degrees it means they're not perpendicular (ninety degrees is one quarter turn of a circle).

Look at Figure 2-5 for examples of parallel vs. non-parallel, and perpendicular vs. non-perpendicular.

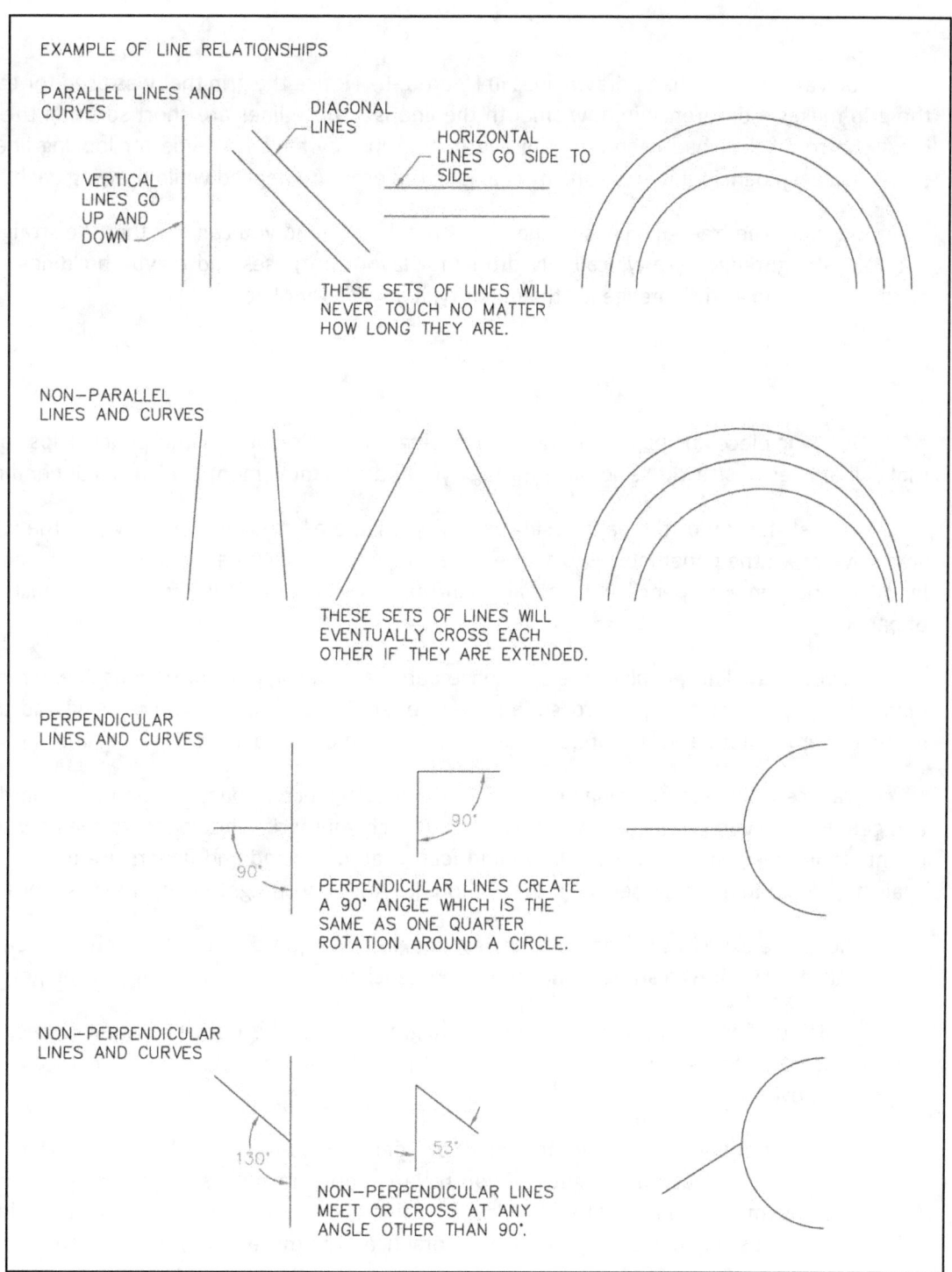

EXAMPLE OF LINE RELATIONSHIPS

PARALLEL LINES AND CURVES

DIAGONAL LINES

HORIZONTAL LINES GO SIDE TO SIDE

VERTICAL LINES GO UP AND DOWN

THESE SETS OF LINES WILL NEVER TOUCH NO MATTER HOW LONG THEY ARE.

NON-PARALLEL LINES AND CURVES

THESE SETS OF LINES WILL EVENTUALLY CROSS EACH OTHER IF THEY ARE EXTENDED.

PERPENDICULAR LINES AND CURVES

90°

90°

PERPENDICULAR LINES CREATE A 90° ANGLE WHICH IS THE SAME AS ONE QUARTER ROTATION AROUND A CIRCLE.

NON-PERPENDICULAR LINES AND CURVES

130°

53°

NON-PERPENDICULAR LINES MEET OR CROSS AT ANY ANGLE OTHER THAN 90°.

Figure 2-5. Line relationships, parallel and perpendicular.

Drawing Lines

Look at the set of hand-drawn lines in Figure 2-6. Notice the grip that was used for each set. As you can see the grip makes a difference in how smooth the line is. These lines are short so using the tight grip will give the most control; if they had been long the overhand grip may have made better looking lines. Notice the range of tone from each pencil; this was done by changing the pressure applied while drawing each line.

Compare the freehand lines to the straightedge lines and you can see that the straightedge lines don't look natural. Straightedges are typically used only for layout purposes and maybe buildings. You will rarely draw a picture relying on a straightedge for the majority, if any, of your lines.

Practice

Get four pieces of paper to practice drawing lines. Use one of the pencil grips for each piece of paper. Make your lines as straight as possible through your natural movement (which will depend on the grip).

Start at the top of the paper using as little pressure as possible, basically just the weight of the pencil. As you move down the paper increase the pressure until your pencil is nearly breaking. Once the tip starts to crack or break, re-sharpen your pencil and start again at the top with light lines. Try to fit at least 100 lines on each piece of paper.

As you draw lines, explore the difference between making one continuous line across the page and making many smaller connected lines across the page. Depending on the grip you're using and the line you're trying to make it's sometimes easier to connect many small lines in order to make one long line.

Practice using a straightedge or ruler on the fourth piece of paper. Don't push hard against it, let it slowly and gently guide you. Draw ten to twenty lines. Watch your wrist and fingers to see how they move. Draw ten to twenty more lines with your eyes closed and feel what your hand and fingers are doing. After drawing the lines against a straightedge draw several more without it. Are they straighter than the first lines you drew?

The above exercises will do three things; one, help you get comfortable with different pencil grips, two, help your mind learn to draw a straight line, and three, teach you the range of tone you can get from your pencil.

Hint: Part of the reason drawing straight lines can be difficult at first is because your fingers, wrist, elbow, and shoulder all rotate around joints, which means they want to do circular motions as you move.

If you only move around one joint your pencil will arc and make a curved line (which we'll talk about next). To make a straight line you have to move more than one joint at a time, this is a compound movement and it's more difficult than a single joint movement. Just like anything else though, drawing a good straight line can be done with practice. The more lines you draw the better you'll get.

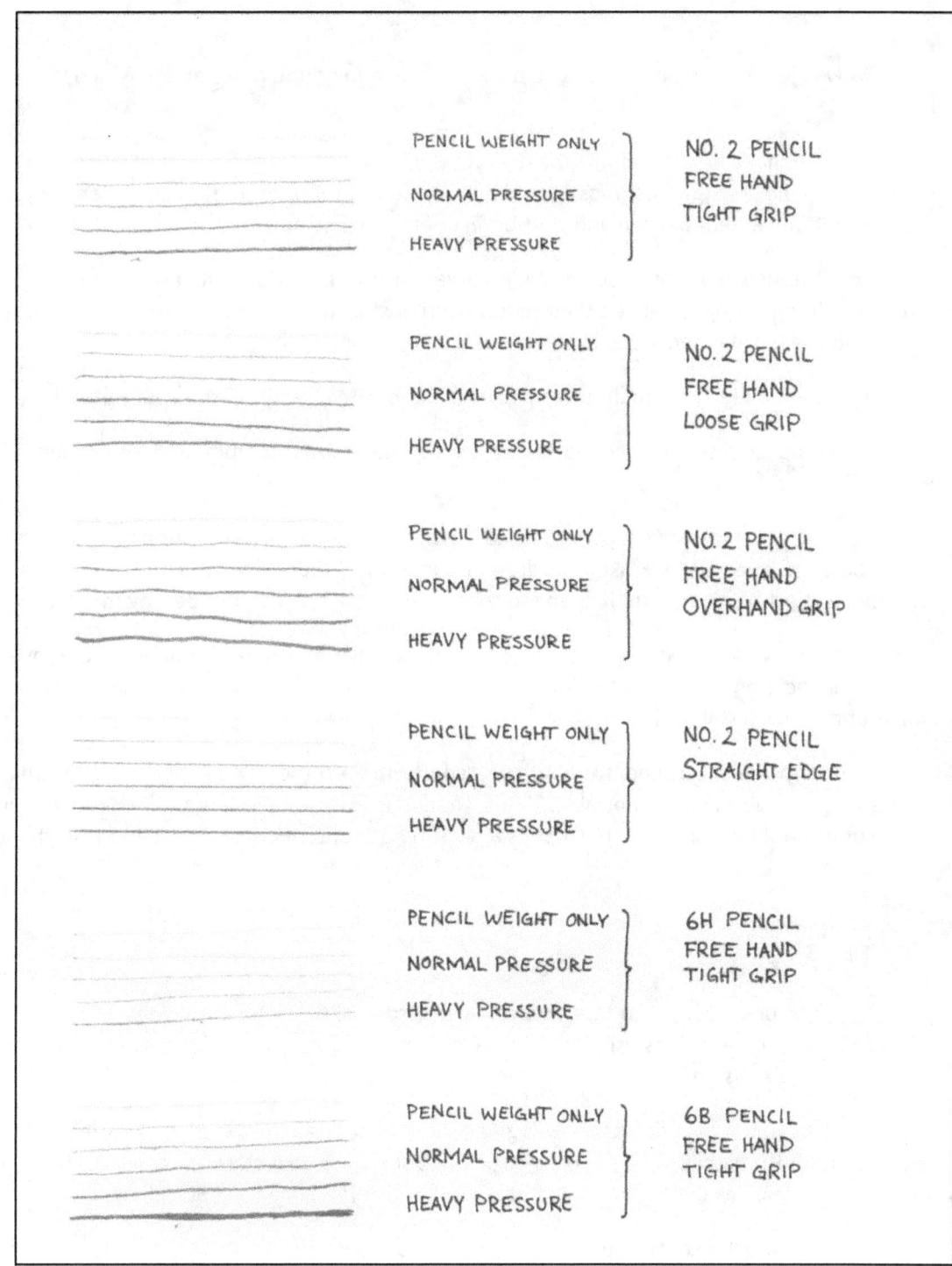

Figure 2-6. Hand-drawn straight lines

Curved Lines

As was just mentioned, when you move around a joint you make an arc which is perfect for drawing curved lines.

You can make an arcing movement at your wrist, elbow, and shoulder. Your fingers can make little arcs too using compound movements; most people are already pretty good at little finger curves because many letters require that movement pattern and your brain already knows how to do it.

You'll notice that it's easy to make curves in one direction but difficult to make them going the other direction. If you're right-handed your natural curve, starting from the bottom of the page, will be up and to the right; if you're left-handed your natural curve is up and to the left.

There are a few ways to draw a curve in the opposite direction from your natural arc.

First, you can use a compound movement (or many small compound movements). This is the most difficult way.

Second, you can turn the paper upside-down and draw a curve in your natural direction. When you turn the paper back over it will look like you drew a curve with your non-dominant hand. This method is easier but sometimes it's difficult to turn the paper over or continue a drawing upside-down.

The third way is to put your elbow or wrist towards the top of the paper and above your pencil, which will change the location of the pivot point. This method is the easiest and will increase the overall length of the curve but your range will still be limited.

Your grip will determine the length of a comfortable curve. Using the tight grip, small curves up to a couple inches long will be most comfortable. Using the loose grip, longer curves from about four to nine inches will be most comfortable (using only the wrist as a pivot point), and of course you can make the longest curves with the overhand grip.

Practice

Get four pieces of paper to practice drawing curves. Using one of the pencil grips for each piece of paper, practice making curved lines using the natural movement from your fingers, wrist, elbow and shoulder, depending on the grip you're using.

Start at the top of the paper using as little pressure as possible. As you move down the paper increase pressure until the pencil is nearly breaking. Once the pencil tip starts to crack or break, re-sharpen it and start again at the top using light lines. Try to fit at least 100 curved lines on each piece of paper.

This again will do three things; one, help you get comfortable with different pencil grips, two, help your mind learn to draw curves, and three, teach you the range of tone you can get from your pencil.

Use the fourth piece of paper to practice drawing curves in the opposite direction as your natural movement. Try all three methods mentioned above so you can learn the advantages and disadvantages of each. If you have a French-curve or stencil with a curve, practice using it the same way you used the straightedge to help you draw straight lines. Feel how it guides your movements and watch how your hand moves to complete different curves.

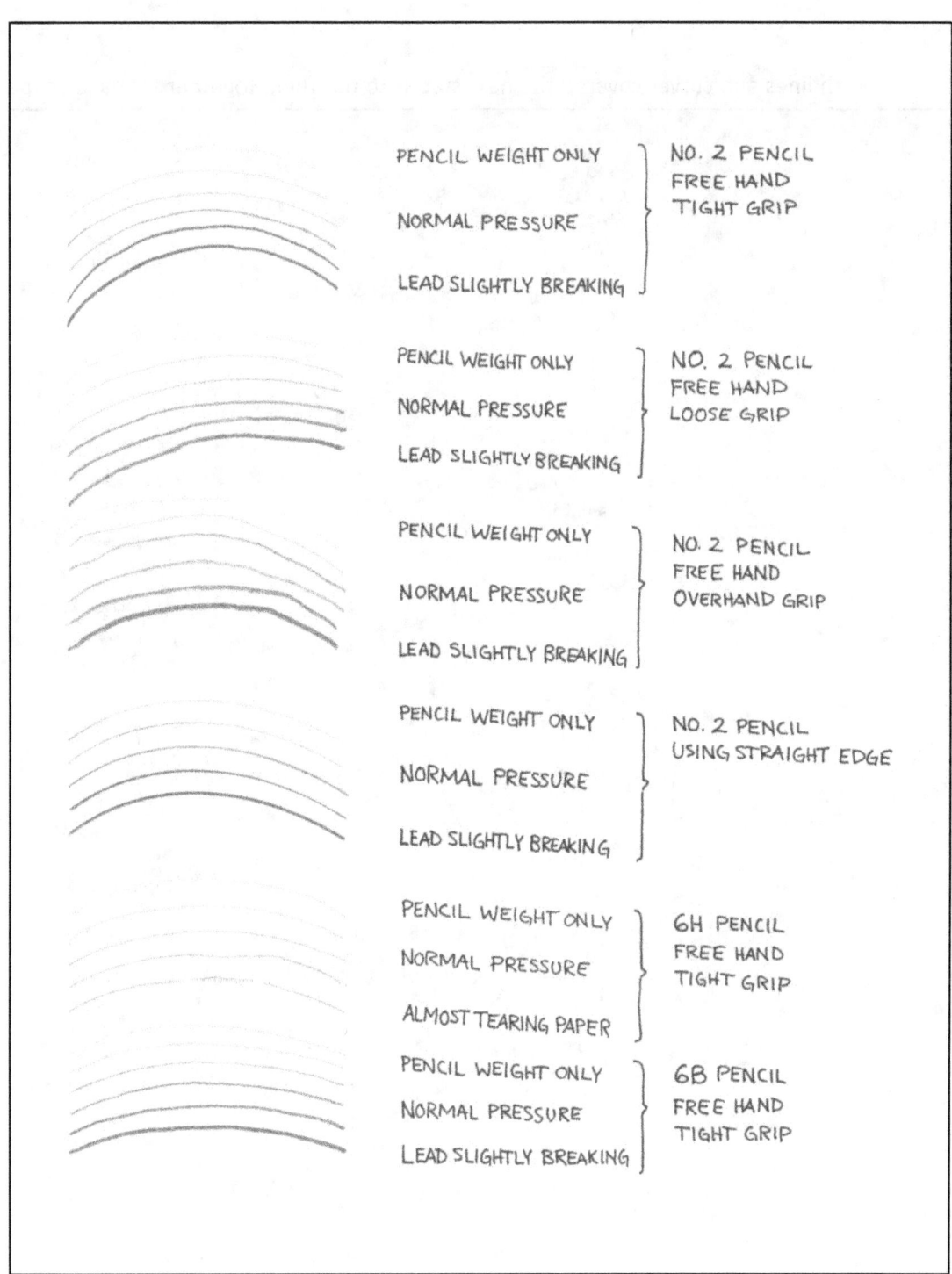

Figure 2-7. Hand-drawn curved lines

Drawing Shapes

With lines and curves covered the next step is to put them together to make shapes. Learning to combine shapes correctly and see the basic shapes of what you are drawing will help you lay out your drawings successfully. There are three basic shapes, the circle, the triangle, and the rectangle.

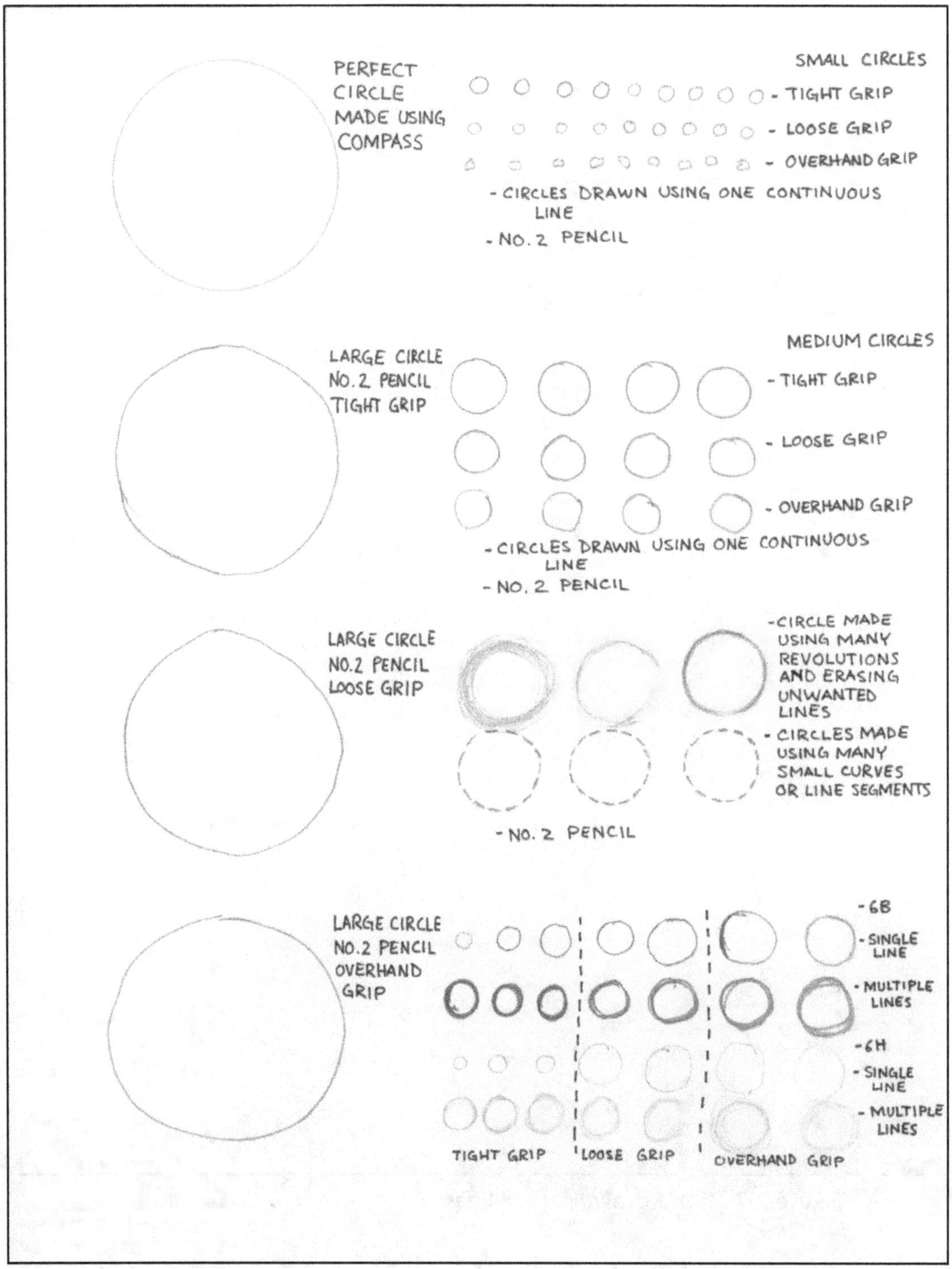

Circles

The circle is difficult to draw. A perfect circle has a center point with all parts of the circle the exact same distance away from the center. A circle has 360 degrees, which basically means it is divided into 360 equal pie-shaped pieces (As was mentioned before, two lines rotated ninety degrees to each other, one quarter of a circle, are perpendicular).

Drawing a perfect circle by hand is challenging, especially trying to do it in one motion, but with practice anyone can at least make a decent circle. Sometimes going

Figure 2-8. Hand-drawn circles

around many times in the same spot will help you be able to see a good circle. This method basically uses the parts of many different circles to make one good circle by erasing what you don't need.

Variations of the circle are called ellipses. An ellipse also has a center point but not all parts of the line are the same distance from the center, it's easiest to think of an ellipse as a circle that's been squashed down a bit. Ellipses are very important when drawing three dimensional drawings because when we see a circle at any angle other than straight on, what we see is an ellipse.

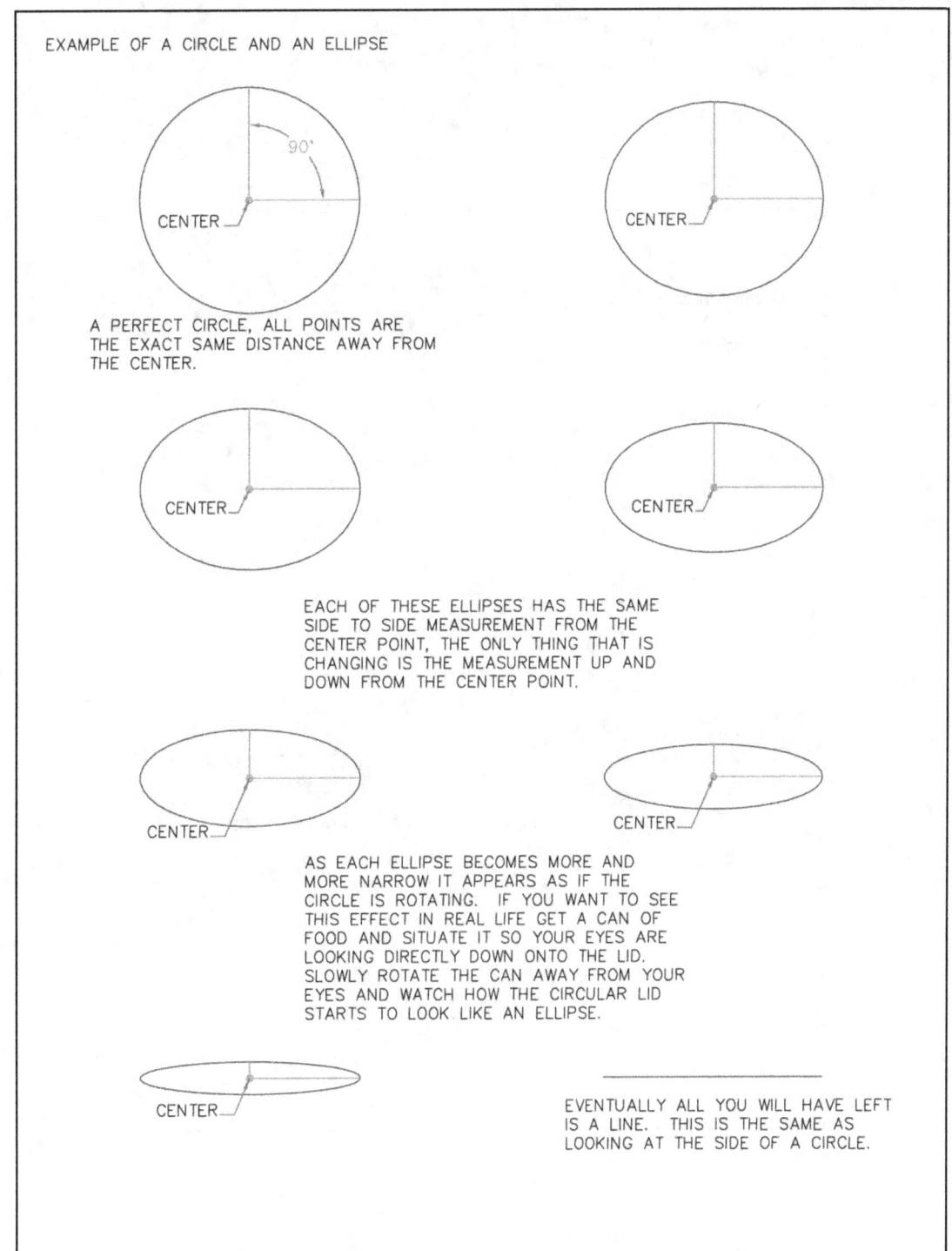

Figure 2-9. Circles and ellipses

Triangles

There are a few types of triangles but all of them have three straight connected lines. The way a triangle is classified depends on the length of its sides, and/or the internal angles. Triangles classified by their sides are equilateral, isosceles, and scalene. Triangles classified by their angles are acute, obtuse and right triangles. For drawing purposes, the name of the triangle doesn't matter as much as being able to see triangular shapes and using triangles to help lay out your drawings.

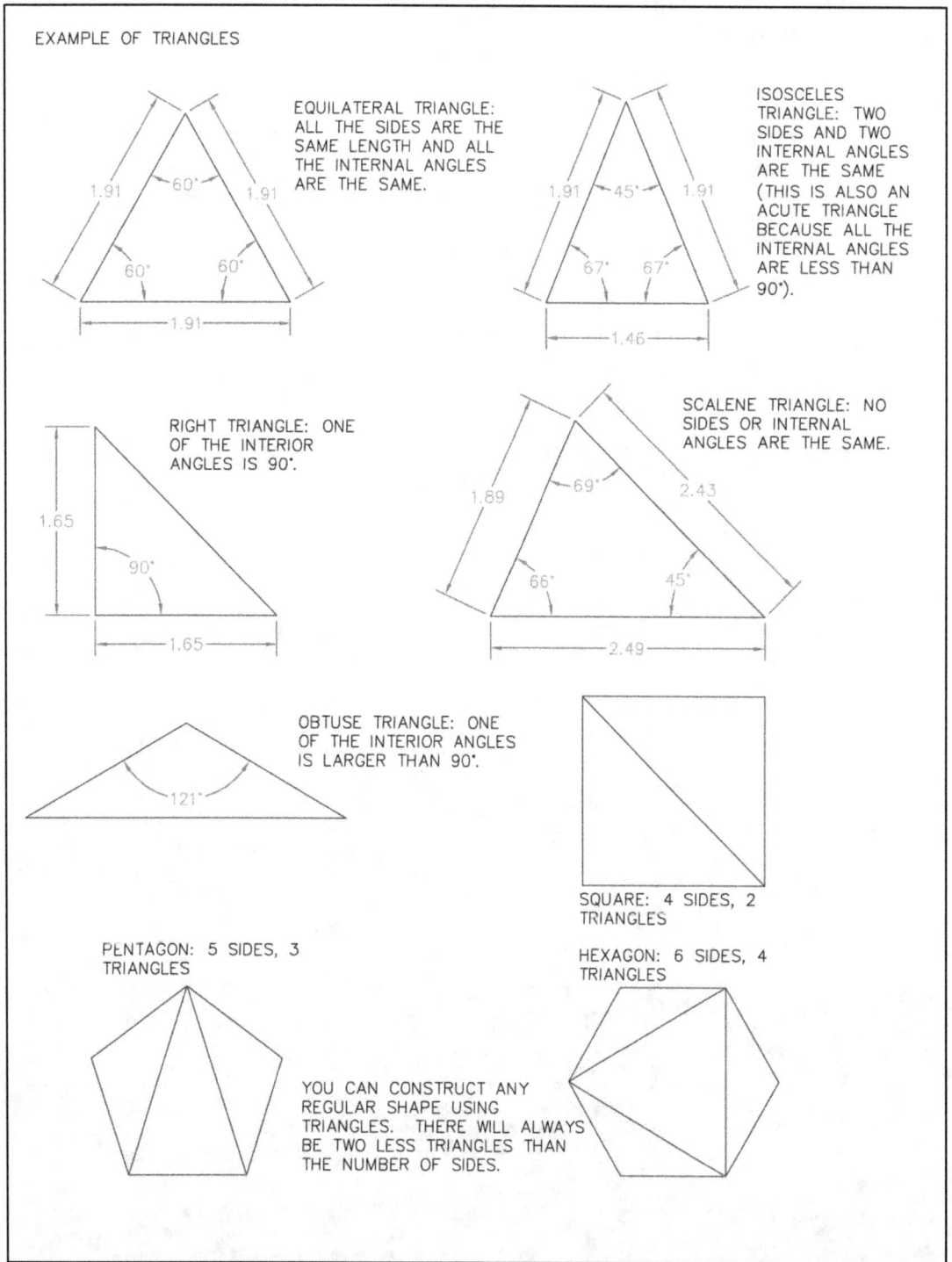

Figure 2-10. Triangles

Rectangles

Rectangles have four lines, two sets of parallel lines perpendicular to each other. Their shapes range from long and skinny, to a perfect square. A cousin to the rectangle is the rhombus or diamond shape. A rhombus has two sets of parallel lines but they are not perpendicular to each other. Another cousin to the rectangle is the trapezoid. The trapezoid has a set of parallel lines and a set of lines that are not parallel. The rhombus and trapezoid are important to rectangles when drawing three dimensional objects the same way ellipses are important to circles.

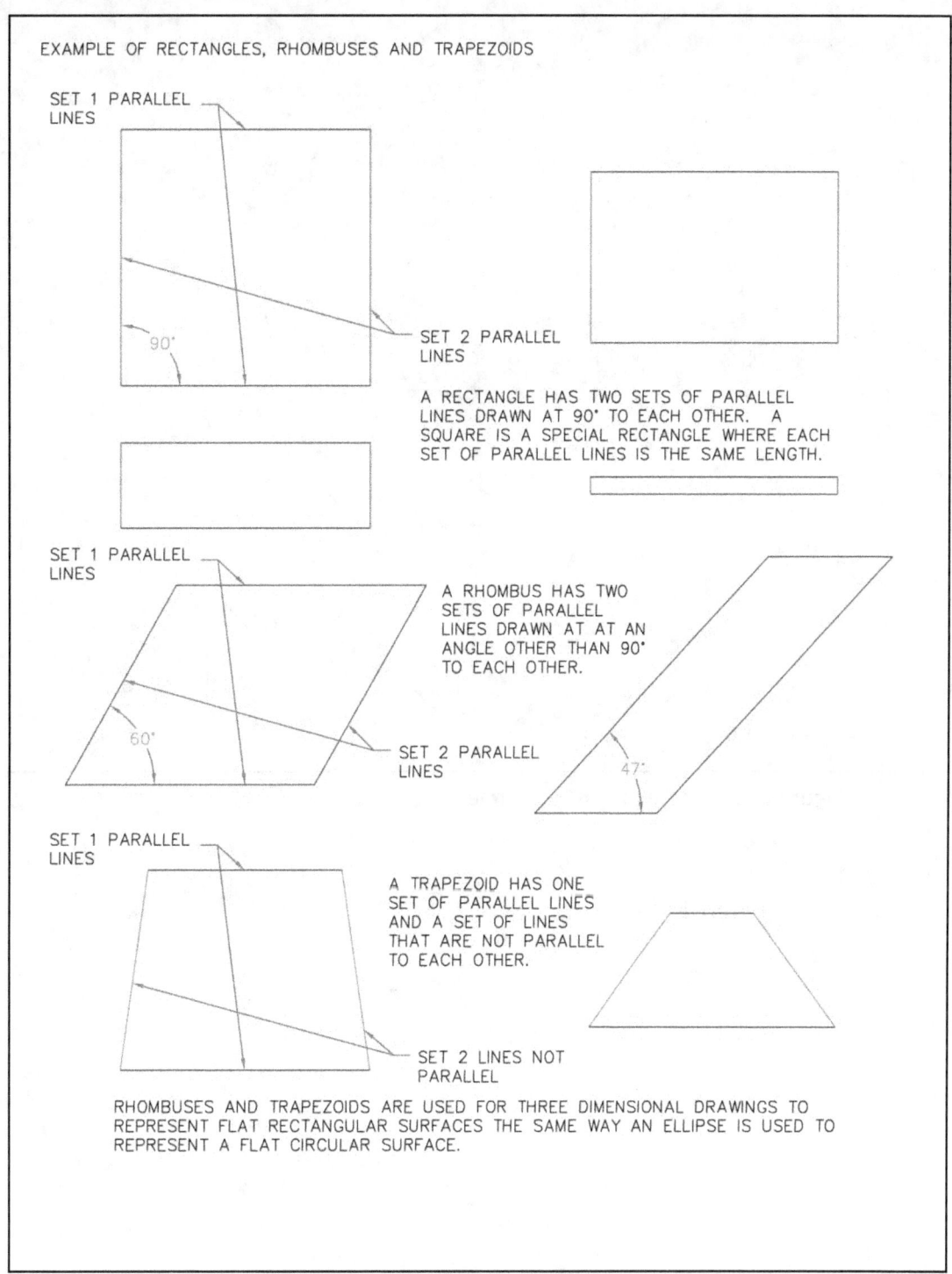

Figure 2-11. Rectangles, rhombuses and trapezoids

Of course there are more shapes than the ones we've just mentioned but there's a reason we aren't discussing them. Any shape with more than four sides can be made with a combination of rectangles, triangles and circles, along with their three dimensional counterparts, rhombuses, trapezoids and ellipses.

Another interesting thing about regular shapes is that the more lines you add, the more it starts to look like a circle. See Figure 2-12, look at the fifteen and twenty sided shapes. They could easily be mistaken as circles if you weren't close enough to see that they're actually made from straight lines.

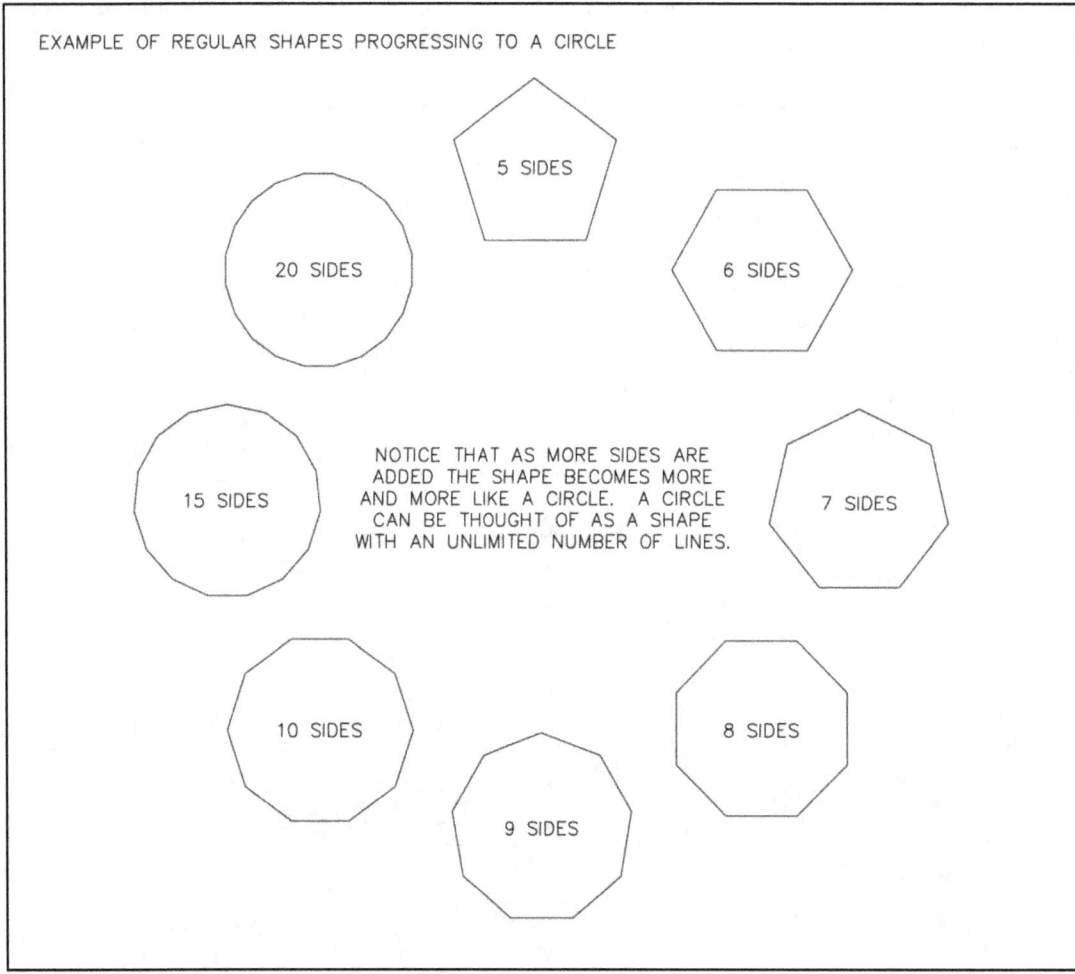

EXAMPLE OF REGULAR SHAPES PROGRESSING TO A CIRCLE

5 SIDES

6 SIDES

20 SIDES

15 SIDES

NOTICE THAT AS MORE SIDES ARE ADDED THE SHAPE BECOMES MORE AND MORE LIKE A CIRCLE. A CIRCLE CAN BE THOUGHT OF AS A SHAPE WITH AN UNLIMITED NUMBER OF LINES.

7 SIDES

10 SIDES

8 SIDES

9 SIDES

Figure 2-12. Progression to a circle

Using Shapes to Draw Objects

Finding the basic shape of an object takes some practice. The trick is to imagine that the object you're looking at is flat and all one color. Doing this, even irregular shapes can be broken down into simple shapes. It may be hard to see at first but with practice you'll learn to easily spot the main shapes of any object.

The examples that follow illustrate that any object can be broken down into basic shapes. The various triangles, rectangles, rhombuses and trapezoids can be used to represent any flat surface with straight edges. If the shape has curves simply add part of a circle or ellipse. You can be as detailed or simple as you want using shapes to describe objects. A rectangle can even be used to represent an ellipse if the level of detail you need is very low and the general idea isn't ruined by the lack of curves, it all depends on how much information you need to convey.

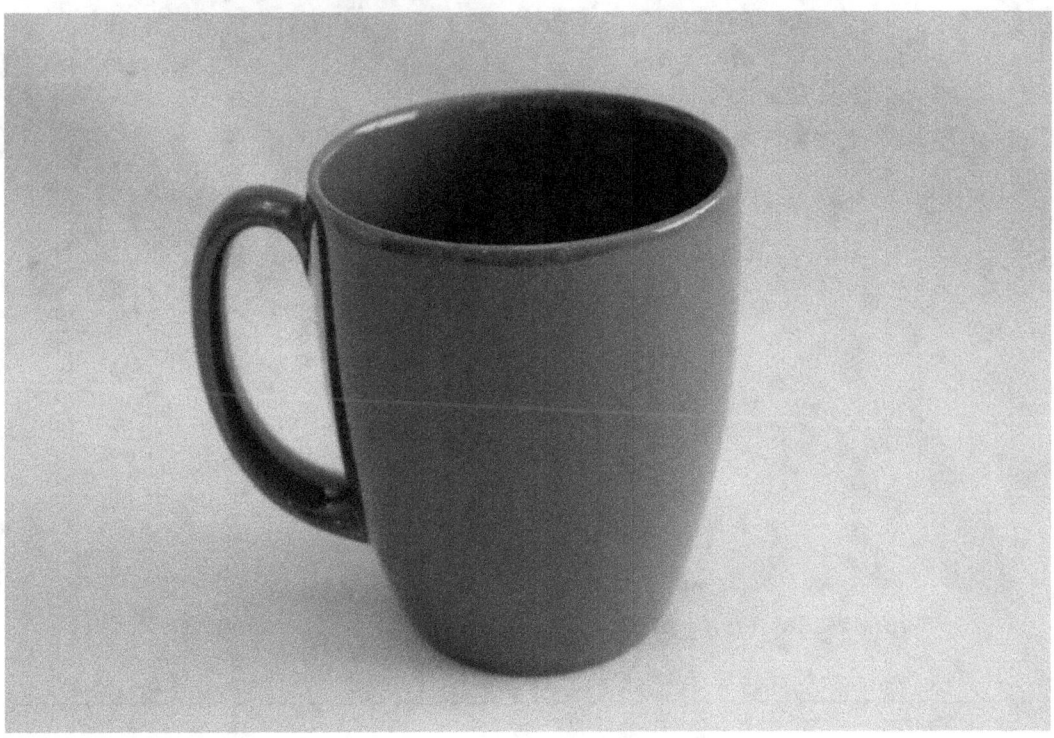

Figure 2-13a. Mug

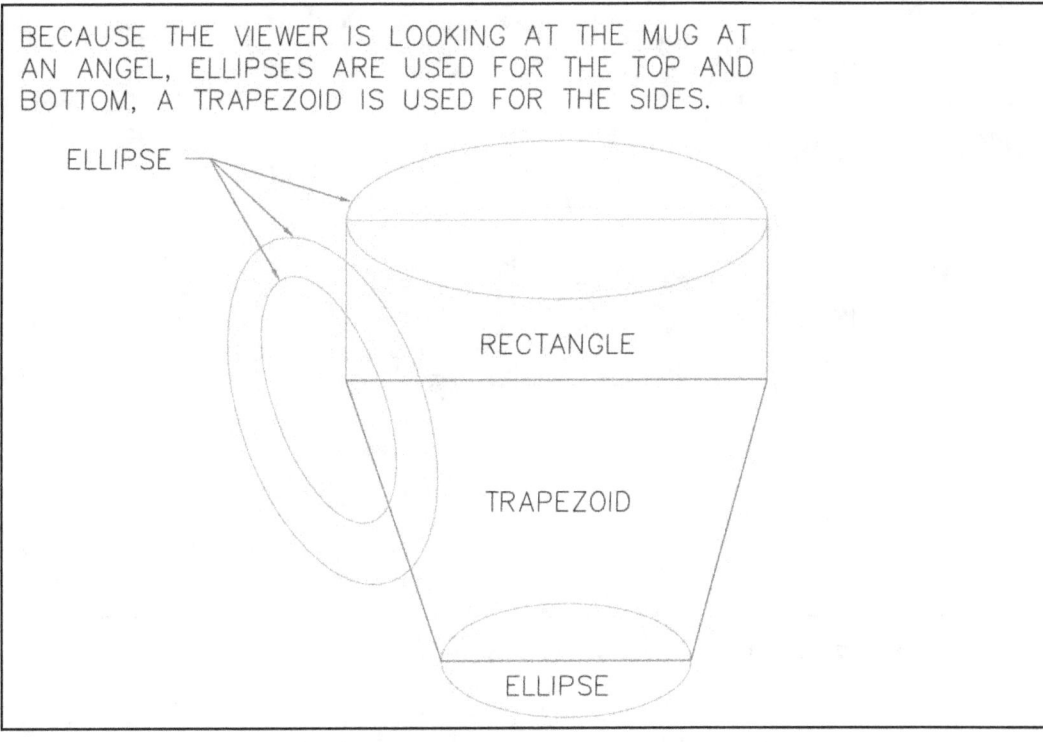

Figure 2-13b. Mug reduced to simple shapes

33

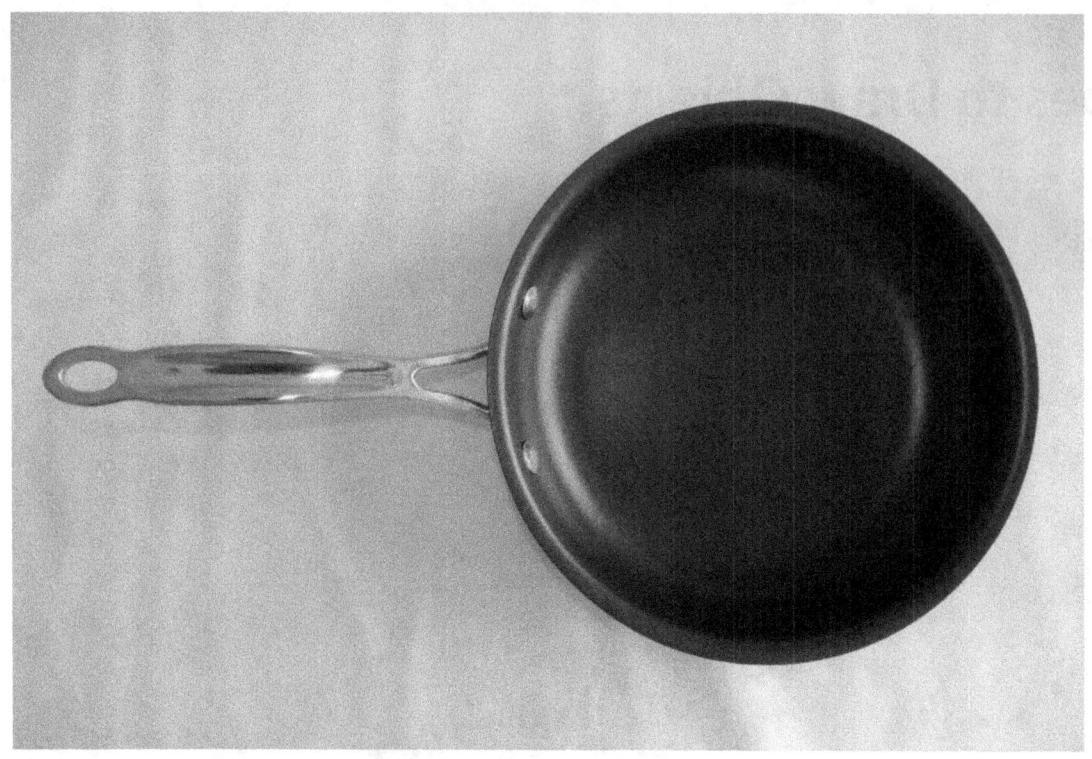

Figure 2-14a. Frying pan

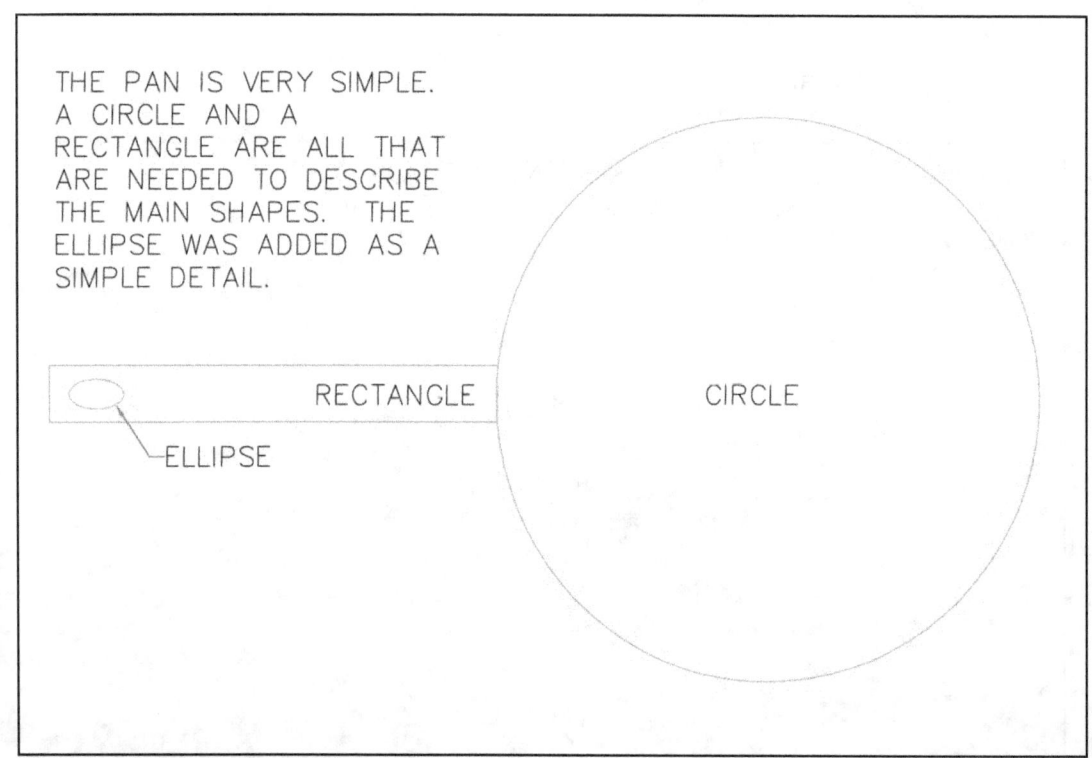

THE PAN IS VERY SIMPLE.
A CIRCLE AND A
RECTANGLE ARE ALL THAT
ARE NEEDED TO DESCRIBE
THE MAIN SHAPES. THE
ELLIPSE WAS ADDED AS A
SIMPLE DETAIL.

RECTANGLE

CIRCLE

ELLIPSE

Figure 2-14b. Frying pan reduced to simple shapes

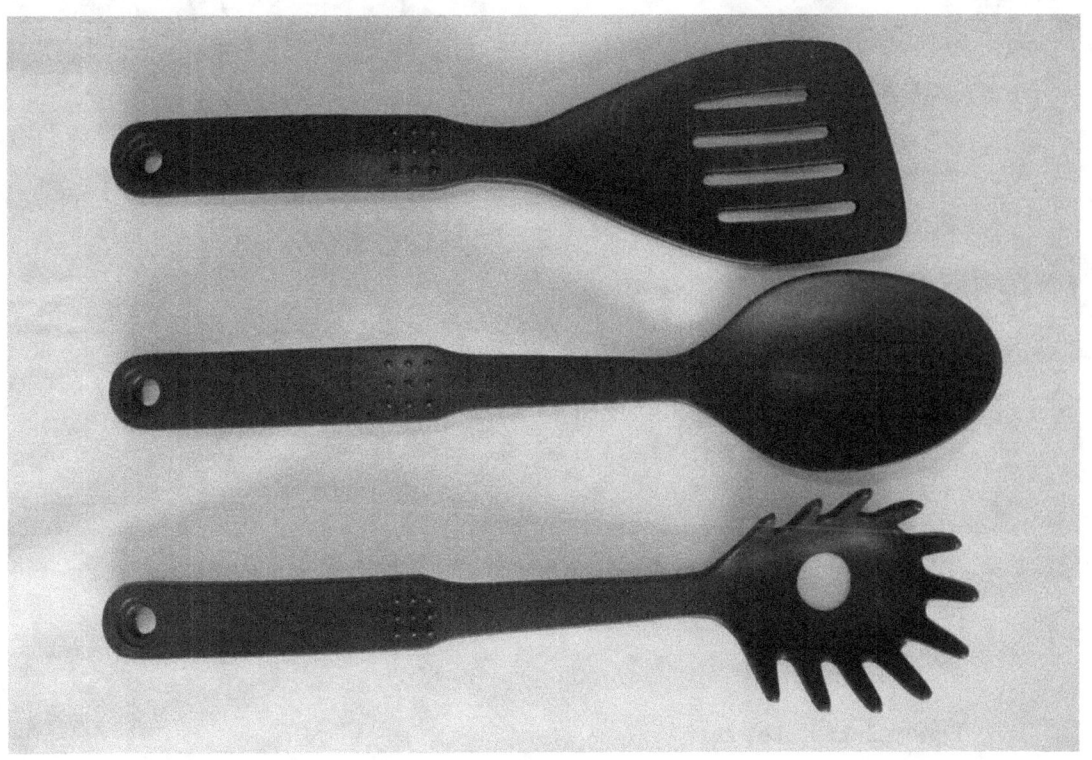

Figure 2-15a. Utensils

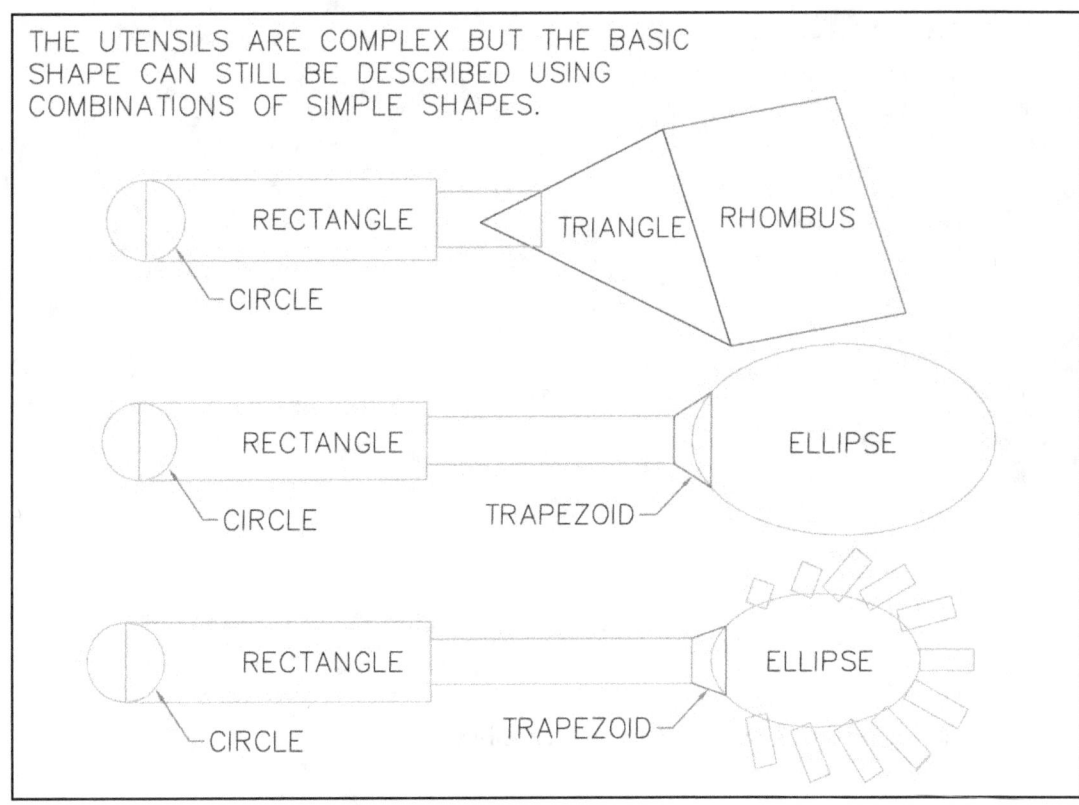

Figure 2-15b. Utensils reduced to simple shapes

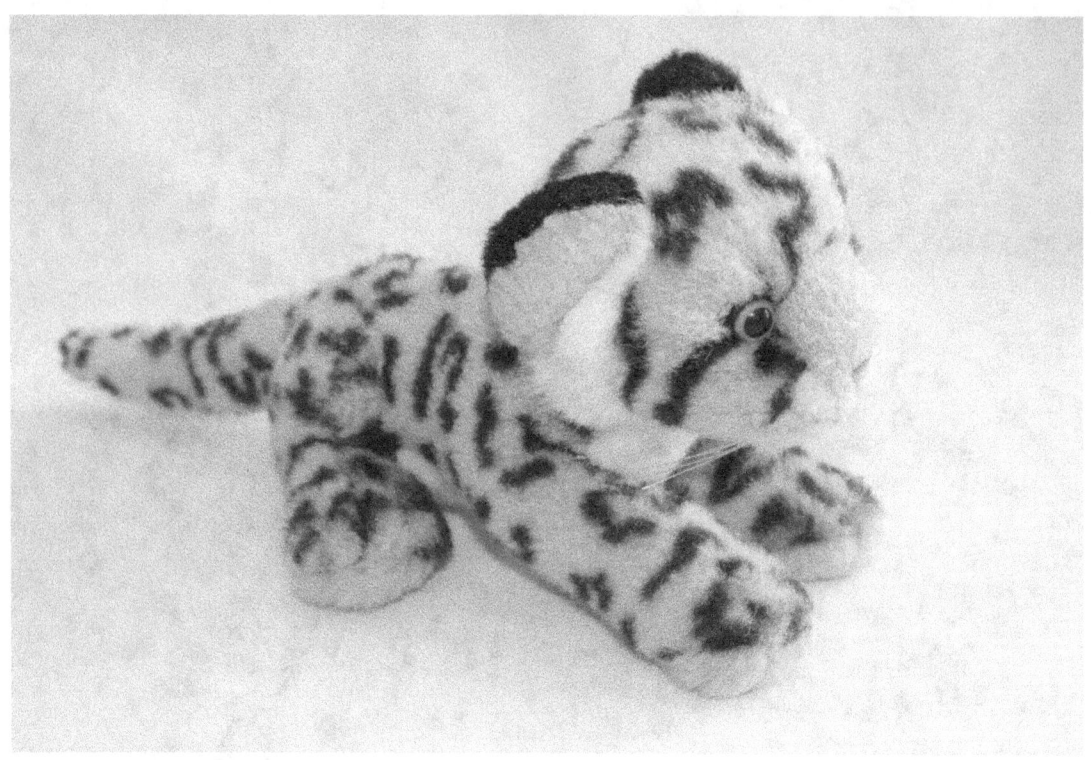

Figure 2-16a. Toy cat

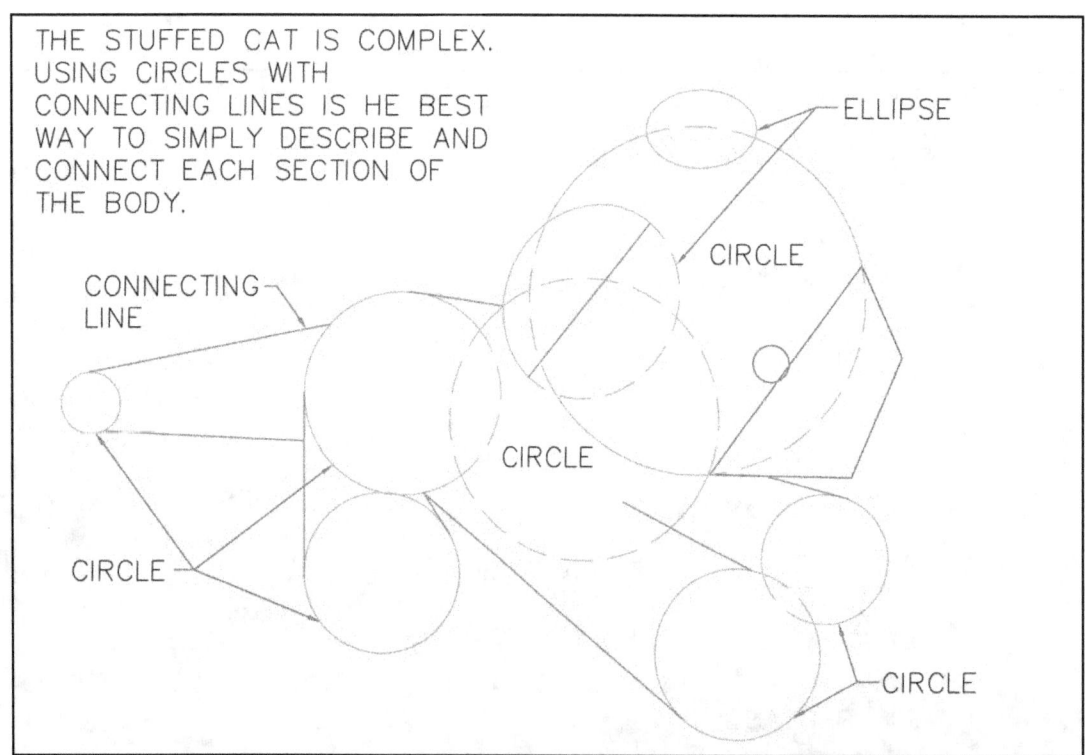

THE STUFFED CAT IS COMPLEX.
USING CIRCLES WITH
CONNECTING LINES IS HE BEST
WAY TO SIMPLY DESCRIBE AND
CONNECT EACH SECTION OF
THE BODY.

ELLIPSE

CIRCLE

CONNECTING
LINE

CIRCLE

CIRCLE

CIRCLE

Figure 2-16b. Toy cat reduced to simple shapes

Practice

Practicing the basic shapes and their variants will help you become more comfortable as you move on to three dimensional shapes. Get a few pieces of paper for each shape, circles, triangles and rectangles.

Start by trying to draw perfect circles of different sizes. Use different grips so you can learn the advantages and challenges of each. Draw circles using a single line, and then make some using many small connected line segments. Finally, place your pencil on the paper and go around many times, stop, and erase lines away to get a perfect circle. When you feel you're making good circles draw some ellipses. Start by drawing wide ellipses and work towards making very skinny ones.

Practice drawing various triangles, use different grips as you do it. Also draw a number of right triangles with lines as close to perpendicular as possible and then attempt some equilateral triangles with all three sides the exact same length.

Practice making all shapes and sizes of rectangles including a perfect square. Also practice trapezoids and rhombuses.

Once you feel good about your shapes go through your house and find four objects you can describe on paper using only shapes. It could be a clock, a spoon, a bed or anything else. Try to see the object as a combination of basic shapes. Imagine the object is flat and all one color. What shape would it be? If you have trouble seeing the shape of the object place a light behind it (if you can), this will highlight the edges of the object and make the side facing you appear darker, you should be able to find the shapes more easily that way. If you still have trouble seeing the shapes, close one eye as you look at the object. This will eliminate some depth perception and make the object appear more two dimensional.

Conclusion

Congratulations, you have finished Volume 2 of the *Drawing Mentor* series. In this lesson you should have developed a proficiency for drawing straight and curved lines, learned how to change the tonal depth of your lines by applying different pencil pressure, and how to describe everyday objects using only shapes. These are foundational skills which you can build on. Volume 3 will take these skills a step further by teaching you how to apply them to create three dimensional objects and add tone and shading.

Perspective, 3-D Shapes and Shading

Welcome to Volume 3. This lesson builds on the skills gained in Volume 2. By now you should know how to draw straight and curved lines and how to use shapes to describe objects. You should also be able to change the tone of your lines by changing the pressure you apply to your pencil. This lesson continues the discussion of lines shapes and tone but takes it a step further, combining these three skills to create 3-D objects.

We see things in three dimensions, height, width, and depth. Height refers to how tall an object is from bottom to top, and width is the measurement from side to side. When drawing that's pretty straight forward because paper also has height and width. The tricky dimension is depth or how far "into" the paper an object goes. We're trying to draw things that have one more dimension than the paper, we have to use some tricks to do this. Two tricks in particular will help you achieve a three dimensional look on a two dimensional surface, they are perspective, and shading/highlighting. Being able to use these techniques effectively will really make the difference between being "okay" at drawing and being a good artist.

Perspective

Perspective refers to the level of the viewer's eye and the direction they're looking in relation to the objects in the drawing. There are three types of perspective, one point, two point and three point. The points are "vanishing points" which basically means the point where parallel lines appear to come together and touch. The more points you use the more complex the drawing gets. There's a time and place to use each type of perspective.

One Point Perspective

One point perspective is the most basic. It can be used when all parallel lines seem to converge at one point, for example, looking down a set of train tracks, or a single road. Another time you could use it is when the focus of a building or object is directly in front of the viewer and you want all attentions to be placed on it.

In a one point perspective drawing, height is shown using vertical lines and width is shown using horizontal lines. Depth is shown using diagonal lines that all meet at the vanishing point. We know that parallel lines never actually touch each other but if you look down a set of train tracks the rails look like they get closer together the further down the tracks you look. This happens because of how our eyes interpret distance. Perspective drawing is how we imitate on paper what our eyes do in real life.

One point perspective drawings will give a feeling of stability. There are usually a lot of horizontal and vertical lines in a one point perspective drawing and our brains will interpret it to be calm, stable and maybe even a little boring.

Follow these steps to make a one point perspective drawing:

1. Draw a horizontal line across the paper, this will be the horizon line and represent the level of the viewer's eye.

2. Make a dot on the horizontal line, this is the vanishing point.

3. Any depth to the drawing is represented by lines drawn from the vanishing point to the edge of the paper.

4. Height and width are represented by vertical and horizontal lines.

5. Circles, cones, and cylinders are not affected by this perspective.

Look at the two examples that follow. Example 3-1 demonstrates step by step how to draw one point perspective rectangular solids from many angles. Example 3-2 demonstrates step by step how to draw a one point perspective drawing of a street.

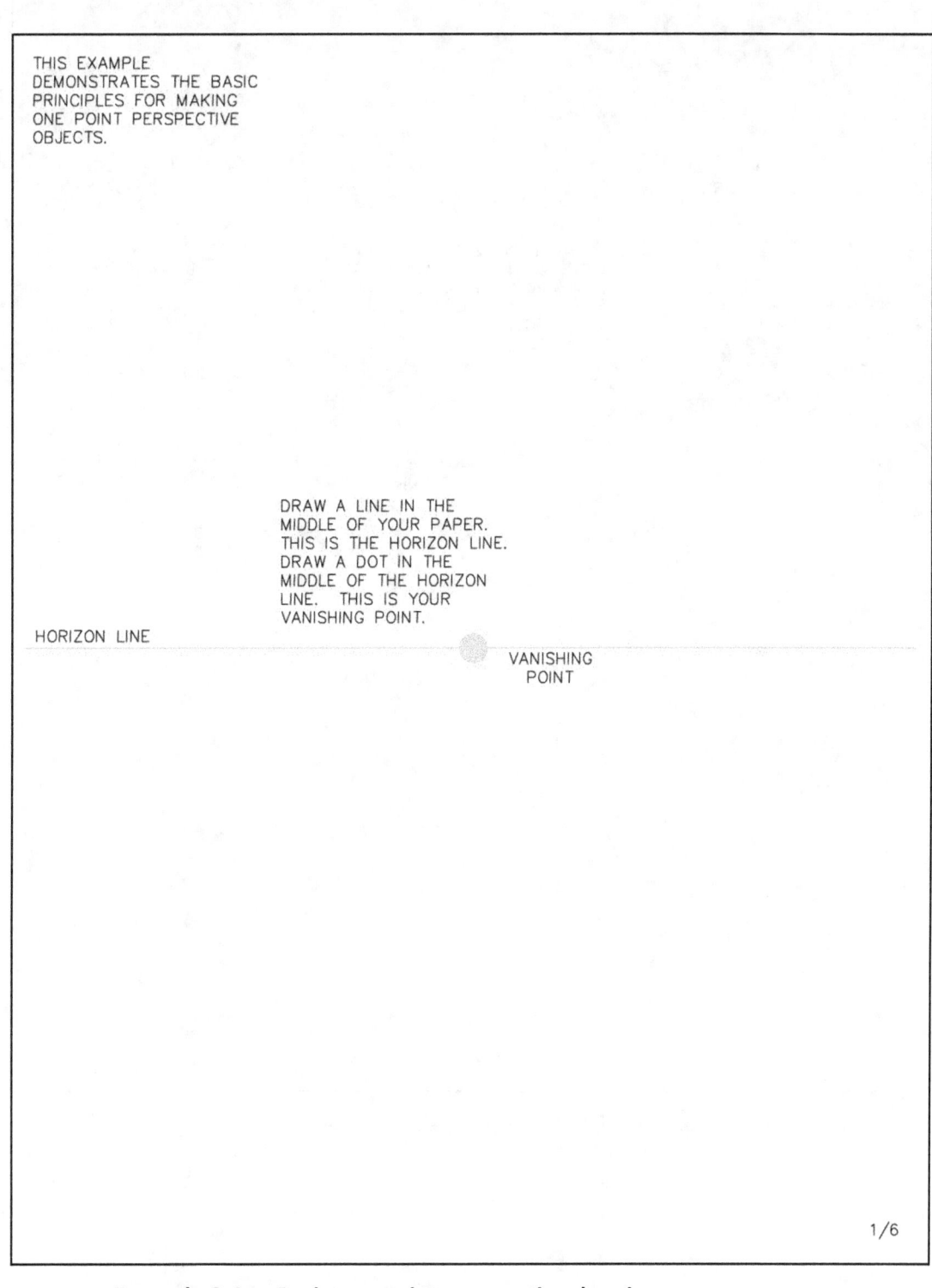

THIS EXAMPLE
DEMONSTRATES THE BASIC
PRINCIPLES FOR MAKING
ONE POINT PERSPECTIVE
OBJECTS.

DRAW A LINE IN THE
MIDDLE OF YOUR PAPER.
THIS IS THE HORIZON LINE.
DRAW A DOT IN THE
MIDDLE OF THE HORIZON
LINE.   THIS IS YOUR
VANISHING POINT.

HORIZON LINE

VANISHING
POINT

1/6

Example 3-1a. Basic one point perspective drawing

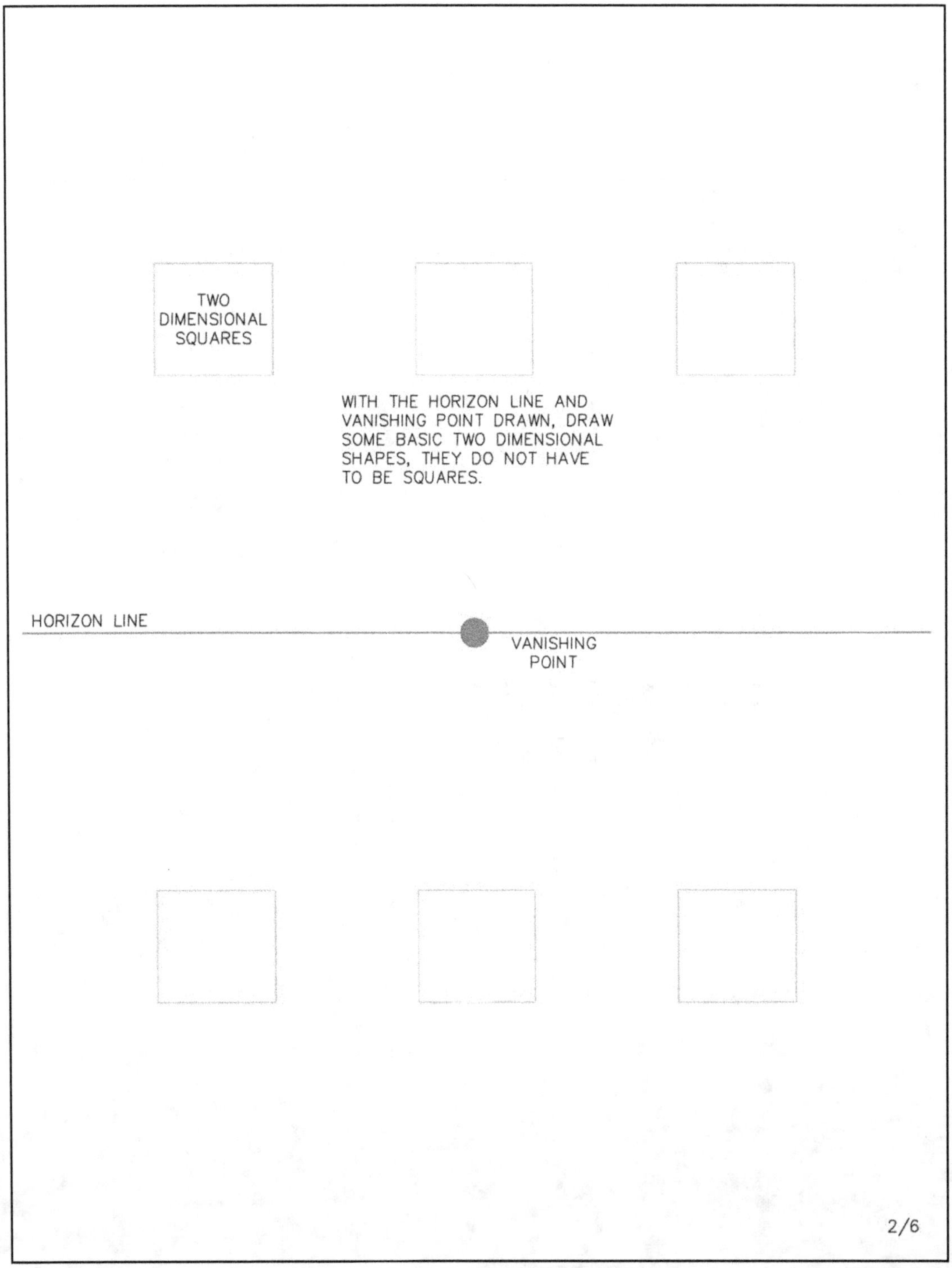

TWO
DIMENSIONAL
SQUARES

WITH THE HORIZON LINE AND
VANISHING POINT DRAWN, DRAW
SOME BASIC TWO DIMENSIONAL
SHAPES, THEY DO NOT HAVE
TO BE SQUARES.

HORIZON LINE

VANISHING
POINT

2/6

Example 3-1b. Basic one point perspective drawing

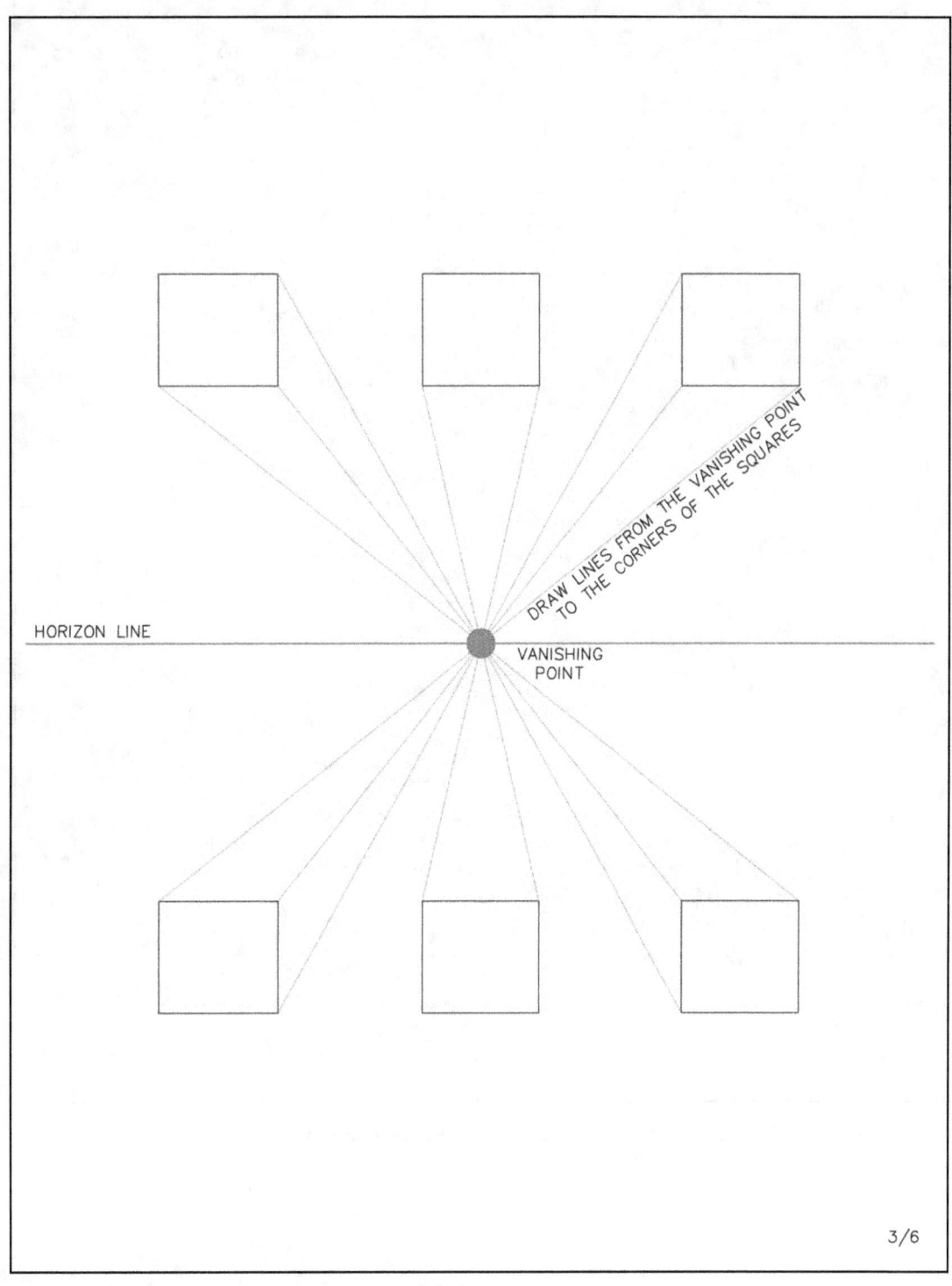

HORIZON LINE

VANISHING POINT

DRAW LINES FROM THE VANISHING POINT TO THE CORNERS OF THE SQUARES

3/6

Example 3-1c. Basic one point perspective drawing

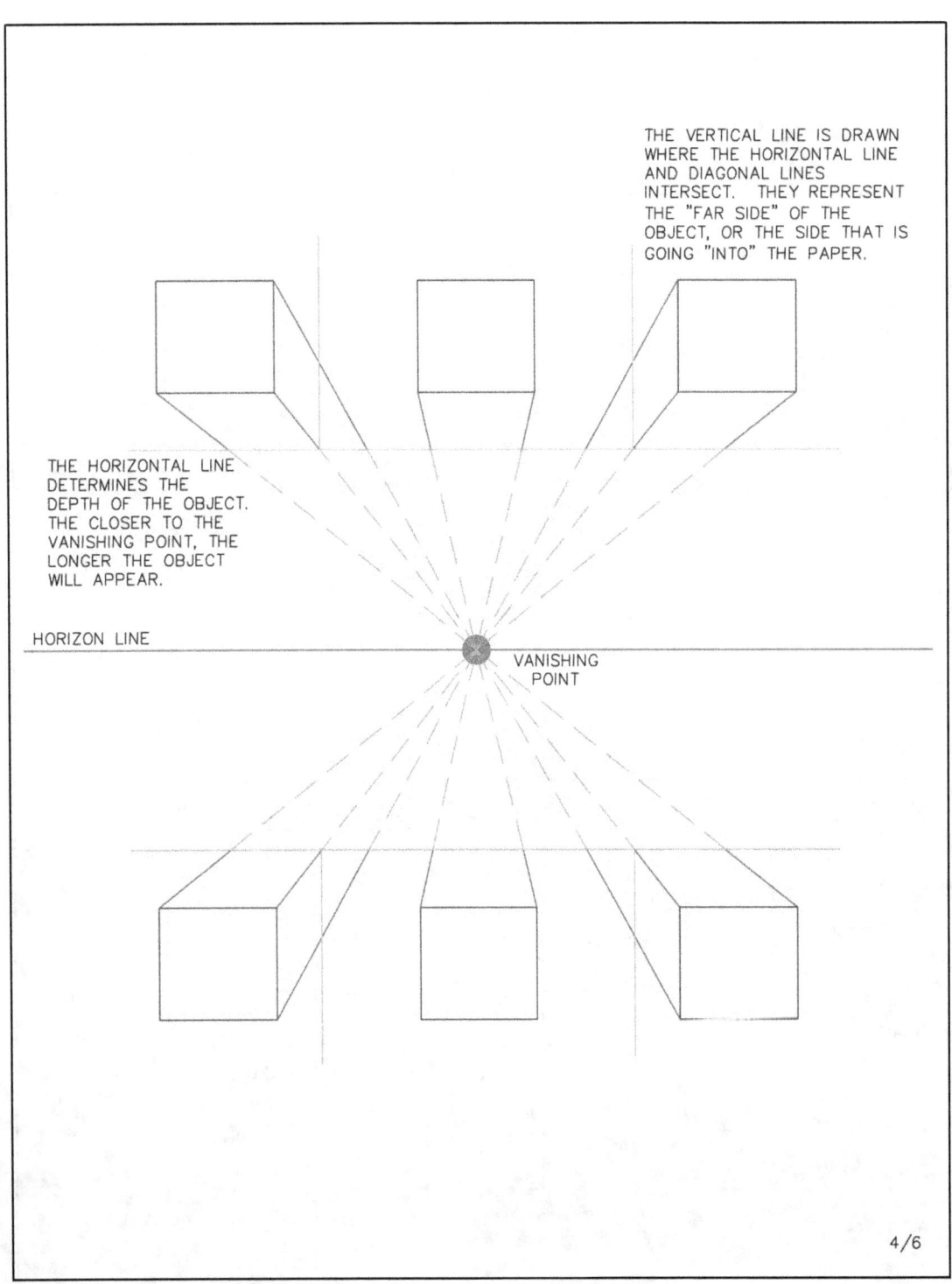

THE VERTICAL LINE IS DRAWN WHERE THE HORIZONTAL LINE AND DIAGONAL LINES INTERSECT. THEY REPRESENT THE "FAR SIDE" OF THE OBJECT, OR THE SIDE THAT IS GOING "INTO" THE PAPER.

THE HORIZONTAL LINE DETERMINES THE DEPTH OF THE OBJECT. THE CLOSER TO THE VANISHING POINT, THE LONGER THE OBJECT WILL APPEAR.

HORIZON LINE

VANISHING POINT

4/6

Example 3-1d. Basic one point perspective drawing

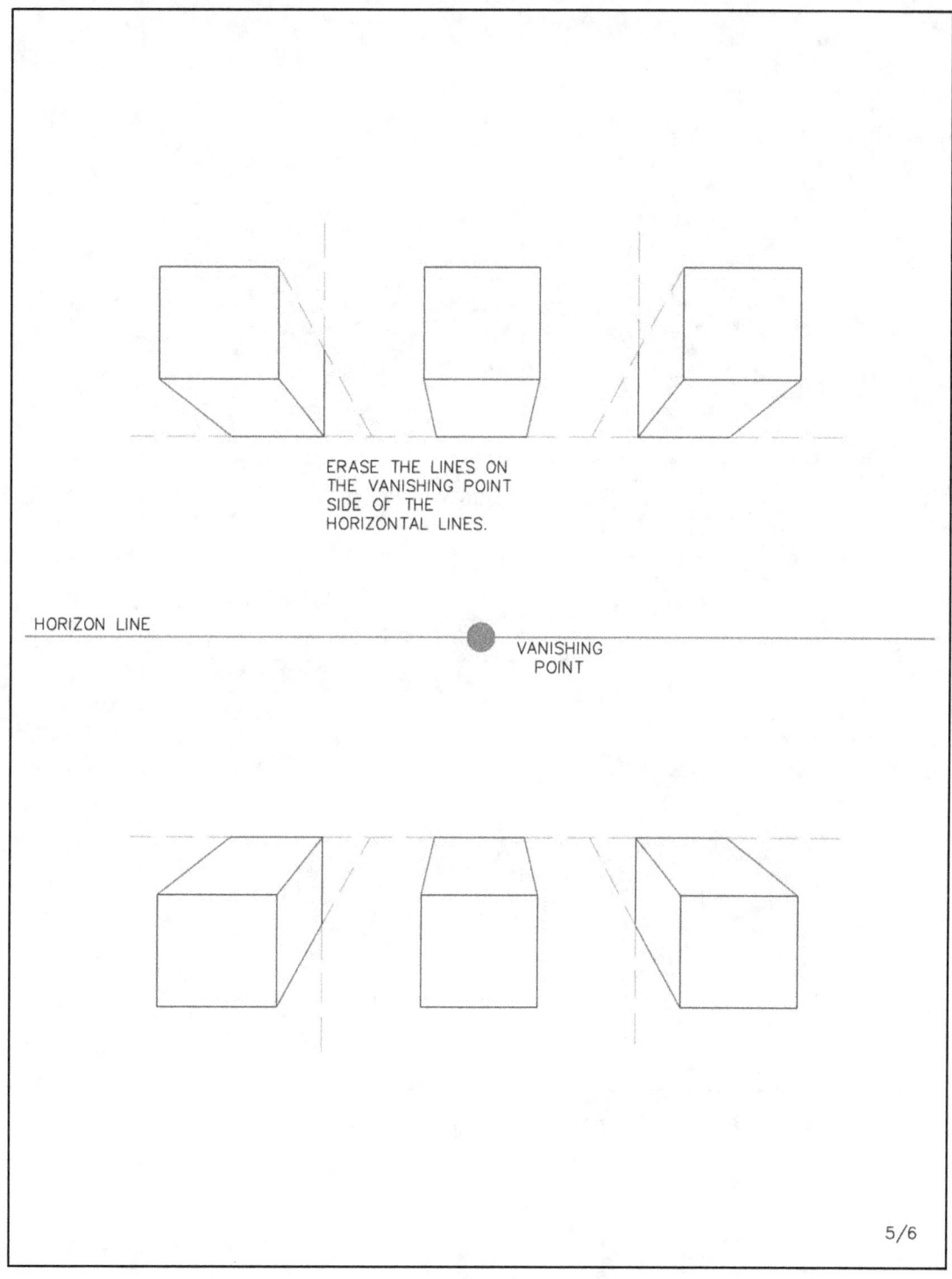

ERASE THE LINES ON
THE VANISHING POINT
SIDE OF THE
HORIZONTAL LINES.

HORIZON LINE

VANISHING
POINT

5/6

Example 3-1e. Basic one point perspective drawing

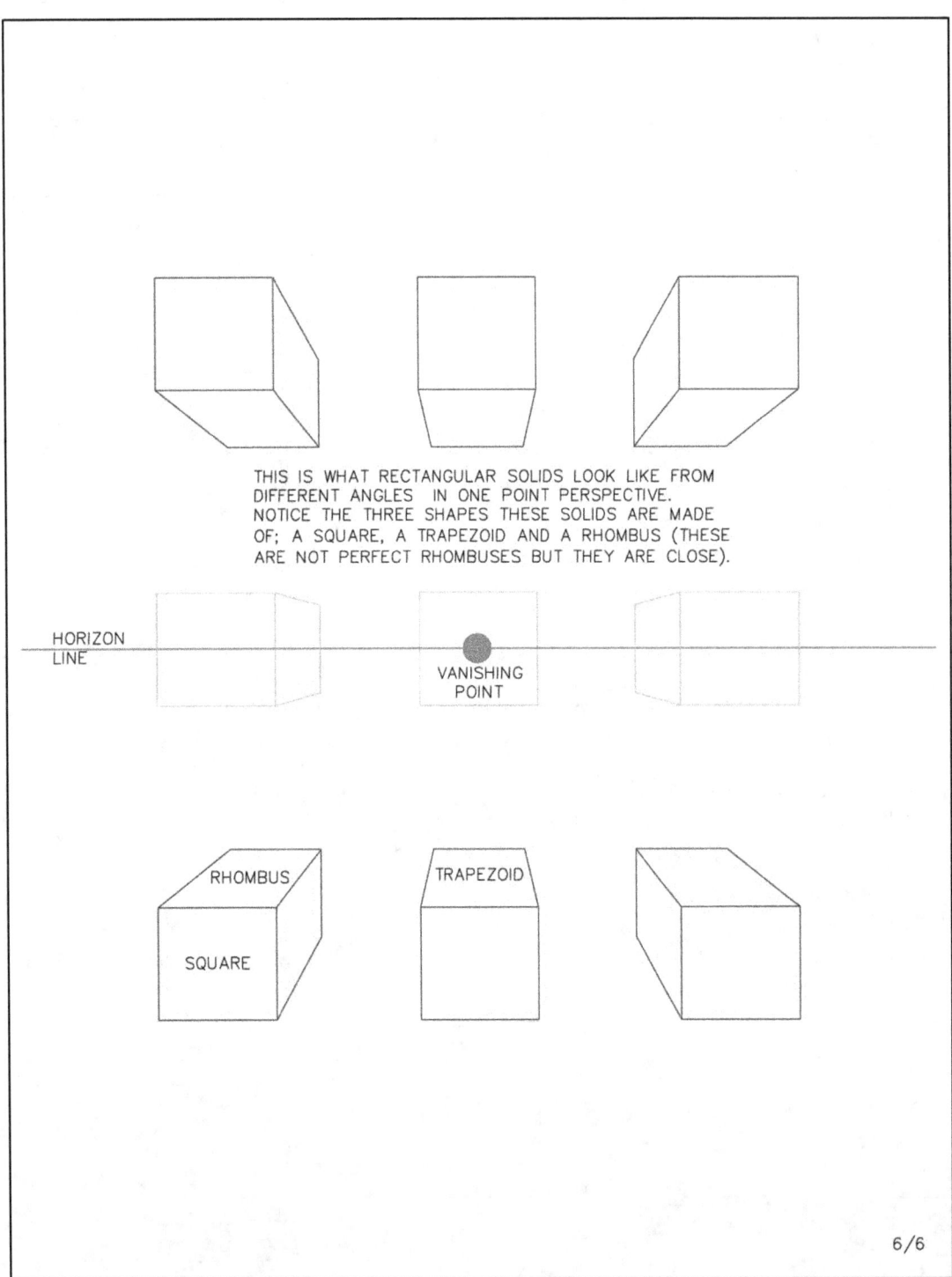

THIS IS WHAT RECTANGULAR SOLIDS LOOK LIKE FROM
DIFFERENT ANGLES IN ONE POINT PERSPECTIVE.
NOTICE THE THREE SHAPES THESE SOLIDS ARE MADE
OF; A SQUARE, A TRAPEZOID AND A RHOMBUS (THESE
ARE NOT PERFECT RHOMBUSES BUT THEY ARE CLOSE).

HORIZON
LINE

VANISHING
POINT

RHOMBUS

SQUARE

TRAPEZOID

6/6

Example 3-1f. Basic one point perspective drawing

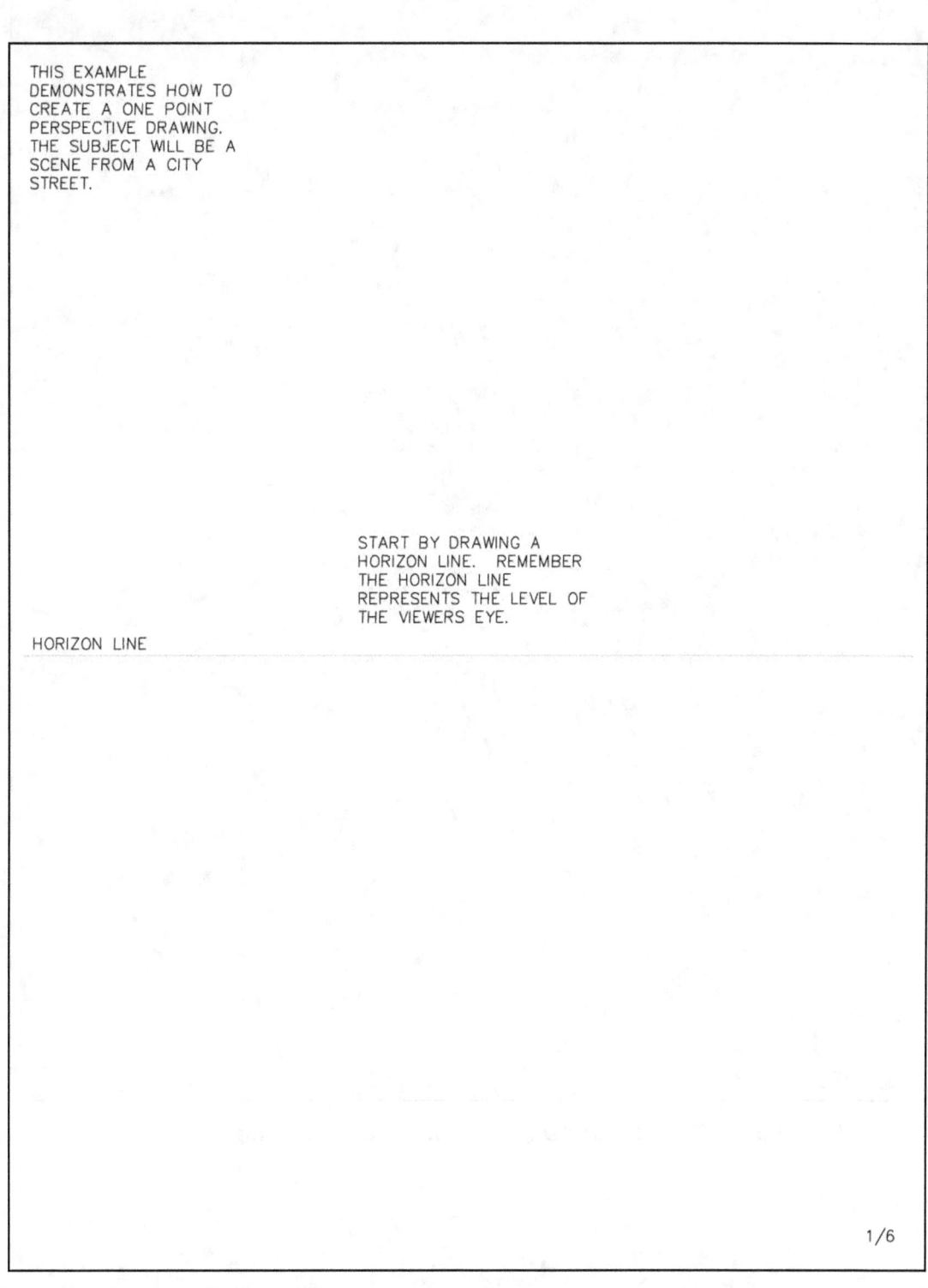

THIS EXAMPLE
DEMONSTRATES HOW TO
CREATE A ONE POINT
PERSPECTIVE DRAWING.
THE SUBJECT WILL BE A
SCENE FROM A CITY
STREET.

START BY DRAWING A
HORIZON LINE. REMEMBER
THE HORIZON LINE
REPRESENTS THE LEVEL OF
THE VIEWERS EYE.

HORIZON LINE

1/6

Example 3-2a. Advanced one point perspective drawing

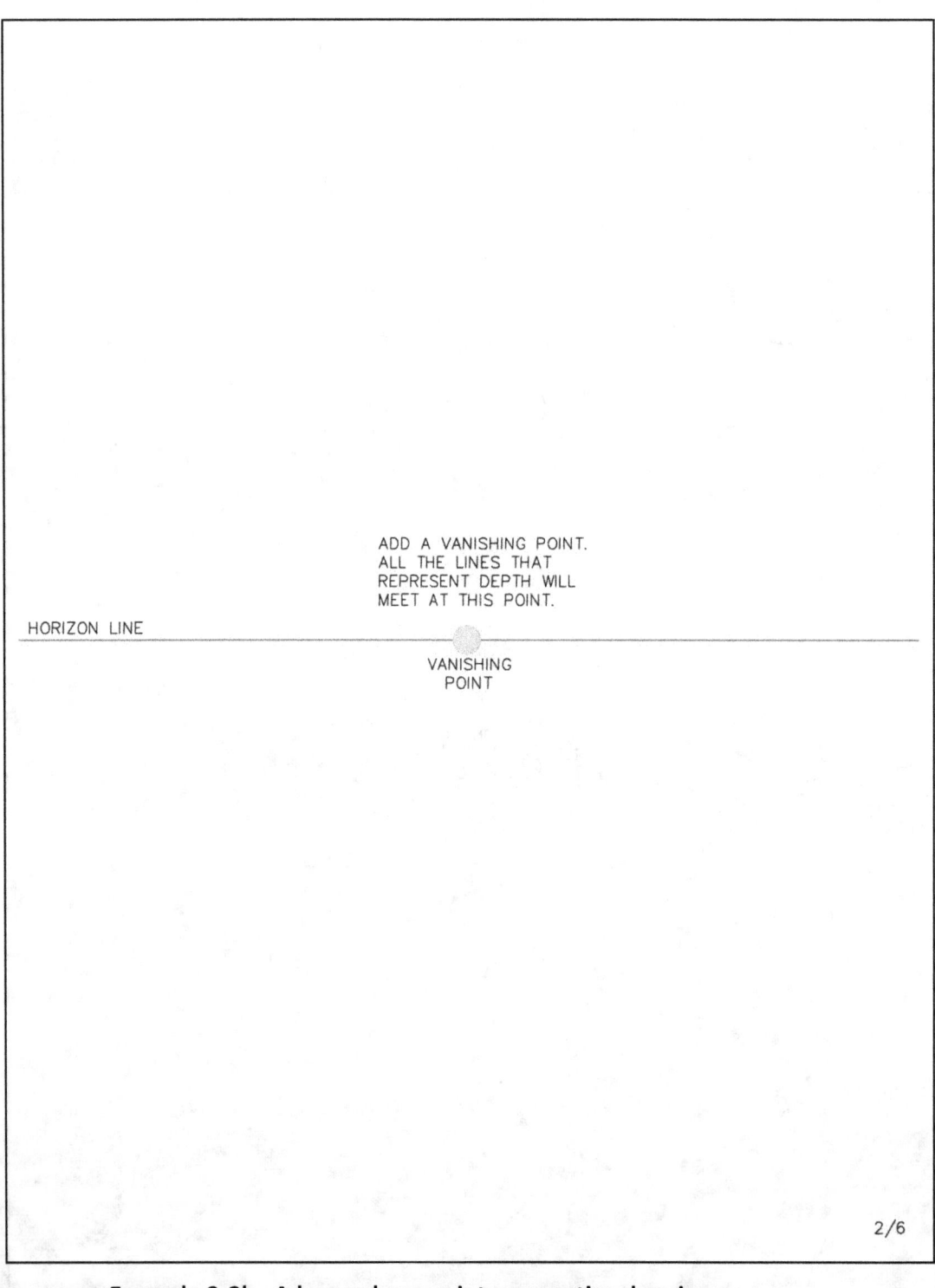

ADD A VANISHING POINT.
ALL THE LINES THAT
REPRESENT DEPTH WILL
MEET AT THIS POINT.

HORIZON LINE

VANISHING
POINT

Example 3-2b. Advanced one point perspective drawing

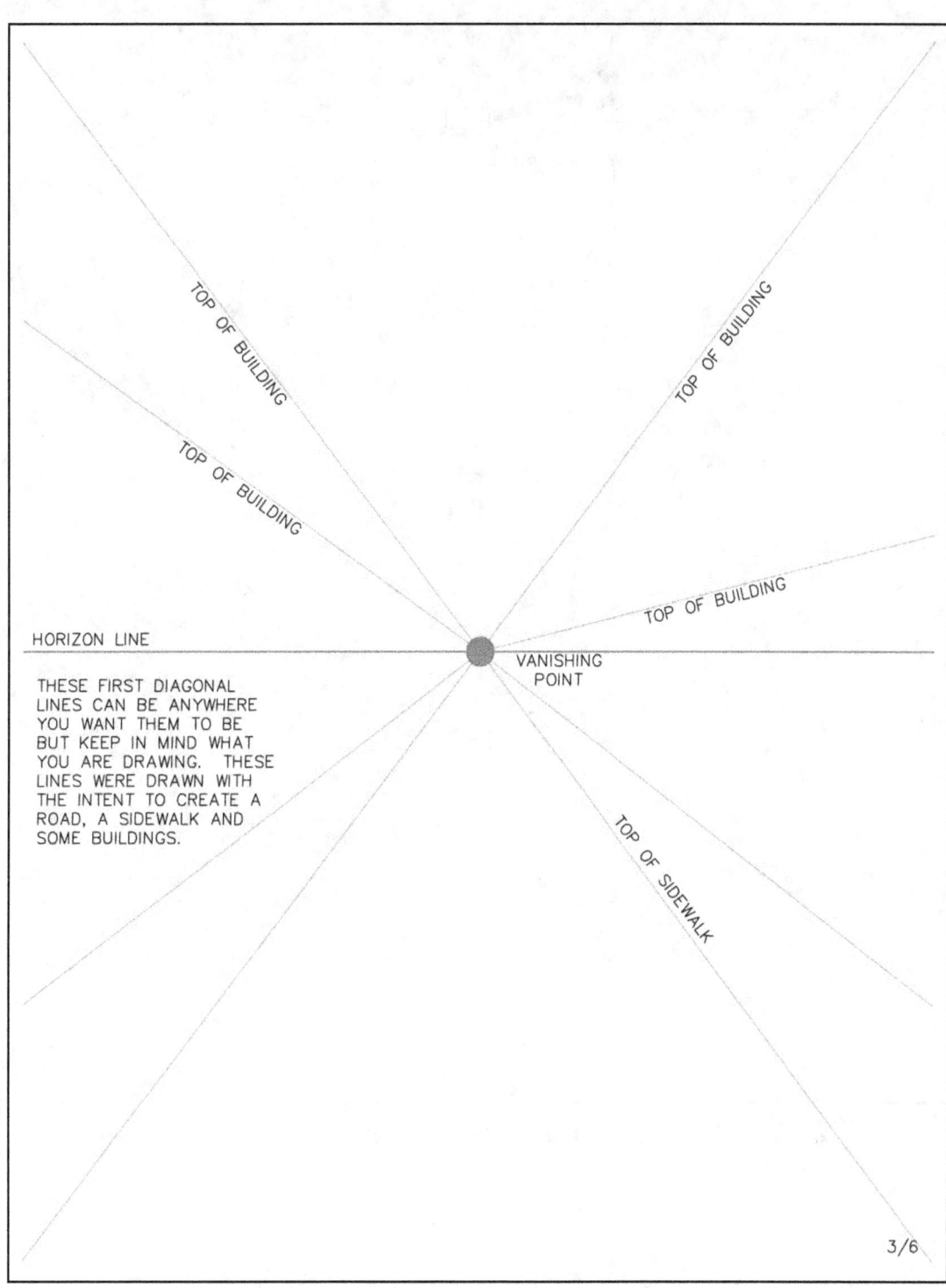

TOP OF BUILDING

TOP OF BUILDING

TOP OF BUILDING

TOP OF BUILDING

HORIZON LINE

VANISHING
POINT

THESE FIRST DIAGONAL
LINES CAN BE ANYWHERE
YOU WANT THEM TO BE
BUT KEEP IN MIND WHAT
YOU ARE DRAWING. THESE
LINES WERE DRAWN WITH
THE INTENT TO CREATE A
ROAD, A SIDEWALK AND
SOME BUILDINGS.

TOP OF SIDEWALK

3/6

Example 3-2c. Advanced one point perspective drawing

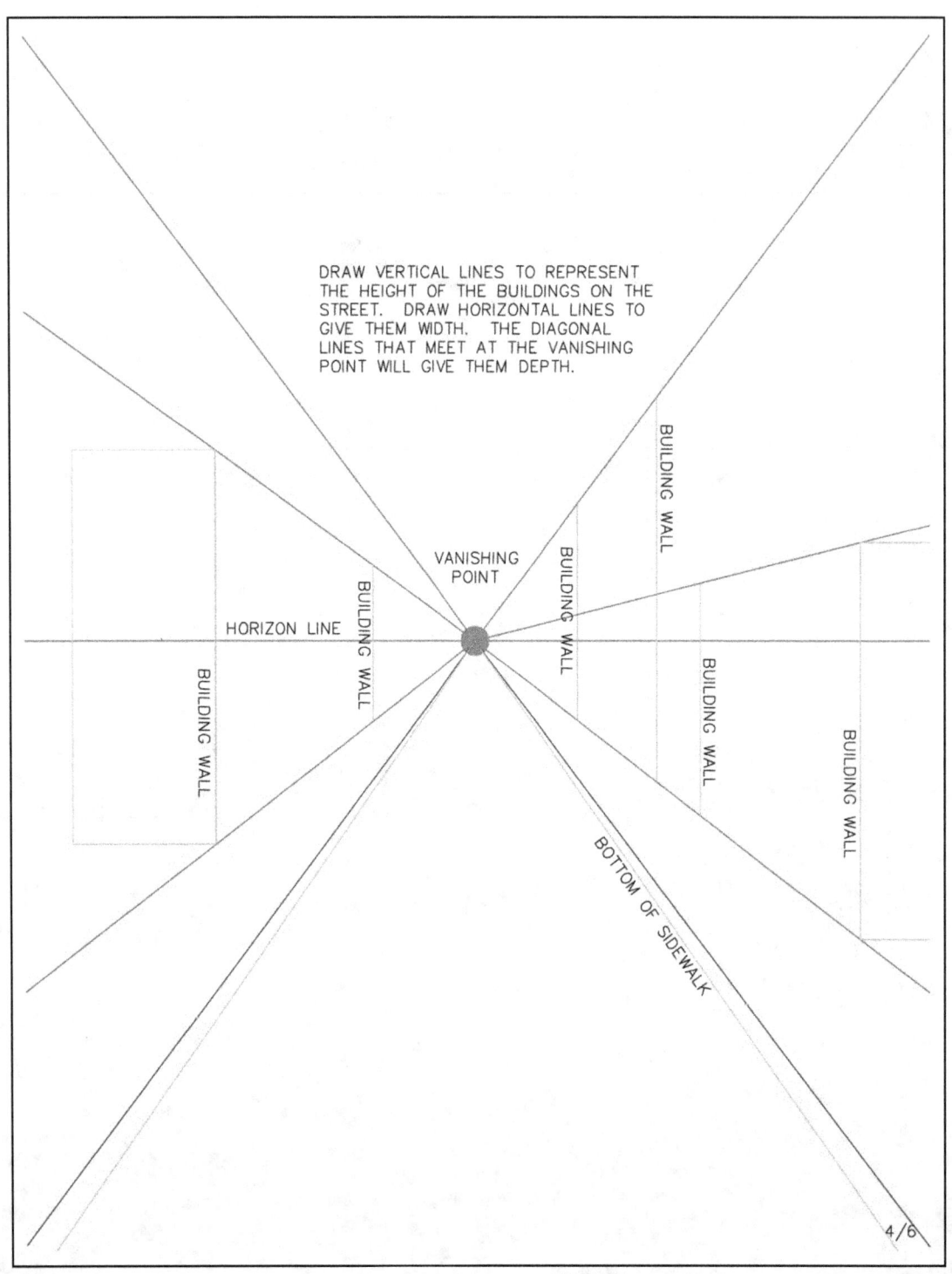

DRAW VERTICAL LINES TO REPRESENT
THE HEIGHT OF THE BUILDINGS ON THE
STREET. DRAW HORIZONTAL LINES TO
GIVE THEM WIDTH. THE DIAGONAL
LINES THAT MEET AT THE VANISHING
POINT WILL GIVE THEM DEPTH.

VANISHING
POINT

HORIZON LINE

BUILDING WALL

BUILDING WALL

BUILDING WALL

BUILDING WALL

BUILDING WALL

BUILDING WALL

BOTTOM OF SIDEWALK

4/6

Example 3-2d. Advanced one point perspective drawing

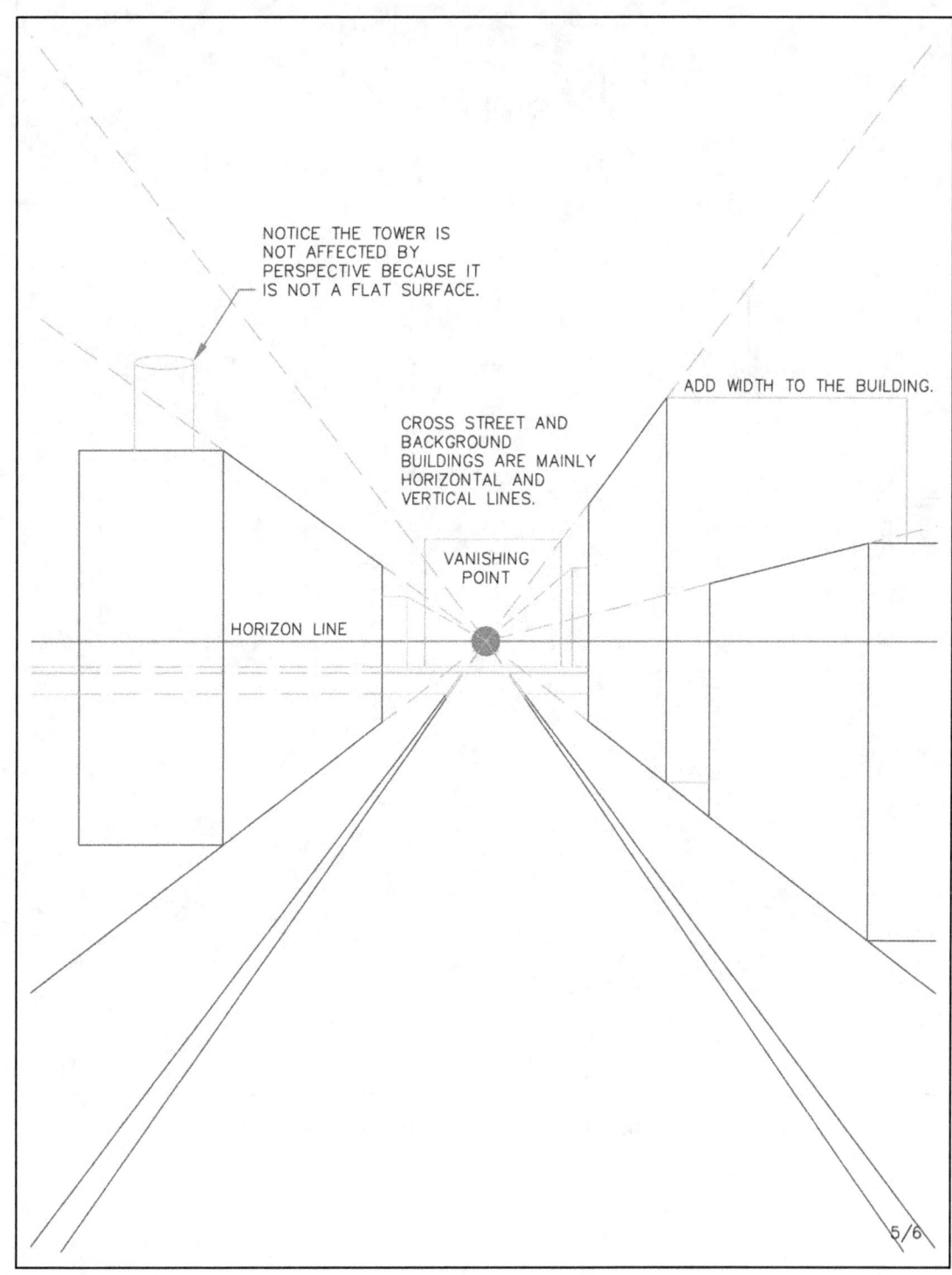

NOTICE THE TOWER IS
NOT AFFECTED BY
PERSPECTIVE BECAUSE IT
IS NOT A FLAT SURFACE.

ADD WIDTH TO THE BUILDING.

CROSS STREET AND
BACKGROUND
BUILDINGS ARE MAINLY
HORIZONTAL AND
VERTICAL LINES.

VANISHING
POINT

HORIZON LINE

5/6

Example 3-2e. Advanced one point perspective drawing

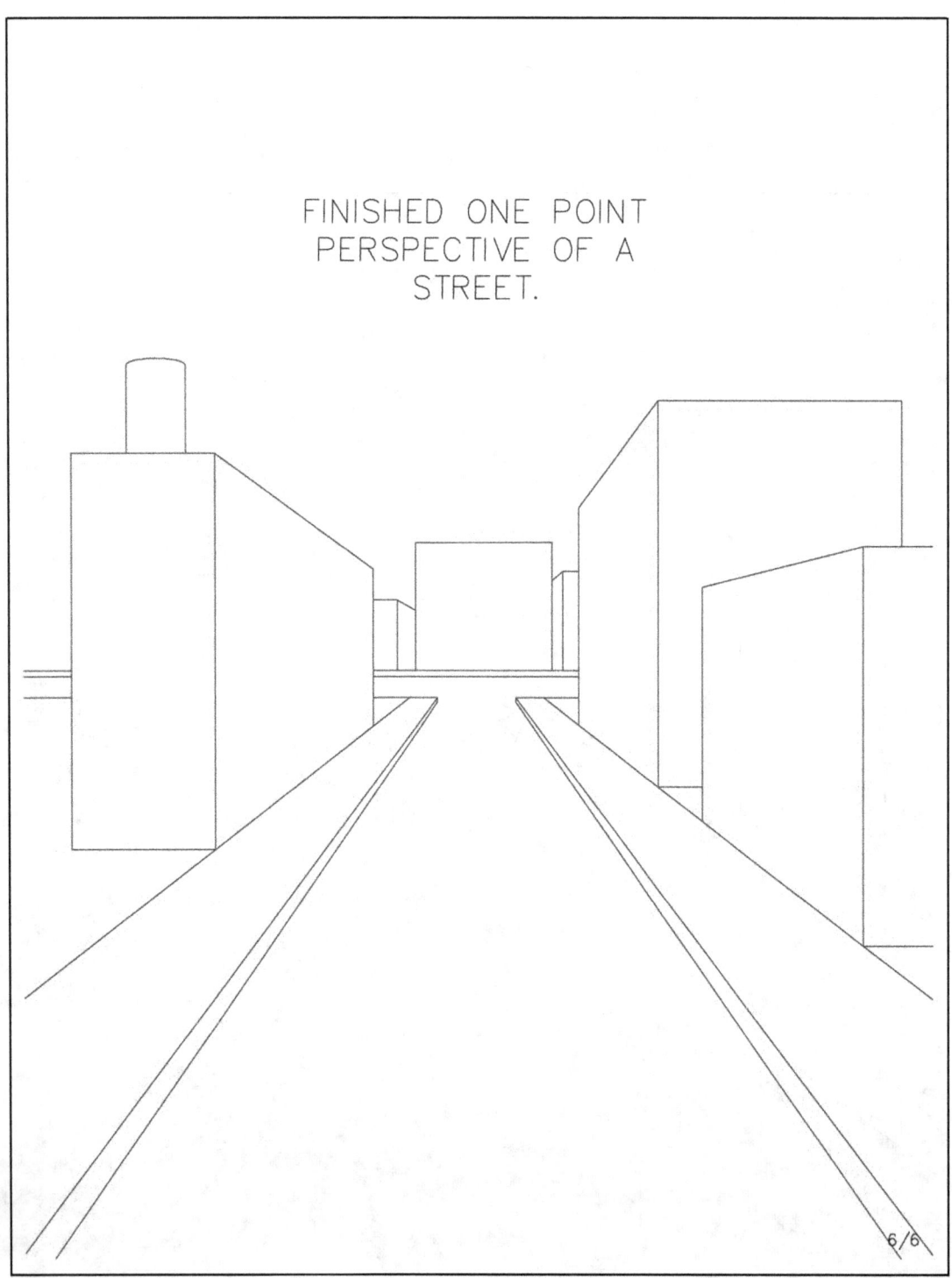

Example 3-2f. Advanced one point perspective drawing

Practice

Draw a one point perspective cube. Follow the steps in Example 3-1. Experiment by drawing cubes at many different locations around the vanishing point.

Draw a one point perspective drawing of a road. Include at least two buildings, each one a different height, and two simple trees that are the same height, one further down the road than the other (hint: the tree further down the road will look smaller even though it's the same height as the one that's closer).

> **Note:** Look at the cubes and buildings in Examples 3-1 and 3-2. Notice how the cubes are made using combinations of shapes. There are squares, rhombuses, and trapezoids placed together so that they look like three dimensional objects on a two dimensional surface. Also notice the tower on the front left building. If we were looking down on the tower from above it would look like a circle, but because we're looking at it from the side, the top of the tower is part of an ellipse. That's why it's important to know the variations of the basic shapes discussed in Volume 2.

Two Point Perspective

A two point perspective is slightly more complicated than a one point perspective. Two point perspective drawings are used when the object you're looking at is not facing you directly. One point perspective is a lot like looking down a single road. Two point perspective is similar to standing on a corner with the ability to look down two roads, one to each side of you.

Each side of the building has its own vanishing point located on the horizon line which again represents the level of the viewer's eye in relation to the objects in the drawing. If the building also has a road on each side, the roads will share the same vanishing point as the side of the building it's on. Height is still represented by vertical lines, but width and depth are combined in the diagonal lines that meet at the vanishing points. Again note that a cylinder or sphere will not change in two point perspective just as it didn't change in the one point perspective.

Two point perspective drawings are generally more interesting to look at than one point perspective drawings. They seem more active because they typically have many diagonal lines and very few horizontal lines but there are still vertical lines which help create a sense of stability.

Follow these steps to make a two point perspective drawing:

1. Draw a horizontal line across the paper, this will be the horizon line and represent the level of the viewer's eye.

2. Draw two dots on the horizon line, one on each side of the paper. These represent the two vanishing points.

3. Draw lines from the vanishing points to the edge of the paper. These lines represent width and depth.

4. Draw vertical lines to represent height.

5. Circles, cones and cylinders are not affected by this perspective.

Look at the examples that follow. Example 3-3 demonstrates step by step how to draw two point perspective rectangular solids from many angles. Notice how the face closest to a vanishing point will look narrower compared to the other faces. Example 3-4 demonstrates step by step how to draw a two point perspective drawing of a street. Notice that the tower on top of the building looks the same as the tower in the one point perspective drawing of Example 3-2.

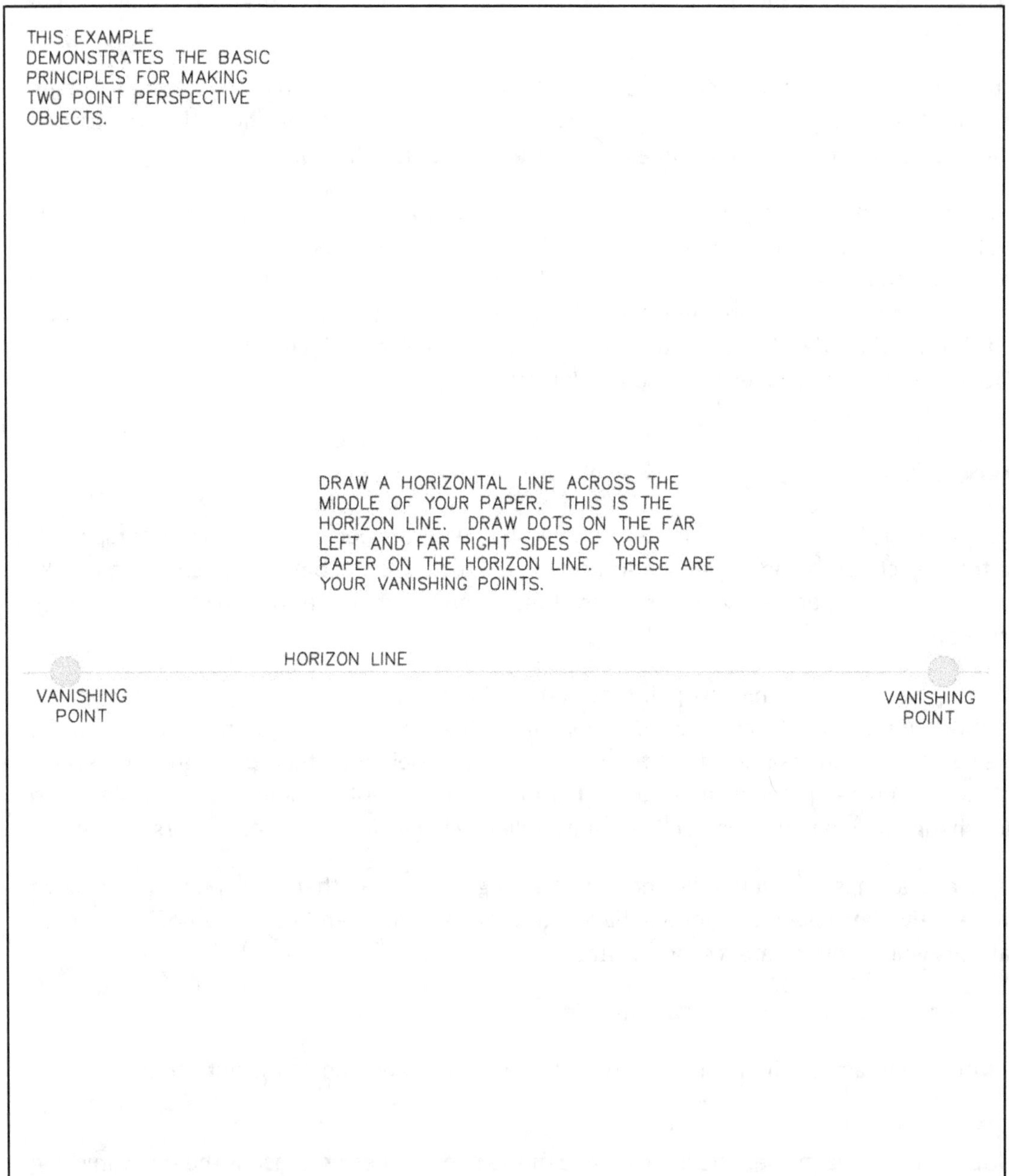

THIS EXAMPLE
DEMONSTRATES THE BASIC
PRINCIPLES FOR MAKING
TWO POINT PERSPECTIVE
OBJECTS.

DRAW A HORIZONTAL LINE ACROSS THE
MIDDLE OF YOUR PAPER. THIS IS THE
HORIZON LINE. DRAW DOTS ON THE FAR
LEFT AND FAR RIGHT SIDES OF YOUR
PAPER ON THE HORIZON LINE. THESE ARE
YOUR VANISHING POINTS.

HORIZON LINE

VANISHING
POINT

VANISHING
POINT

1/6

Example 3-3a. Basic two point perspective drawing

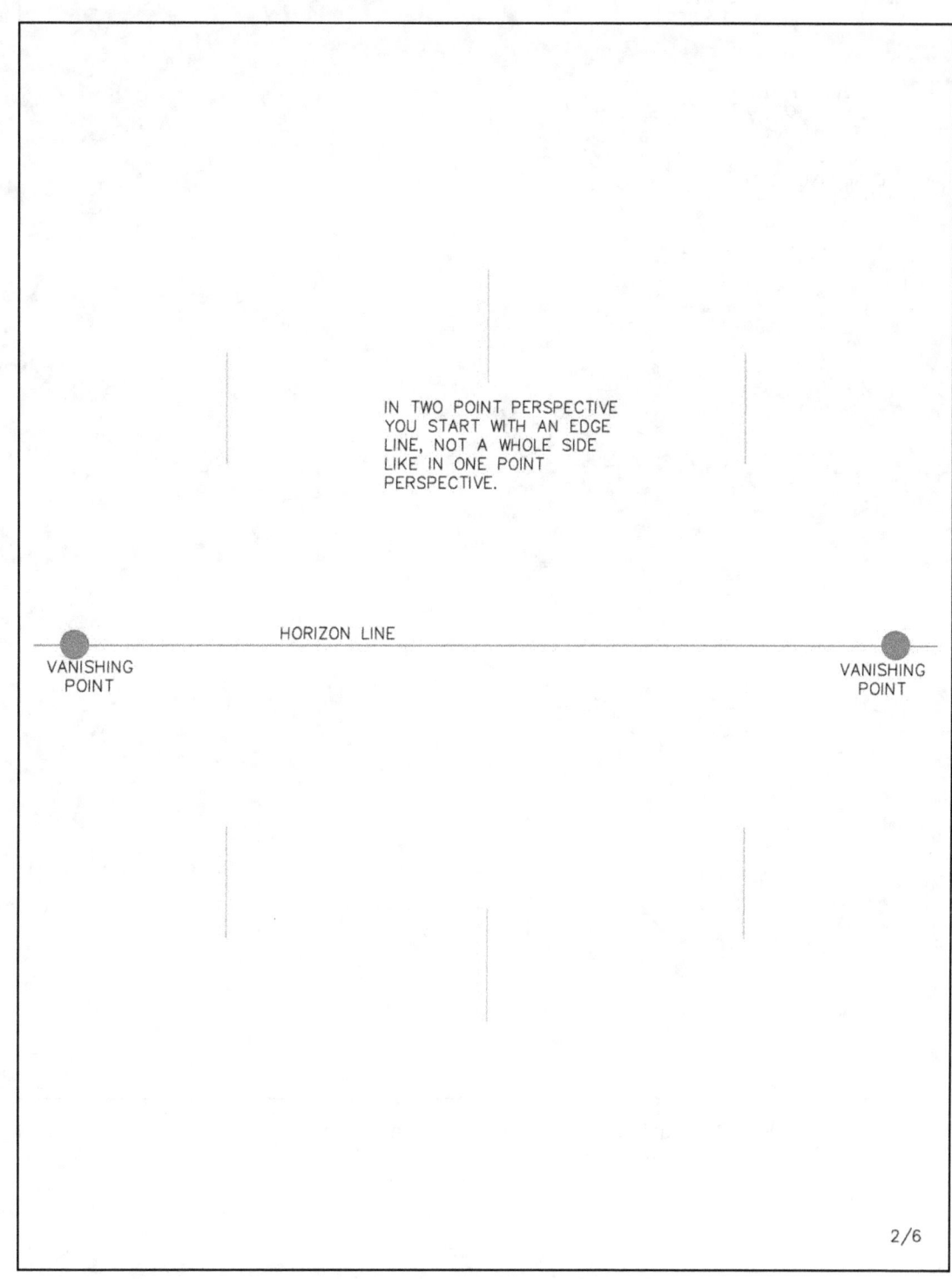

Example 3-3b. Basic two point perspective drawing

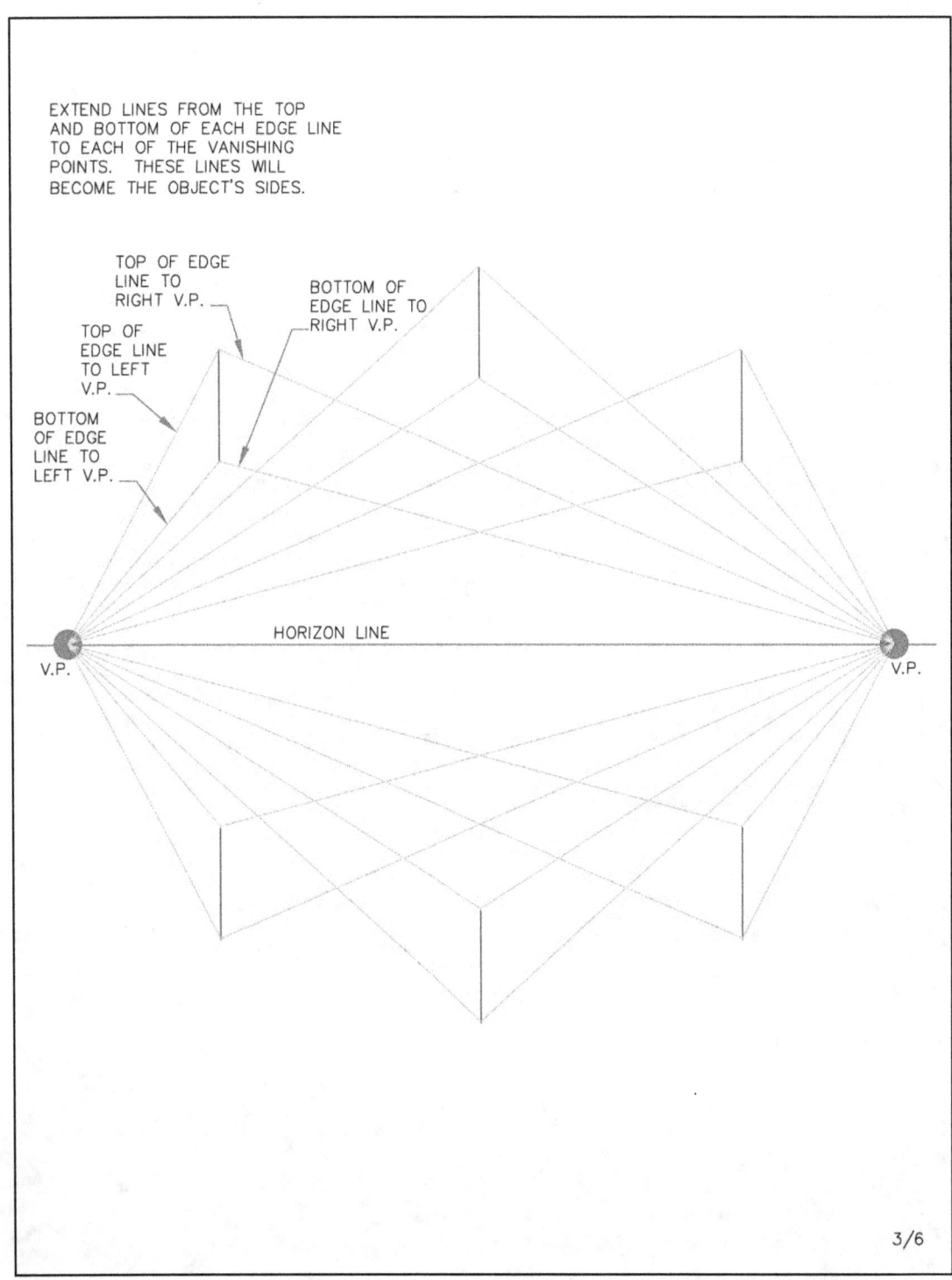

EXTEND LINES FROM THE TOP
AND BOTTOM OF EACH EDGE LINE
TO EACH OF THE VANISHING
POINTS. THESE LINES WILL
BECOME THE OBJECT'S SIDES.

TOP OF EDGE
LINE TO
RIGHT V.P.

BOTTOM OF
EDGE LINE TO
RIGHT V.P.

TOP OF
EDGE LINE
TO LEFT
V.P.

BOTTOM
OF EDGE
LINE TO
LEFT V.P.

HORIZON LINE

V.P.

V.P.

3/6

Example 3-3c. Basic two point perspective drawing

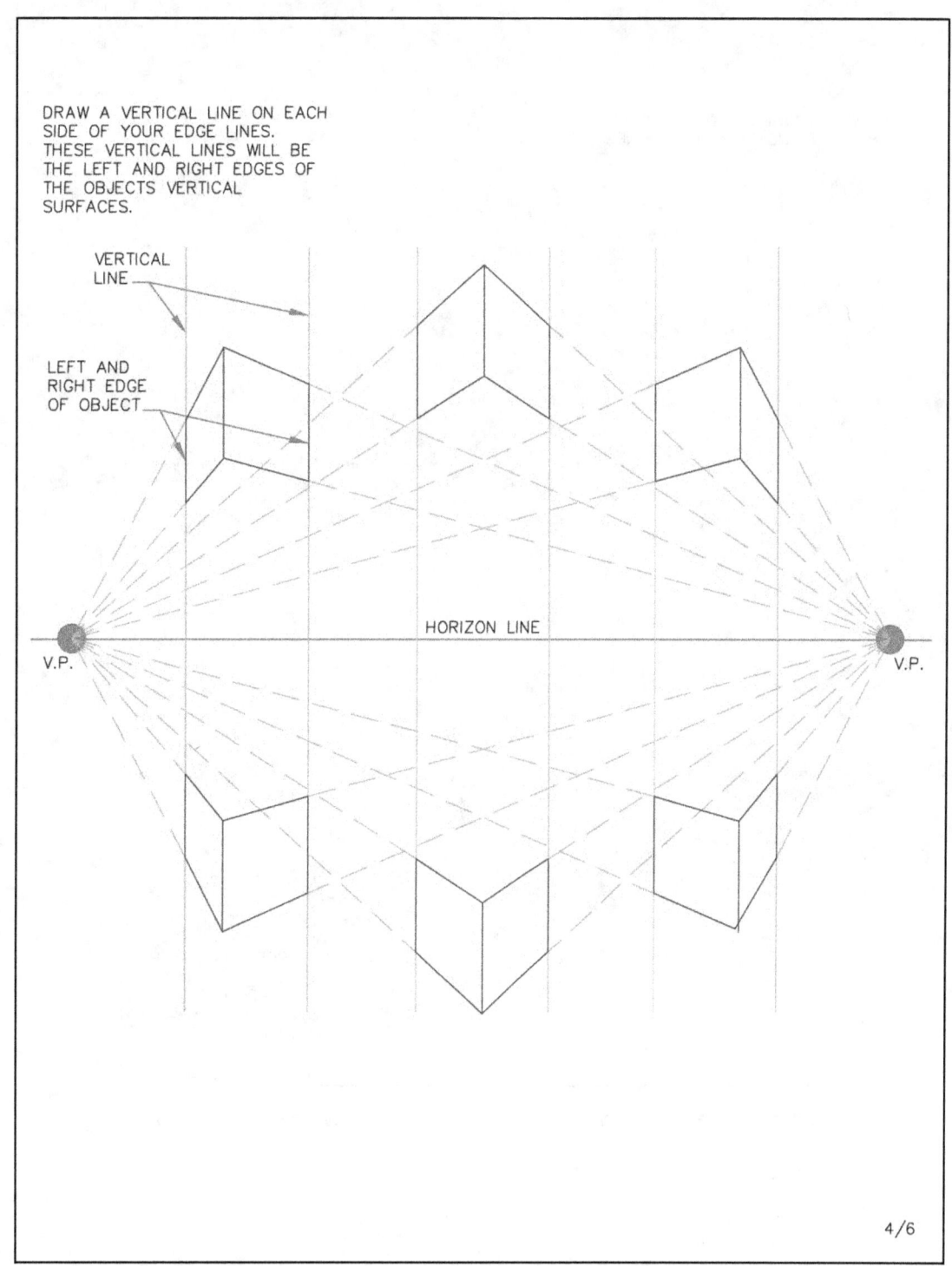

DRAW A VERTICAL LINE ON EACH
SIDE OF YOUR EDGE LINES.
THESE VERTICAL LINES WILL BE
THE LEFT AND RIGHT EDGES OF
THE OBJECTS VERTICAL
SURFACES.

VERTICAL
LINE

LEFT AND
RIGHT EDGE
OF OBJECT

HORIZON LINE

V.P.

V.P.

4/6

Example 3-3d. Basic two point perspective drawing

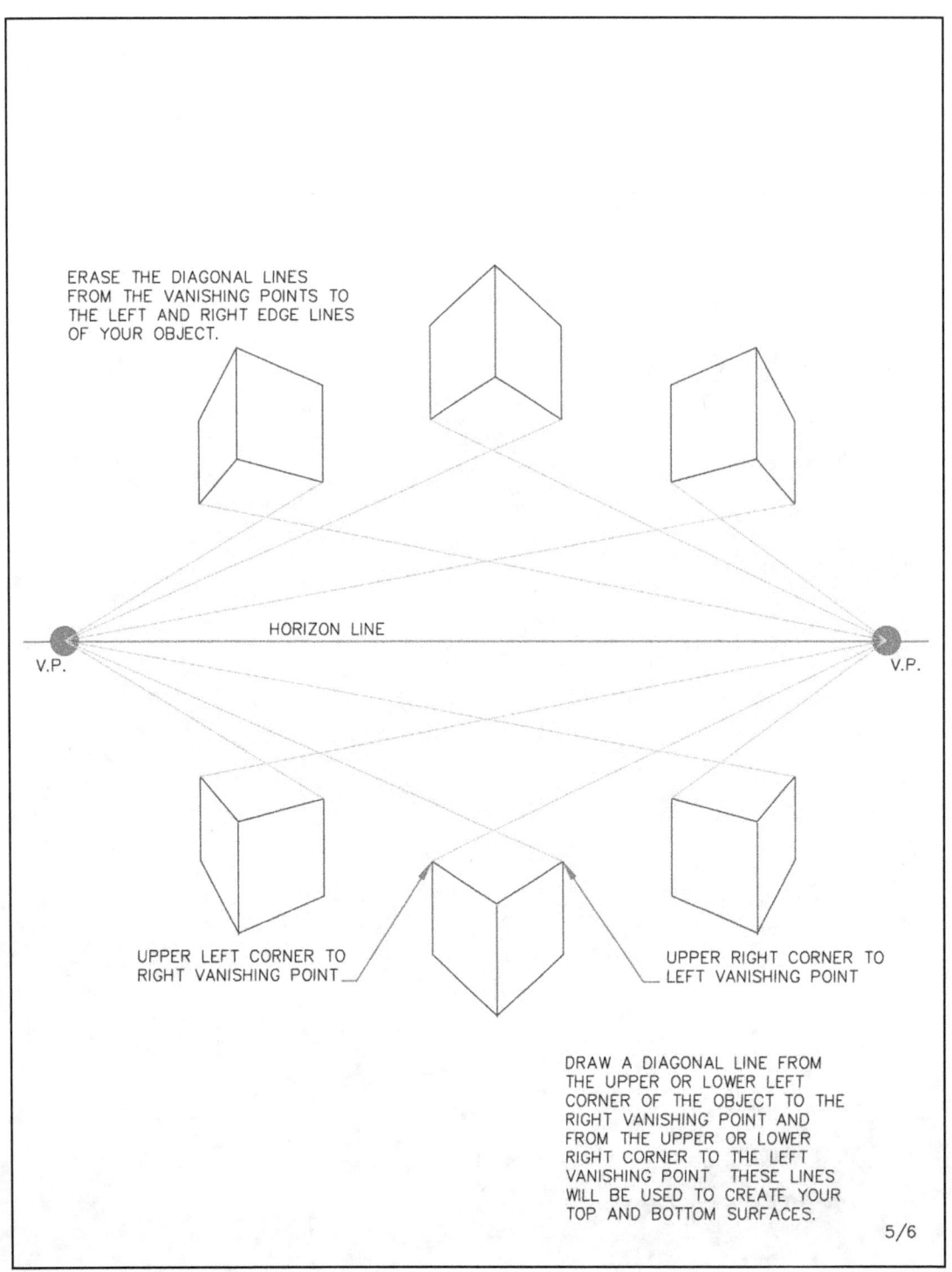

ERASE THE DIAGONAL LINES
FROM THE VANISHING POINTS TO
THE LEFT AND RIGHT EDGE LINES
OF YOUR OBJECT.

HORIZON LINE

V.P.

V.P.

UPPER LEFT CORNER TO
RIGHT VANISHING POINT

UPPER RIGHT CORNER TO
LEFT VANISHING POINT

DRAW A DIAGONAL LINE FROM
THE UPPER OR LOWER LEFT
CORNER OF THE OBJECT TO THE
RIGHT VANISHING POINT AND
FROM THE UPPER OR LOWER
RIGHT CORNER TO THE LEFT
VANISHING POINT THESE LINES
WILL BE USED TO CREATE YOUR
TOP AND BOTTOM SURFACES.

5/6

Example 3-3e. Basic two point perspective drawing

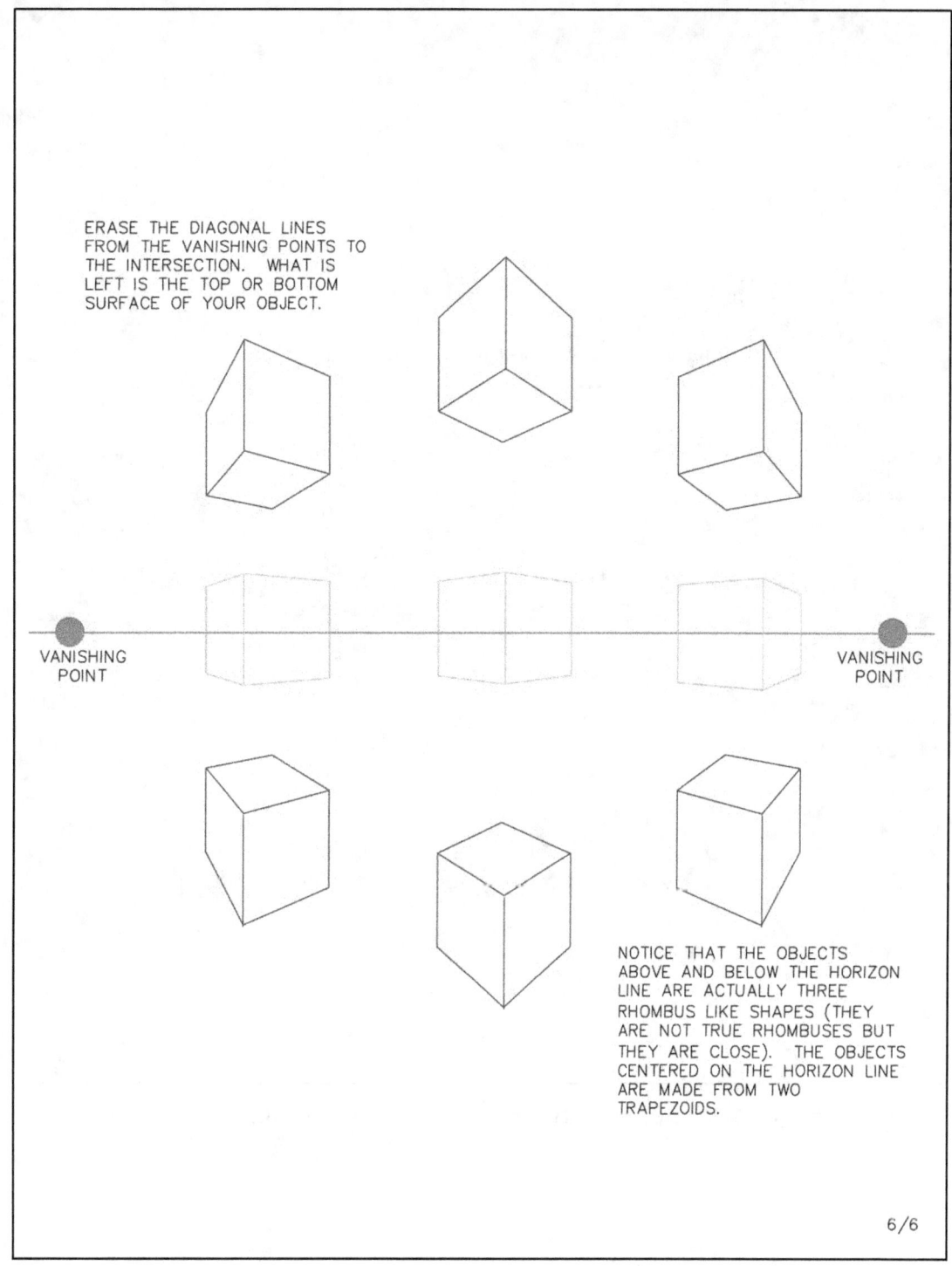

ERASE THE DIAGONAL LINES
FROM THE VANISHING POINTS TO
THE INTERSECTION. WHAT IS
LEFT IS THE TOP OR BOTTOM
SURFACE OF YOUR OBJECT.

VANISHING
POINT

VANISHING
POINT

NOTICE THAT THE OBJECTS
ABOVE AND BELOW THE HORIZON
LINE ARE ACTUALLY THREE
RHOMBUS LIKE SHAPES (THEY
ARE NOT TRUE RHOMBUSES BUT
THEY ARE CLOSE). THE OBJECTS
CENTERED ON THE HORIZON LINE
ARE MADE FROM TWO
TRAPEZOIDS.

6/6

Example 3-3f. Basic two point perspective drawing

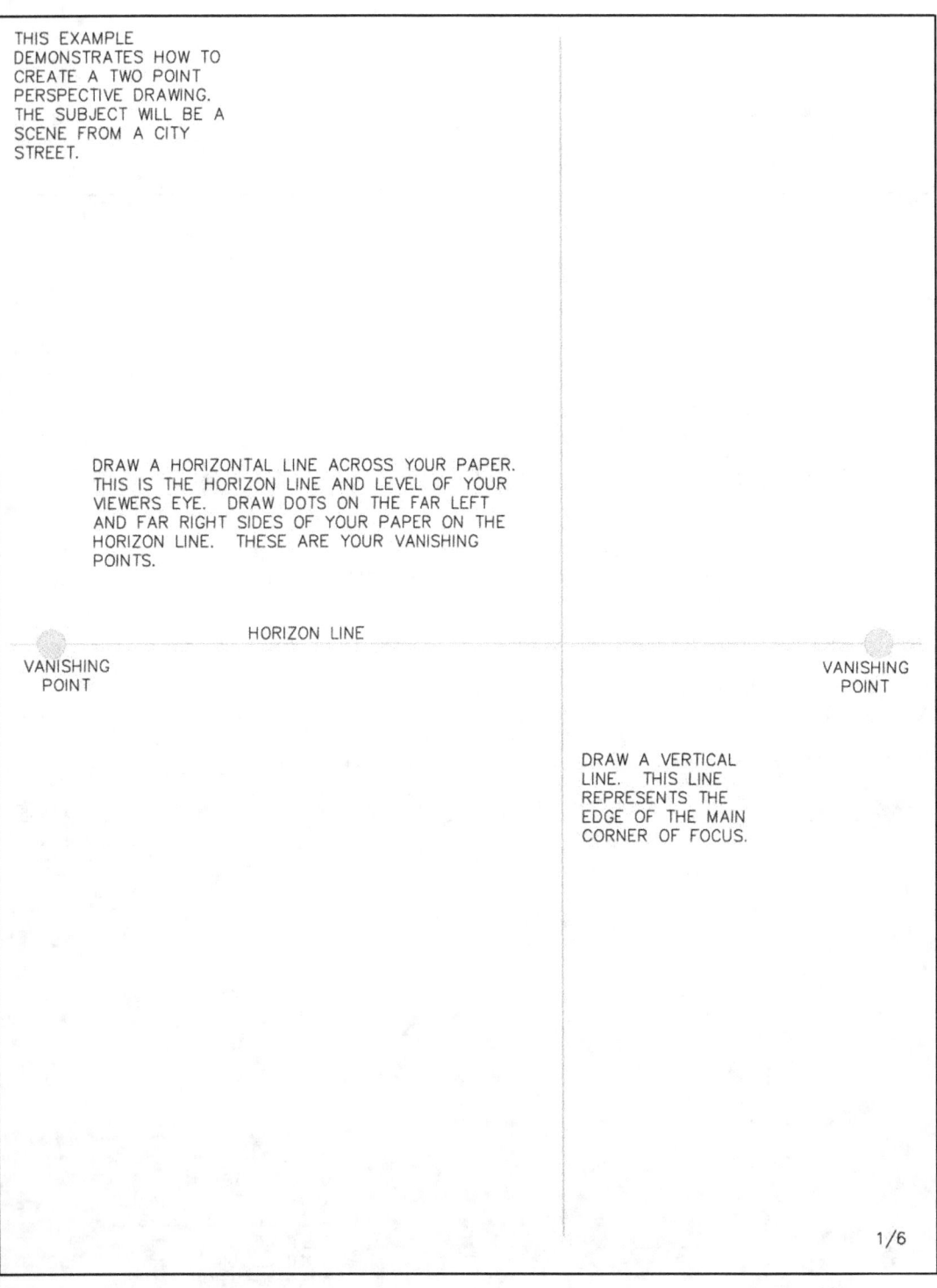

THIS EXAMPLE
DEMONSTRATES HOW TO
CREATE A TWO POINT
PERSPECTIVE DRAWING.
THE SUBJECT WILL BE A
SCENE FROM A CITY
STREET.

DRAW A HORIZONTAL LINE ACROSS YOUR PAPER.
THIS IS THE HORIZON LINE AND LEVEL OF YOUR
VIEWERS EYE. DRAW DOTS ON THE FAR LEFT
AND FAR RIGHT SIDES OF YOUR PAPER ON THE
HORIZON LINE. THESE ARE YOUR VANISHING
POINTS.

HORIZON LINE

VANISHING
POINT

VANISHING
POINT

DRAW A VERTICAL
LINE. THIS LINE
REPRESENTS THE
EDGE OF THE MAIN
CORNER OF FOCUS.

1/6

Example 3-4a. Advanced two point perspective drawing

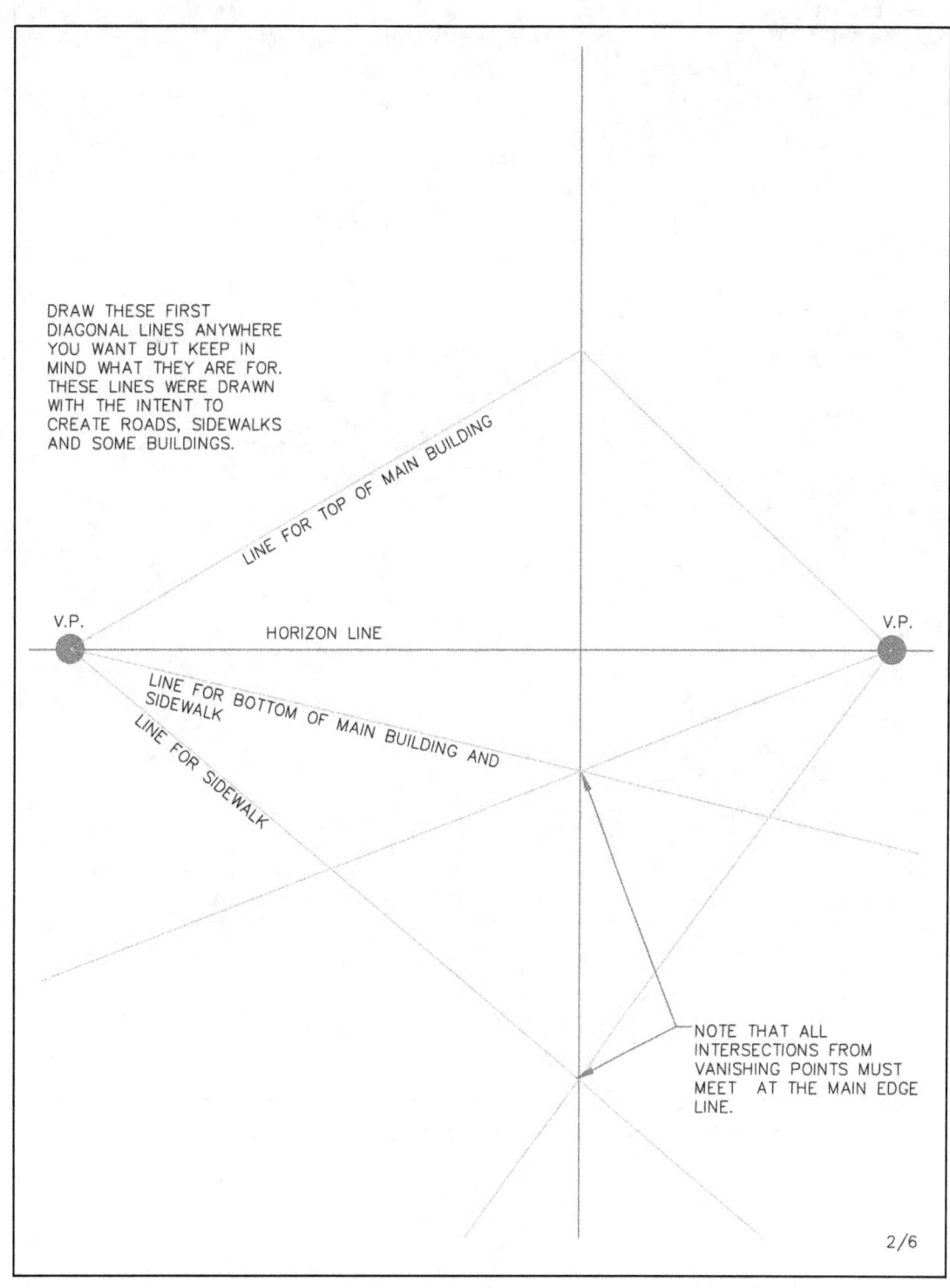

DRAW THESE FIRST
DIAGONAL LINES ANYWHERE
YOU WANT BUT KEEP IN
MIND WHAT THEY ARE FOR.
THESE LINES WERE DRAWN
WITH THE INTENT TO
CREATE ROADS, SIDEWALKS
AND SOME BUILDINGS.

LINE FOR TOP OF MAIN BUILDING

V.P.

HORIZON LINE

V.P.

LINE FOR BOTTOM OF MAIN BUILDING AND
SIDEWALK

LINE FOR SIDEWALK

NOTE THAT ALL
INTERSECTIONS FROM
VANISHING POINTS MUST
MEET AT THE MAIN EDGE
LINE.

2/6

Example 3-4b. Advanced two point perspective drawing

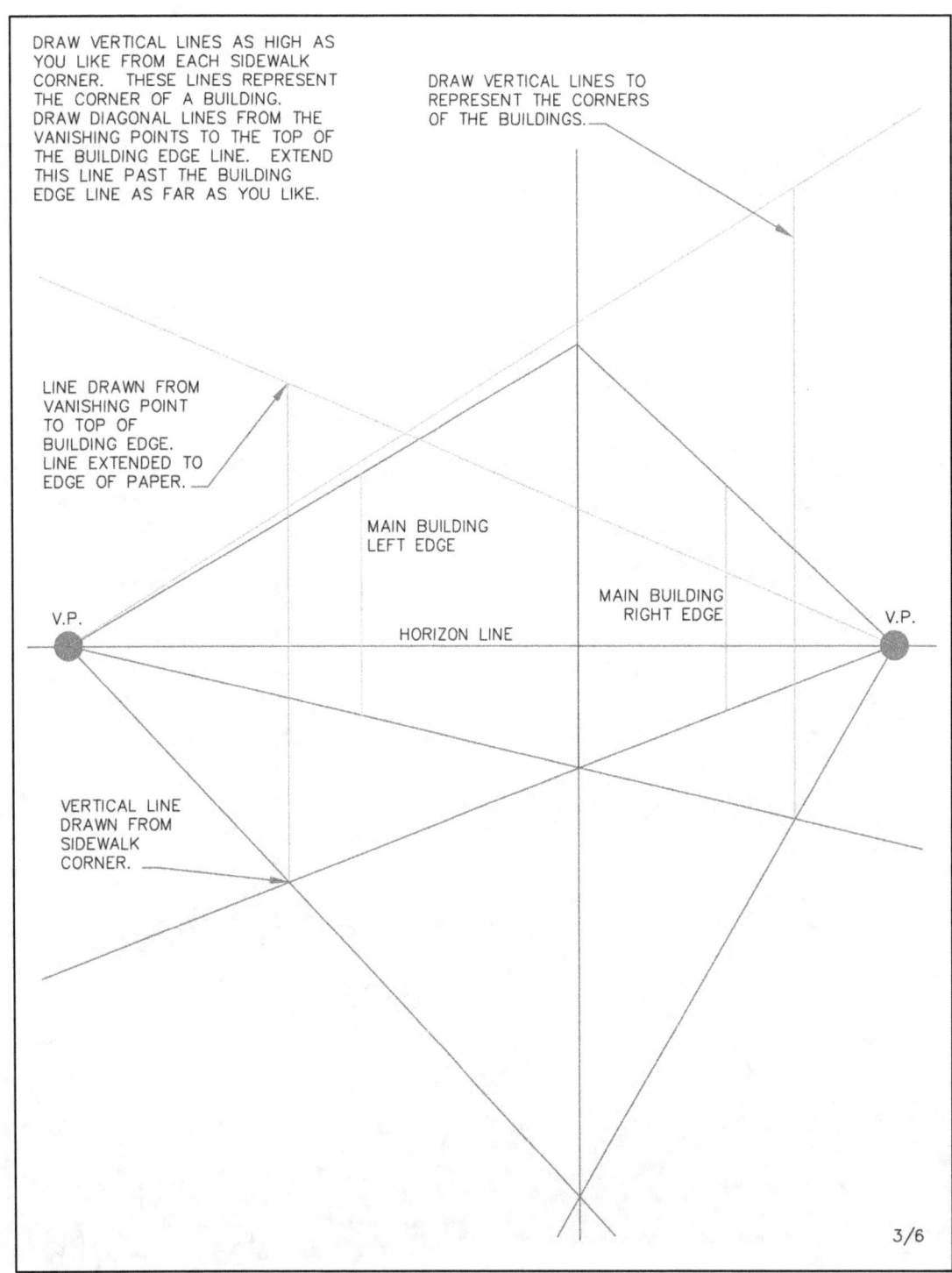

DRAW VERTICAL LINES AS HIGH AS
YOU LIKE FROM EACH SIDEWALK
CORNER.   THESE LINES REPRESENT
THE CORNER OF A BUILDING.
DRAW DIAGONAL LINES FROM THE
VANISHING POINTS TO THE TOP OF
THE BUILDING EDGE LINE.   EXTEND
THIS LINE PAST THE BUILDING
EDGE LINE AS FAR AS YOU LIKE.

DRAW VERTICAL LINES TO
REPRESENT THE CORNERS
OF THE BUILDINGS.

LINE DRAWN FROM
VANISHING POINT
TO TOP OF
BUILDING EDGE.
LINE EXTENDED TO
EDGE OF PAPER.

MAIN BUILDING
LEFT EDGE

MAIN BUILDING
RIGHT EDGE

V.P.

HORIZON LINE

V.P.

VERTICAL LINE
DRAWN FROM
SIDEWALK
CORNER.

3/6

Example 3-4c. Advanced two point perspective drawing

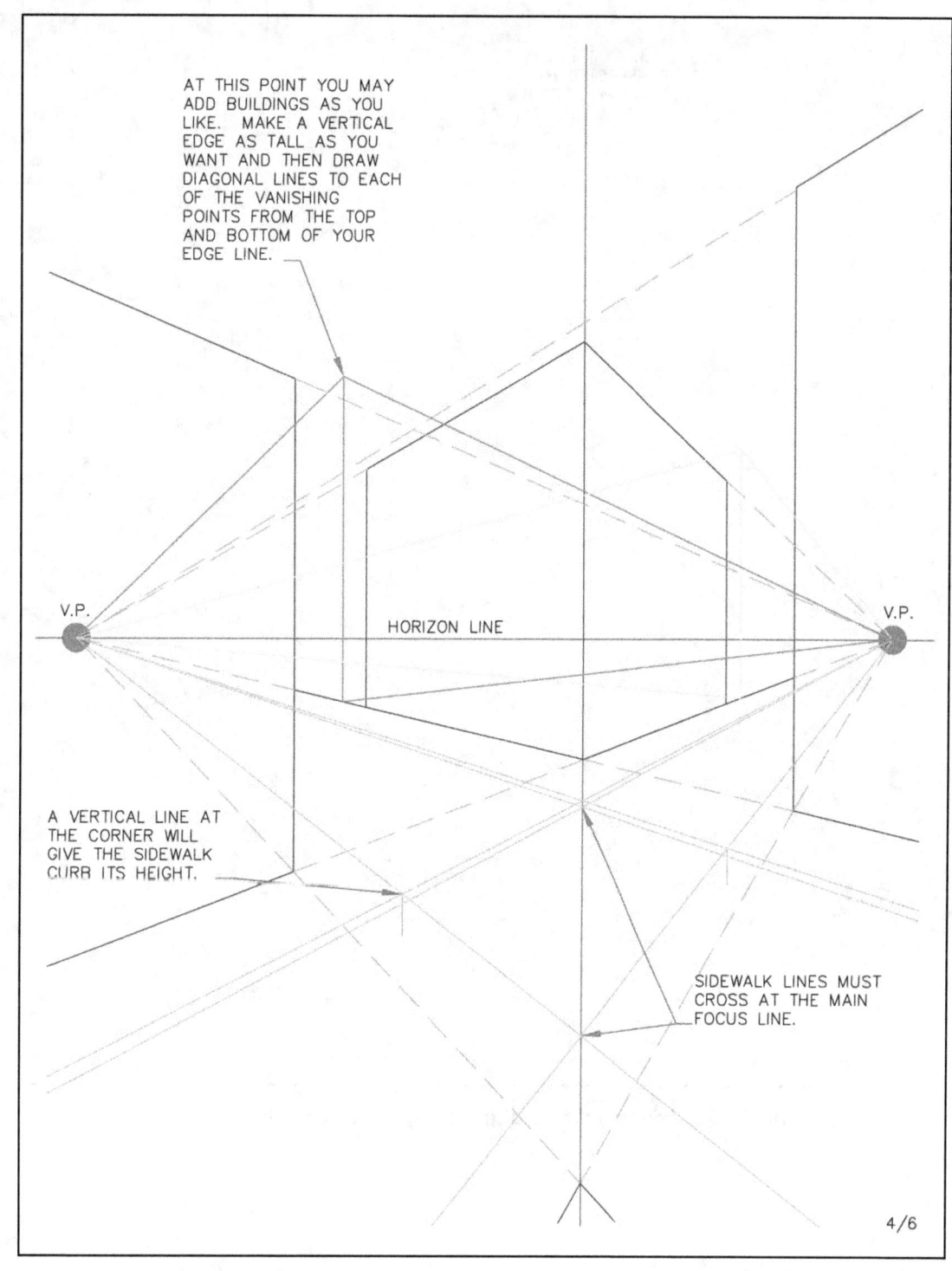

AT THIS POINT YOU MAY
ADD BUILDINGS AS YOU
LIKE. MAKE A VERTICAL
EDGE AS TALL AS YOU
WANT AND THEN DRAW
DIAGONAL LINES TO EACH
OF THE VANISHING
POINTS FROM THE TOP
AND BOTTOM OF YOUR
EDGE LINE.

V.P.

HORIZON LINE

V.P.

A VERTICAL LINE AT
THE CORNER WILL
GIVE THE SIDEWALK
CURB ITS HEIGHT.

SIDEWALK LINES MUST
CROSS AT THE MAIN
FOCUS LINE.

4/6

Example 3-4d. Advanced two point perspective drawing

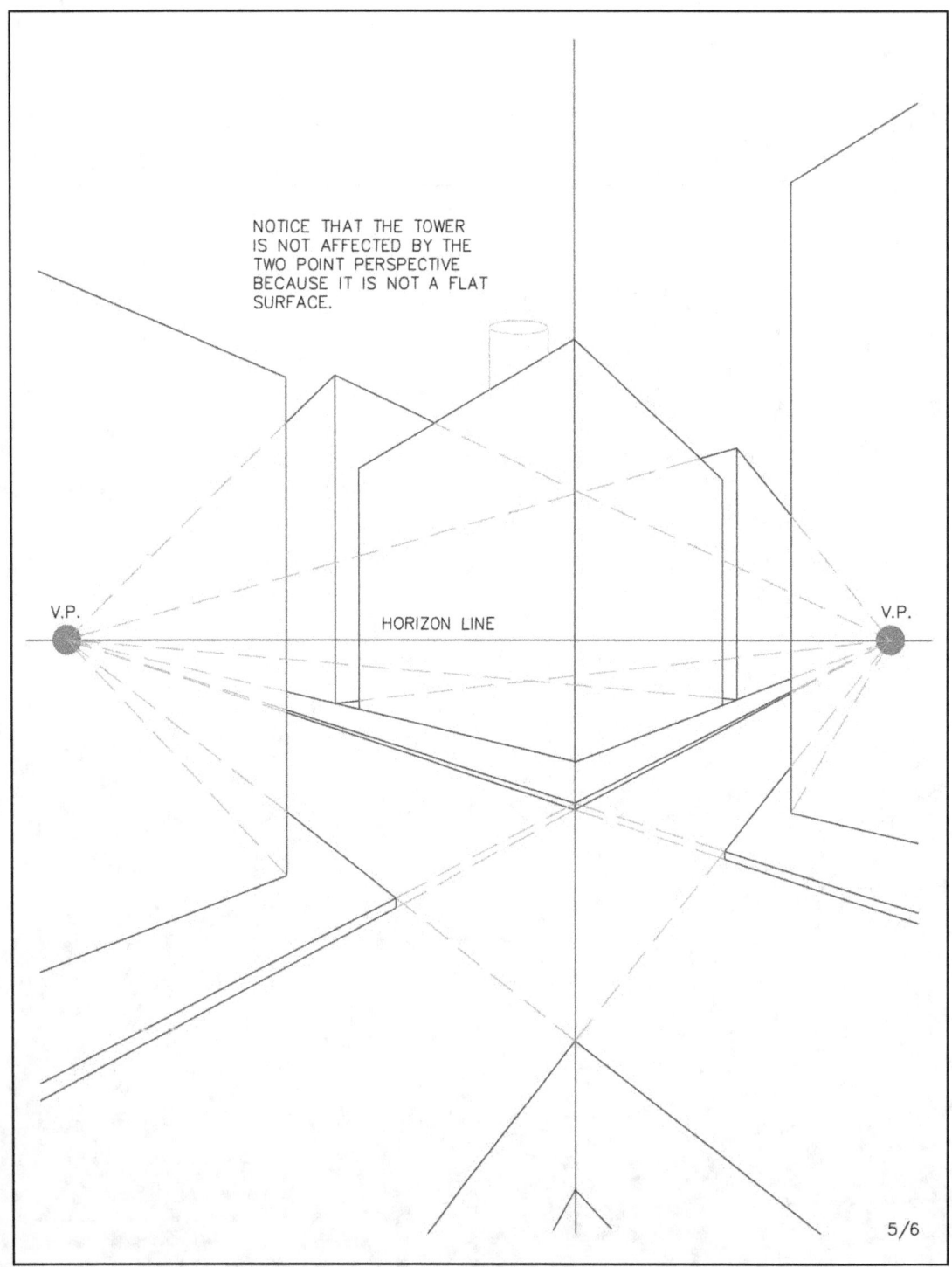

NOTICE THAT THE TOWER
IS NOT AFFECTED BY THE
TWO POINT PERSPECTIVE
BECAUSE IT IS NOT A FLAT
SURFACE.

V.P.

V.P.

HORIZON LINE

5/6

Example 3-4e. Advanced two point perspective drawing

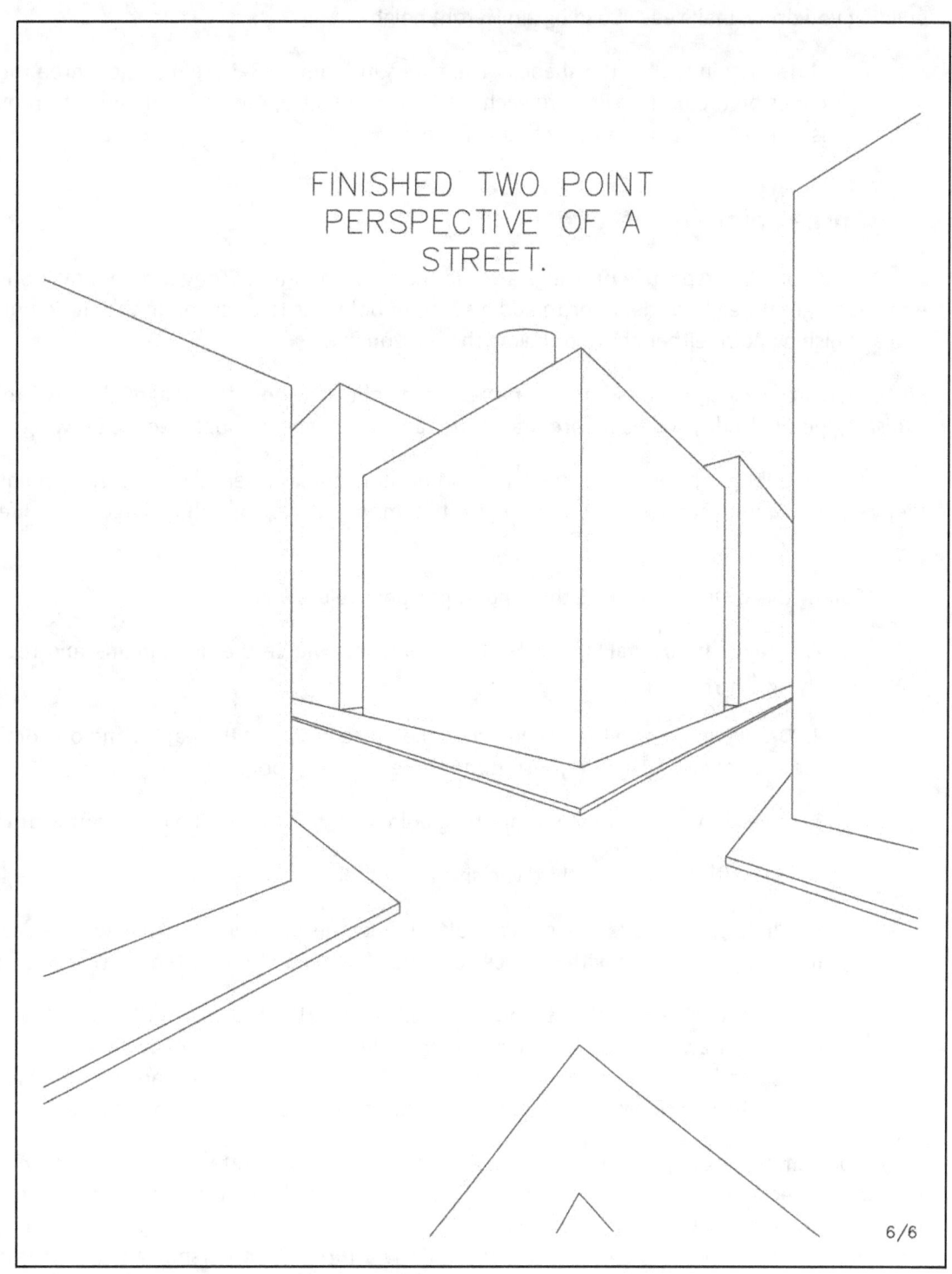

FINISHED TWO POINT
PERSPECTIVE OF A
STREET.

6/6

Example 3-4f. Advanced two point perspective drawing

Practice

Draw two point perspective cubes. Follow the steps in Example 3-3. Experiment by drawing cubes at many different locations.

Draw a two point perspective drawing. Draw a three story building with at least six windows, two windows on each floor (it doesn't matter which side of the building the windows are on). Draw two trees that are the same height, place them both on the same side of the building. Finish by drawing a building on each side of the first building you drew, make each building a different height.

> **Note:** Again look at the shapes. The cubes in Example 3-3 are made of three rhombus-like shapes; the cubes on the horizon line are each made using two trapezoids. Sketching out rhombuses and trapezoids is a very quick and easy way to draw cubes.

Three Point Perspective

Three point perspective drawings are the most complicated. They are generally only used when trying to emphasize great height or depth or to add a sense of boldness to a scene. In the three point perspective you will add a vanishing point either above or below the horizon line.

Instead of using vertical lines to represent height, you now use diagonal lines projecting from the third vanishing point. Width and depth are drawn the same as a two point perspective drawing.

Because there are only diagonal lines and no horizontal or vertical lines, three point perspective drawings feel very bold and dynamic. They tend to give the impression of something larger than life, high energy, or even scary.

Follow these steps to make a three point perspective drawing:

> **1.** Draw a horizontal line across the paper, this will be the horizon line and represent the level of the viewer's eye.
>
> **2.** Draw two dots on the horizon line, one on each side of the paper, and one dot either above or below the horizon line. These represent the three vanishing points.
>
> **3.** Lines drawn from the two vanishing points on the horizon line represent width and depth.
>
> **4.** Lines drawn from the third vanishing point (either above or below the horizon line) represent height.
>
> **5.** Circles, cones, and cylinders are affected by this perspective. They will be skewed and require a grid to draw properly but with practice you'll be able to add them without using a full grid.
>
> **Note:** The closer an object is to a vanishing point the more distorted it will look because the angle of the line drawn from that vanishing point increases. You can avoid extreme angles by placing the vanishing points off the paper's surface. To do this, tape the paper to a table or smooth board and locate the vanishing points on the table above (or below) and to each side of the paper.

Look at the examples that follow. Example 3-5 demonstrates step by step how to draw three point perspective rectangular solids from many angles. Notice how the blocks start to look distorted on the far left and right. Notice also that the blocks drawn above and below the upper and lower vanishing points look very tall. Example 3-6 demonstrates step by step how to draw a three point perspective drawing of a street. Notice how these buildings look very tall, and how it makes the viewer feel small.

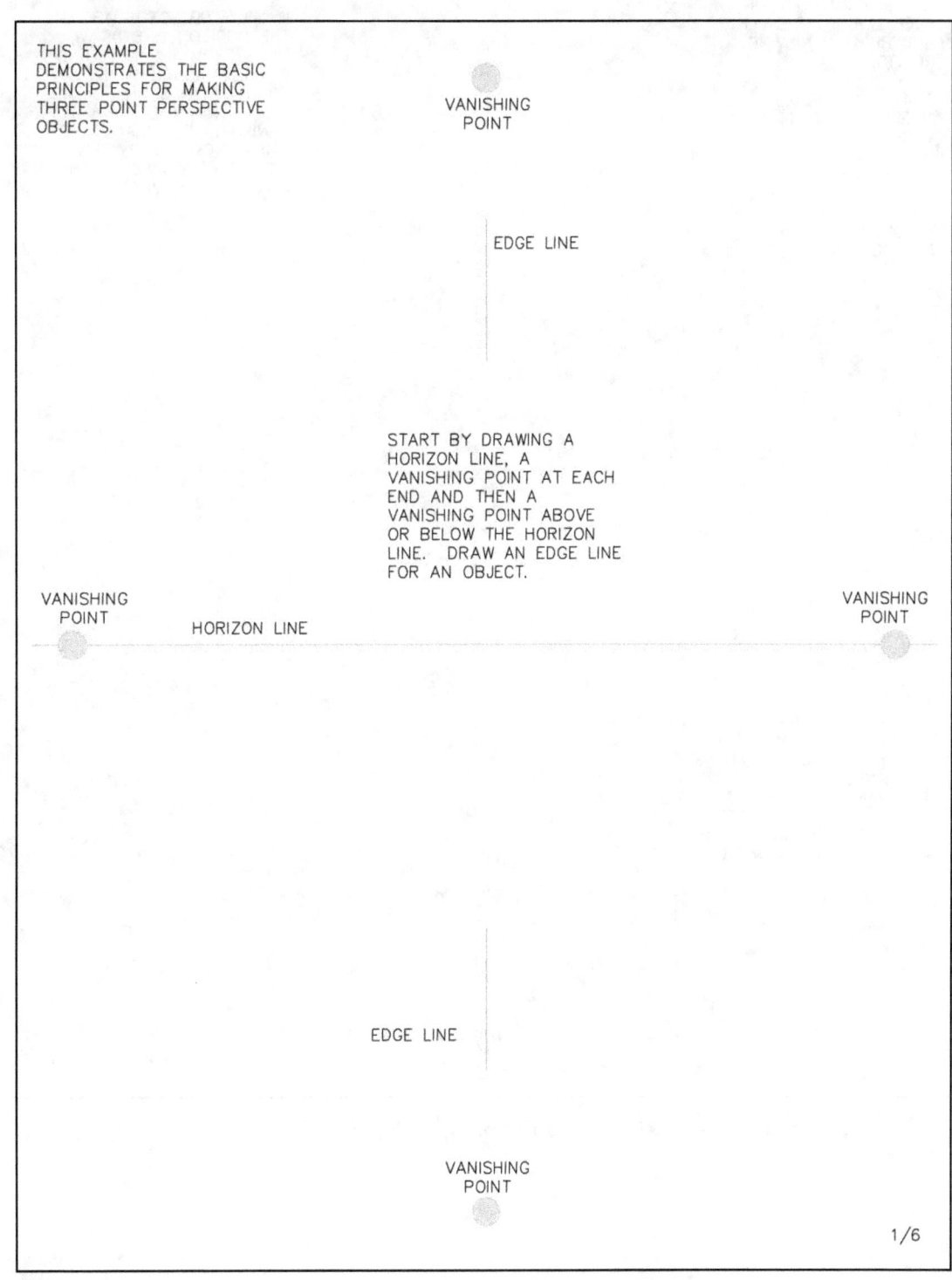

THIS EXAMPLE
DEMONSTRATES THE BASIC
PRINCIPLES FOR MAKING
THREE POINT PERSPECTIVE
OBJECTS.

VANISHING
POINT

EDGE LINE

START BY DRAWING A
HORIZON LINE, A
VANISHING POINT AT EACH
END AND THEN A
VANISHING POINT ABOVE
OR BELOW THE HORIZON
LINE. DRAW AN EDGE LINE
FOR AN OBJECT.

VANISHING
POINT

VANISHING
POINT

HORIZON LINE

EDGE LINE

VANISHING
POINT

1/6

Example 3-5a. Basic three point perspective drawing

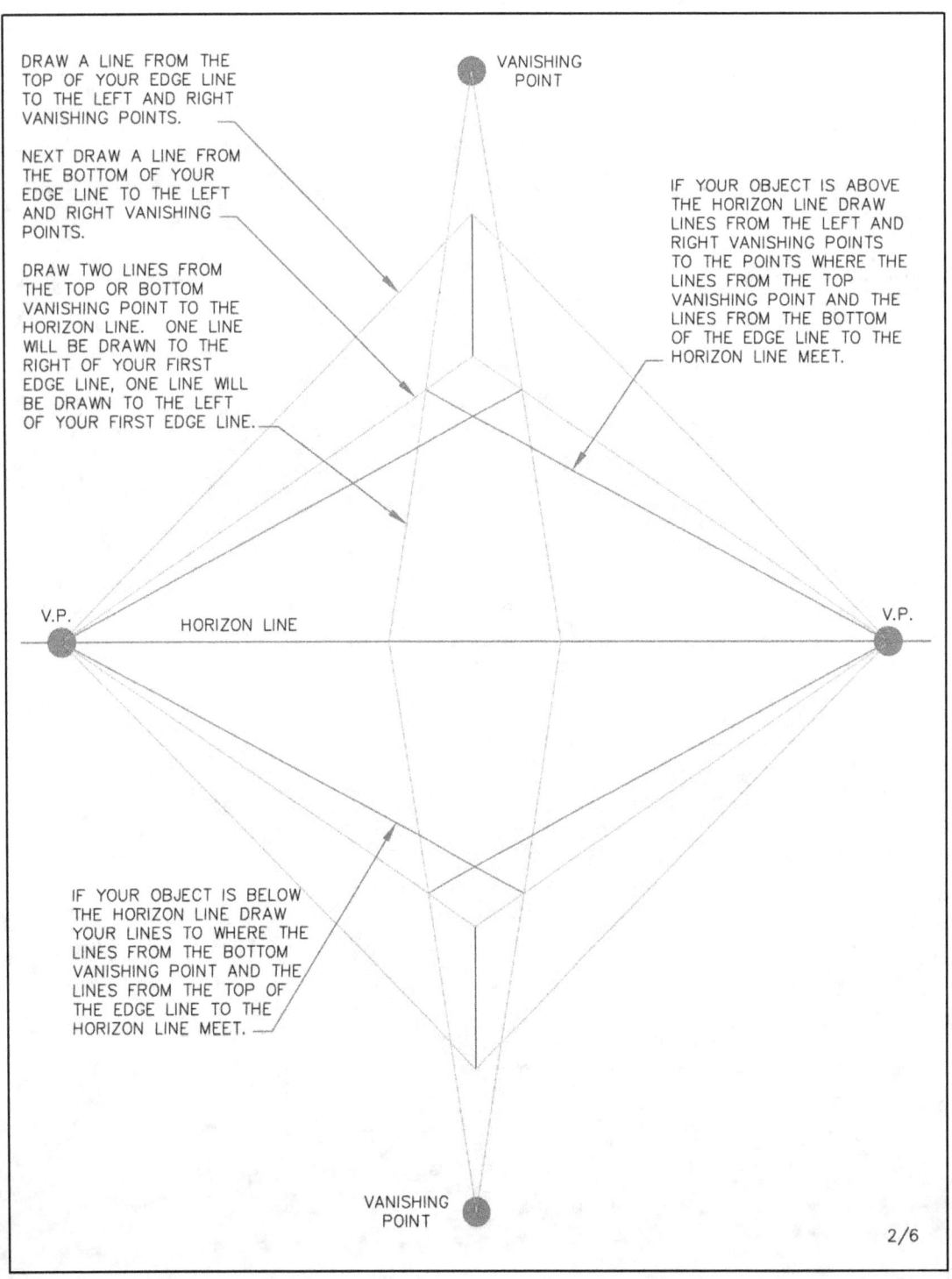

DRAW A LINE FROM THE
TOP OF YOUR EDGE LINE
TO THE LEFT AND RIGHT
VANISHING POINTS.

NEXT DRAW A LINE FROM
THE BOTTOM OF YOUR
EDGE LINE TO THE LEFT
AND RIGHT VANISHING
POINTS.

DRAW TWO LINES FROM
THE TOP OR BOTTOM
VANISHING POINT TO THE
HORIZON LINE.   ONE LINE
WILL BE DRAWN TO THE
RIGHT OF YOUR FIRST
EDGE LINE, ONE LINE WILL
BE DRAWN TO THE LEFT
OF YOUR FIRST EDGE LINE.

VANISHING
POINT

IF YOUR OBJECT IS ABOVE
THE HORIZON LINE DRAW
LINES FROM THE LEFT AND
RIGHT VANISHING POINTS
TO THE POINTS WHERE THE
LINES FROM THE TOP
VANISHING POINT AND THE
LINES FROM THE BOTTOM
OF THE EDGE LINE TO THE
HORIZON LINE MEET.

V.P.

HORIZON LINE

V.P.

IF YOUR OBJECT IS BELOW
THE HORIZON LINE DRAW
YOUR LINES TO WHERE THE
LINES FROM THE BOTTOM
VANISHING POINT AND THE
LINES FROM THE TOP OF
THE EDGE LINE TO THE
HORIZON LINE MEET.

VANISHING
POINT

2/6

Example 3-5b. Basic three point perspective drawing

68

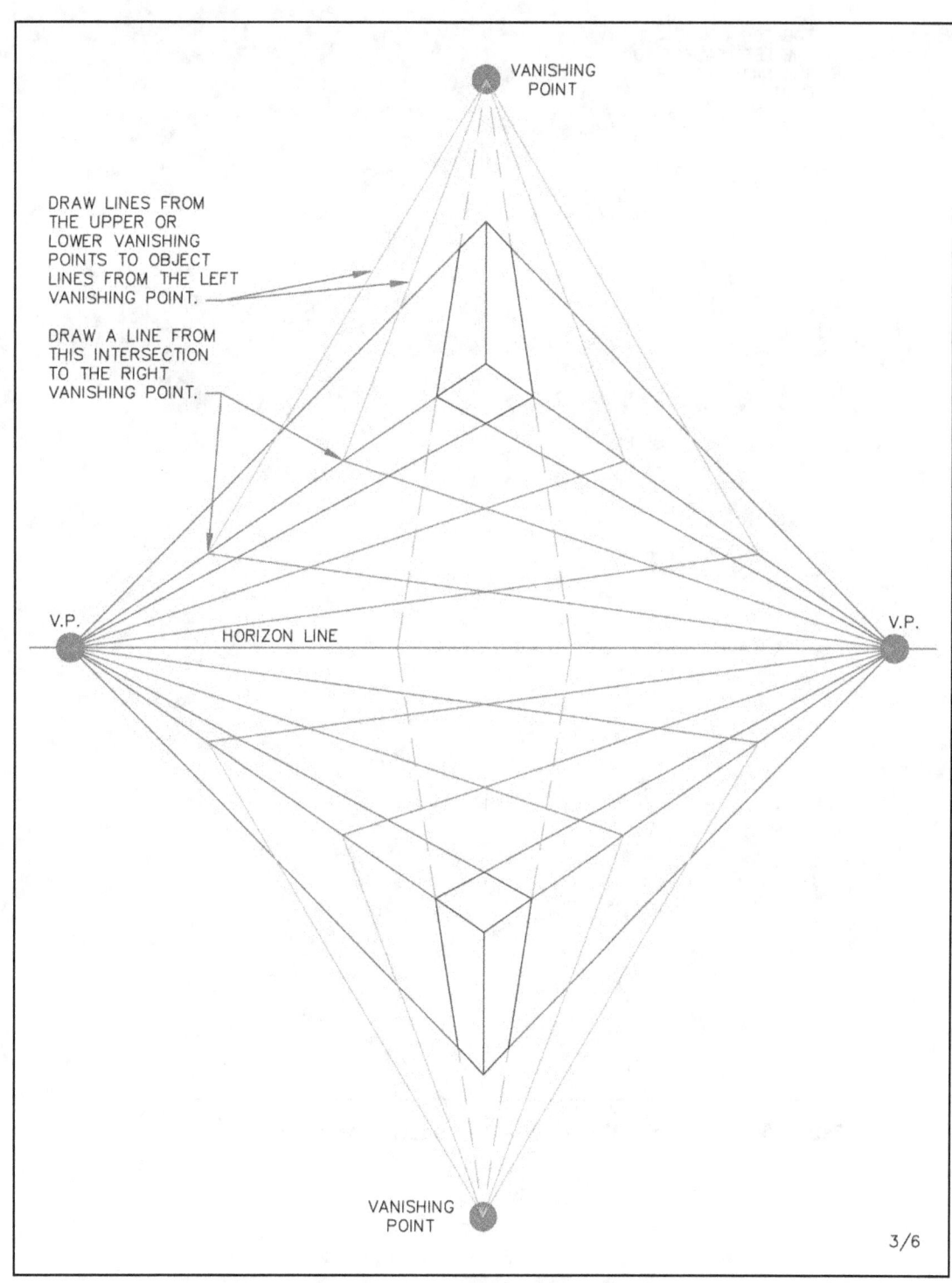

Example 3-5c. Basic three point perspective drawing

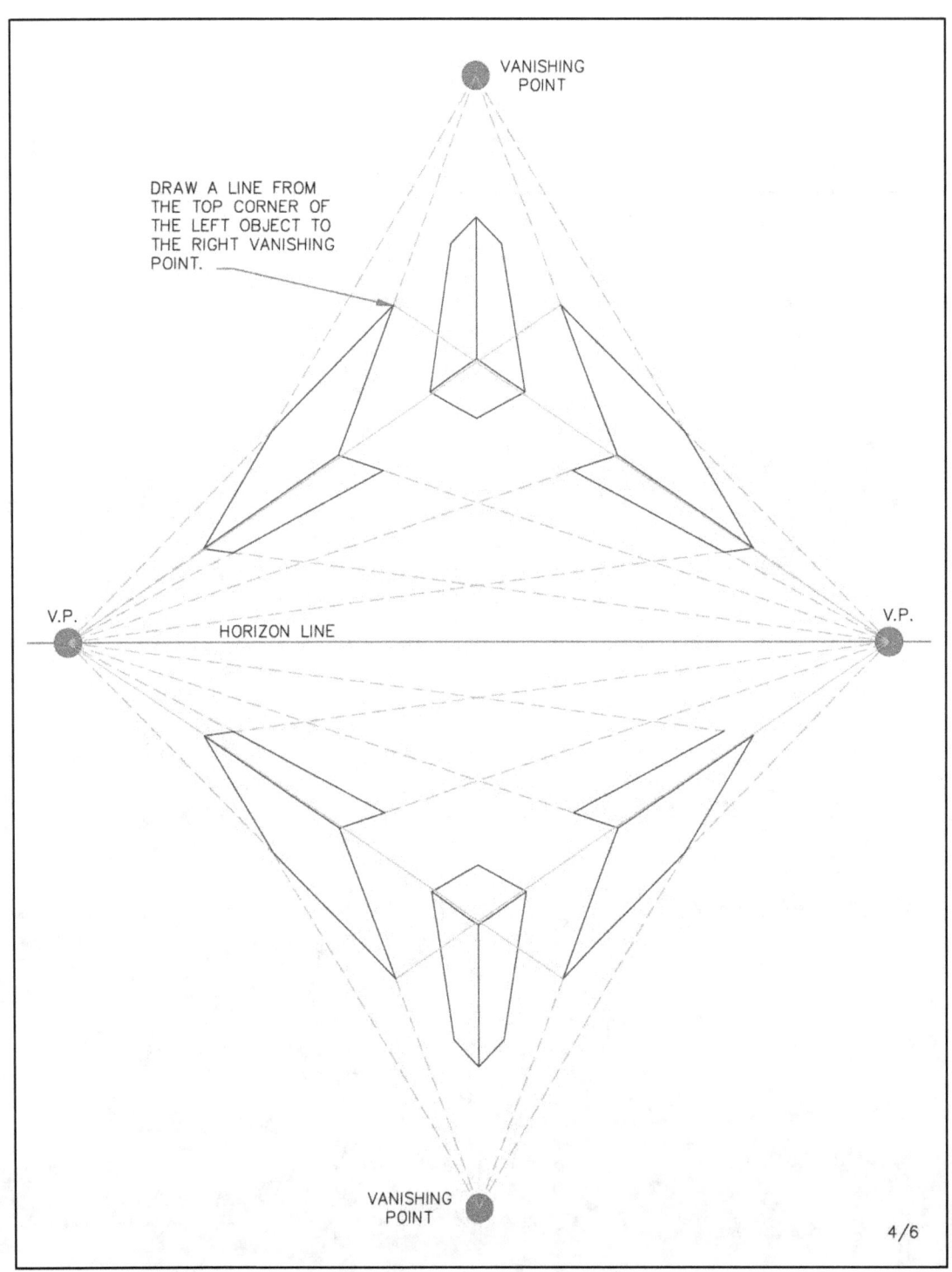

VANISHING POINT

DRAW A LINE FROM THE TOP CORNER OF THE LEFT OBJECT TO THE RIGHT VANISHING POINT.

V.P.

HORIZON LINE

V.P.

VANISHING POINT

4/6

Example 3-5d. Basic three point perspective drawing

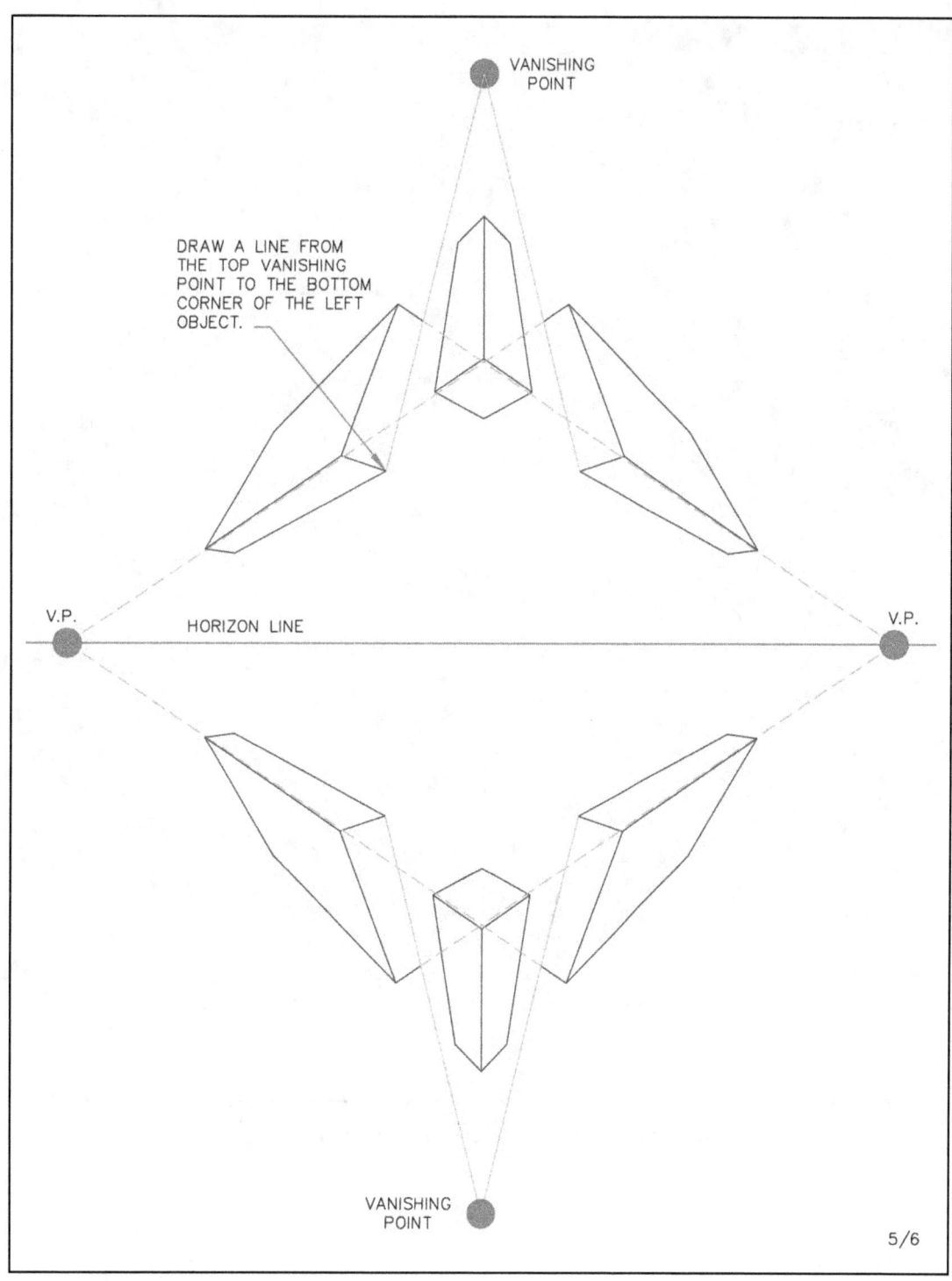

Example 3-5e. Basic three point perspective drawing

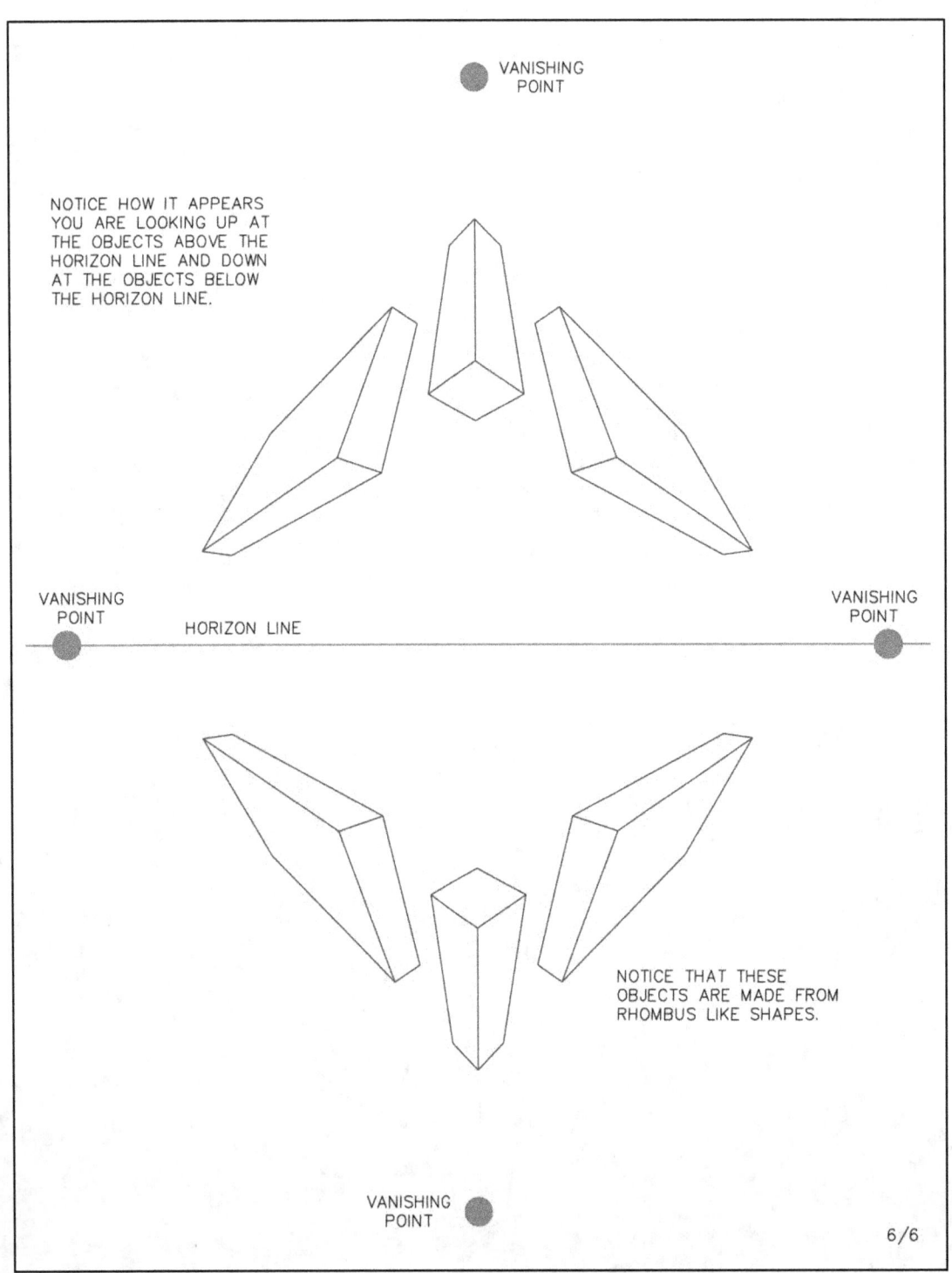

VANISHING
POINT

NOTICE HOW IT APPEARS
YOU ARE LOOKING UP AT
THE OBJECTS ABOVE THE
HORIZON LINE AND DOWN
AT THE OBJECTS BELOW
THE HORIZON LINE.

VANISHING
POINT

HORIZON LINE

VANISHING
POINT

NOTICE THAT THESE
OBJECTS ARE MADE FROM
RHOMBUS LIKE SHAPES.

VANISHING
POINT

6/6

Example 3-5f. Basic three point perspective drawing

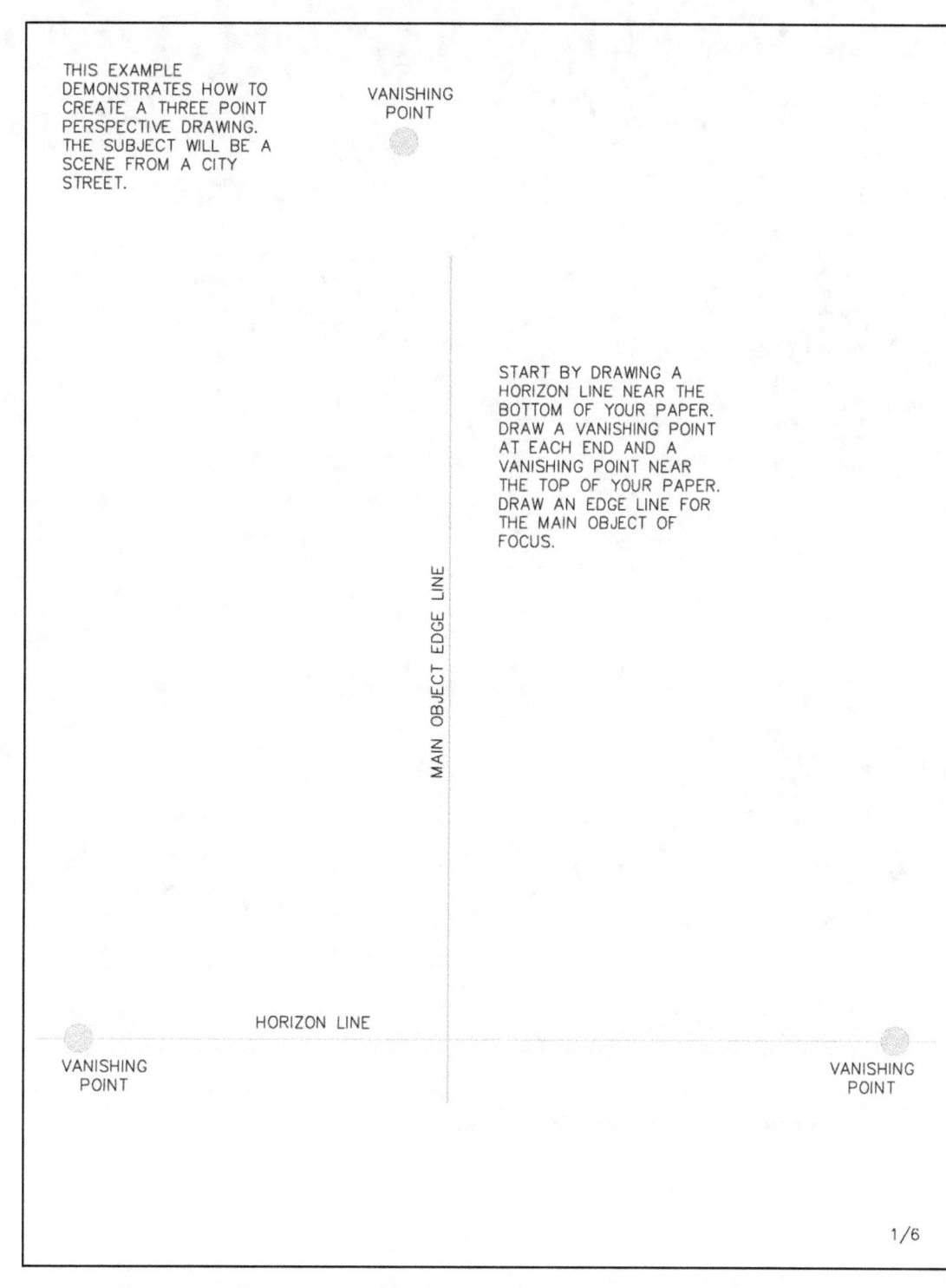

THIS EXAMPLE
DEMONSTRATES HOW TO
CREATE A THREE POINT
PERSPECTIVE DRAWING.
THE SUBJECT WILL BE A
SCENE FROM A CITY
STREET.

VANISHING
POINT

START BY DRAWING A
HORIZON LINE NEAR THE
BOTTOM OF YOUR PAPER.
DRAW A VANISHING POINT
AT EACH END AND A
VANISHING POINT NEAR
THE TOP OF YOUR PAPER.
DRAW AN EDGE LINE FOR
THE MAIN OBJECT OF
FOCUS.

MAIN OBJECT EDGE LINE

HORIZON LINE

VANISHING
POINT

VANISHING
POINT

1/6

Example 3-6a. Advanced three point perspective drawing

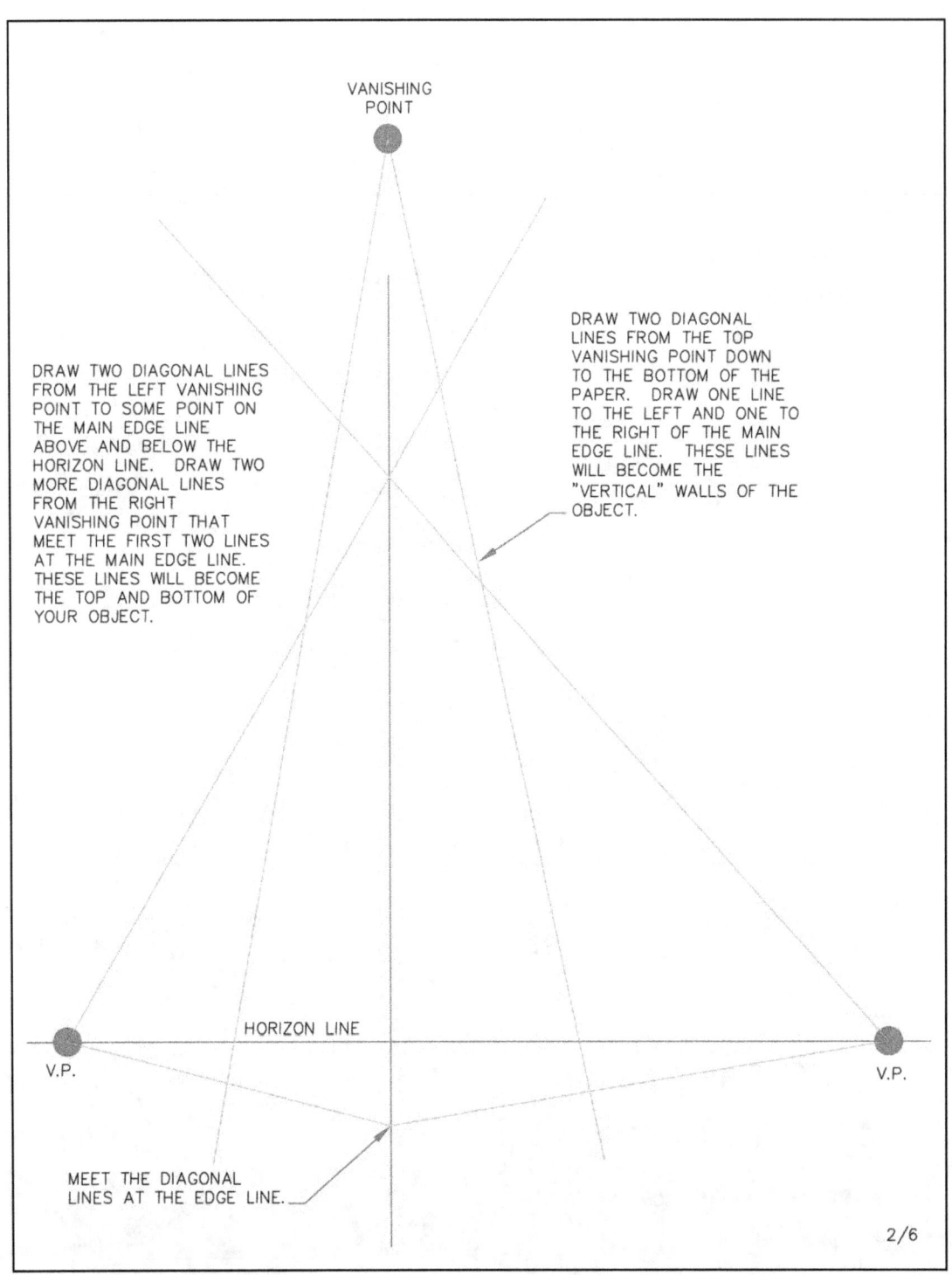

VANISHING POINT

DRAW TWO DIAGONAL LINES FROM THE TOP VANISHING POINT DOWN TO THE BOTTOM OF THE PAPER. DRAW ONE LINE TO THE LEFT AND ONE TO THE RIGHT OF THE MAIN EDGE LINE. THESE LINES WILL BECOME THE "VERTICAL" WALLS OF THE OBJECT.

DRAW TWO DIAGONAL LINES FROM THE LEFT VANISHING POINT TO SOME POINT ON THE MAIN EDGE LINE ABOVE AND BELOW THE HORIZON LINE. DRAW TWO MORE DIAGONAL LINES FROM THE RIGHT VANISHING POINT THAT MEET THE FIRST TWO LINES AT THE MAIN EDGE LINE. THESE LINES WILL BECOME THE TOP AND BOTTOM OF YOUR OBJECT.

HORIZON LINE

V.P.

V.P.

MEET THE DIAGONAL LINES AT THE EDGE LINE.

2/6

Example 3-6b. Advanced three point perspective drawing

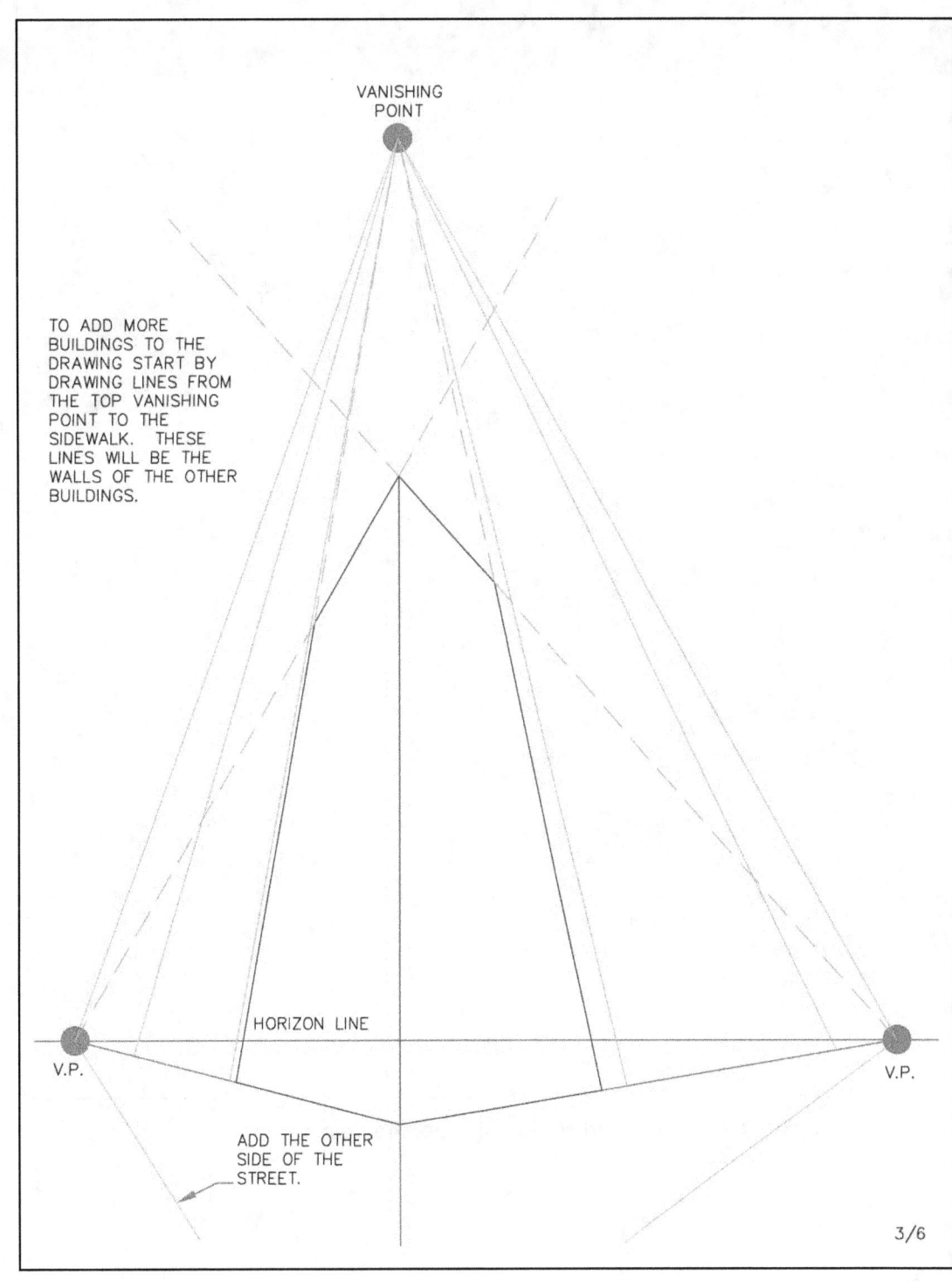

VANISHING
POINT

TO ADD MORE
BUILDINGS TO THE
DRAWING START BY
DRAWING LINES FROM
THE TOP VANISHING
POINT TO THE
SIDEWALK. THESE
LINES WILL BE THE
WALLS OF THE OTHER
BUILDINGS.

HORIZON LINE

V.P.

V.P.

ADD THE OTHER
SIDE OF THE
STREET.

3/6

Example 3-6c. Advanced three point perspective drawing

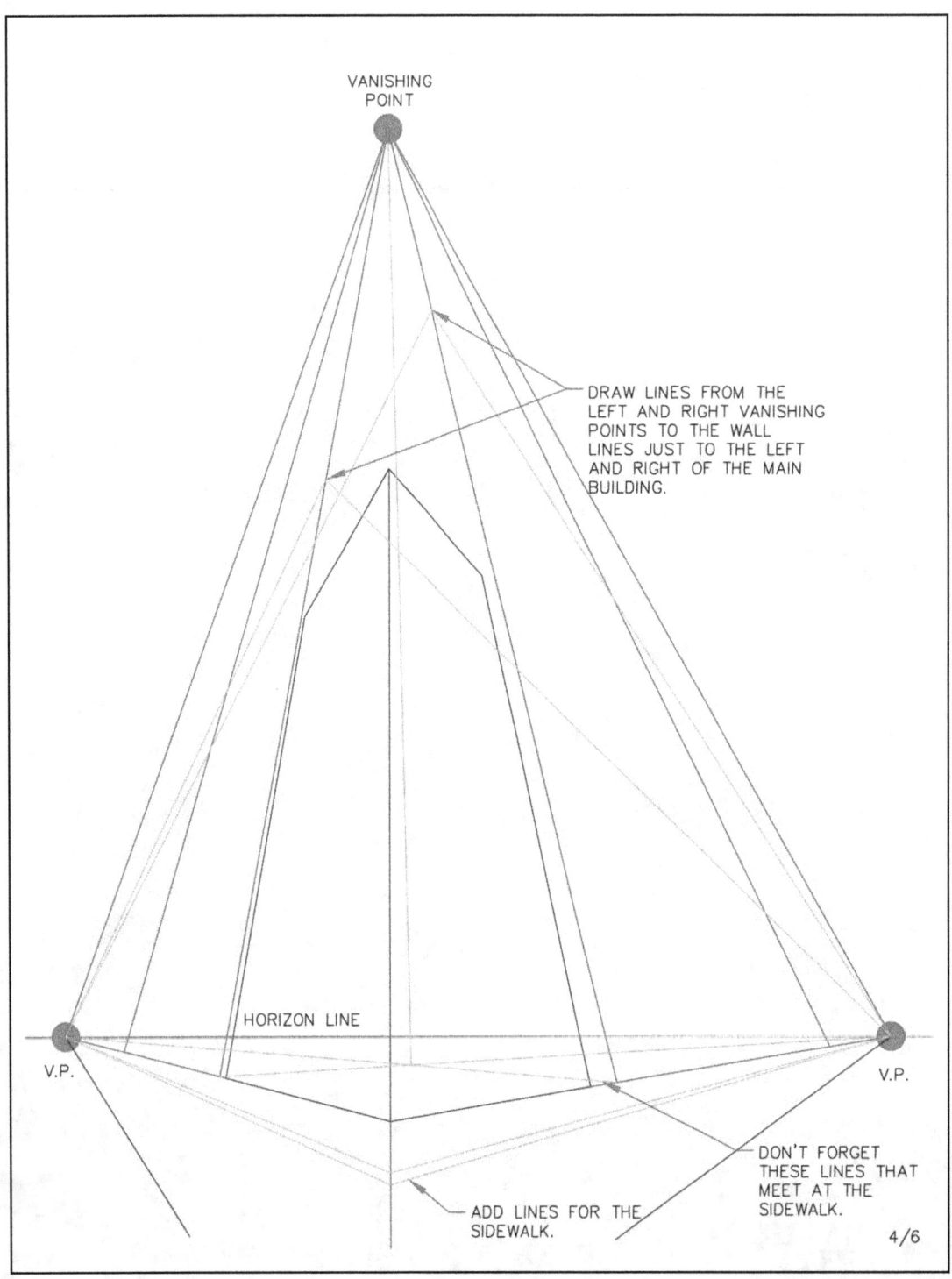

VANISHING
POINT

DRAW LINES FROM THE
LEFT AND RIGHT VANISHING
POINTS TO THE WALL
LINES JUST TO THE LEFT
AND RIGHT OF THE MAIN
BUILDING.

HORIZON LINE

V.P.

V.P.

DON'T FORGET
THESE LINES THAT
MEET AT THE
SIDEWALK.

ADD LINES FOR THE
SIDEWALK.

4/6

Example 3-6d. Advanced three point perspective drawing

76

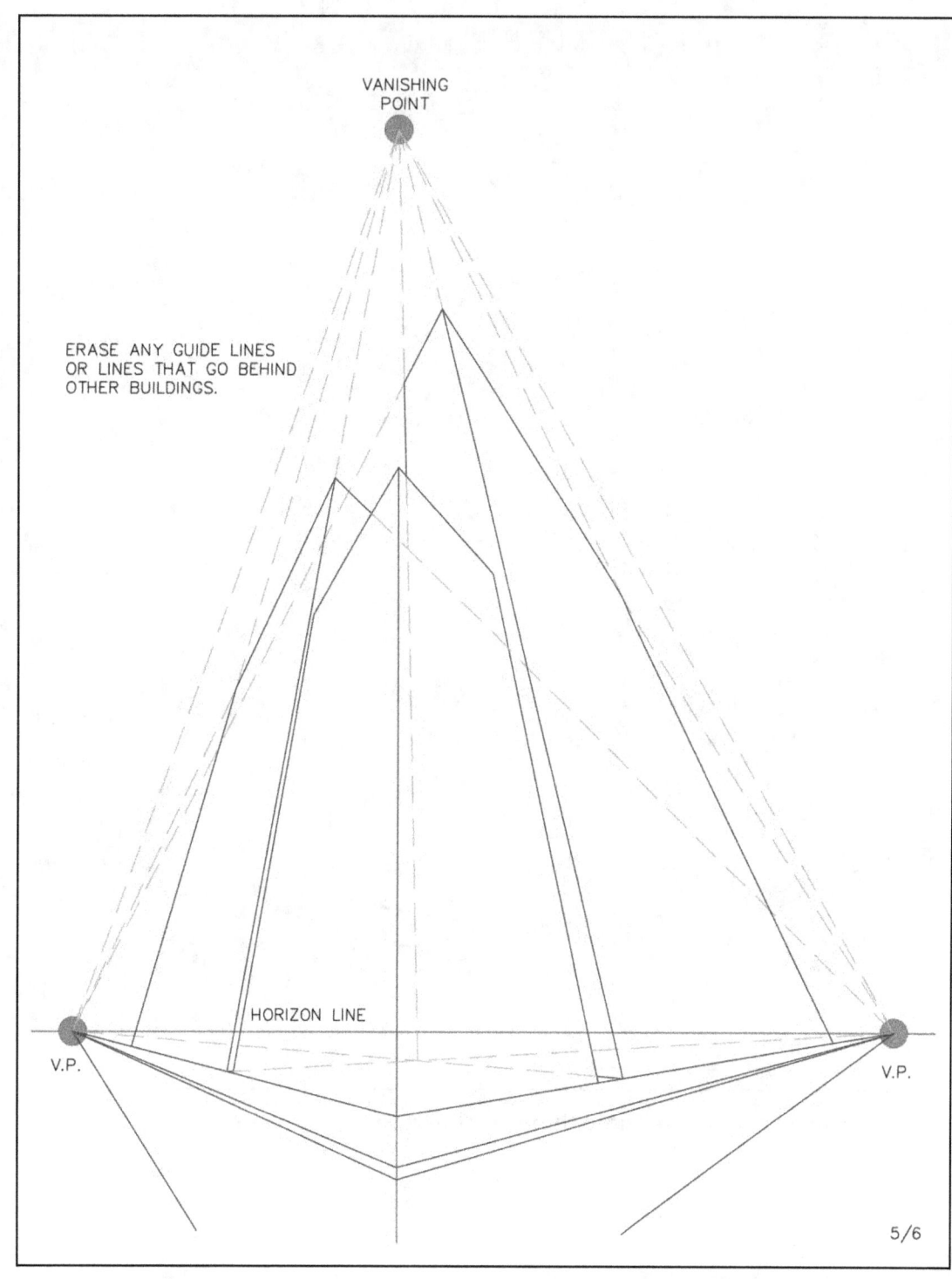

VANISHING
POINT

ERASE ANY GUIDE LINES
OR LINES THAT GO BEHIND
OTHER BUILDINGS.

HORIZON LINE

V.P.

V.P.

5/6

Example 3-6e. Advanced three point perspective drawing

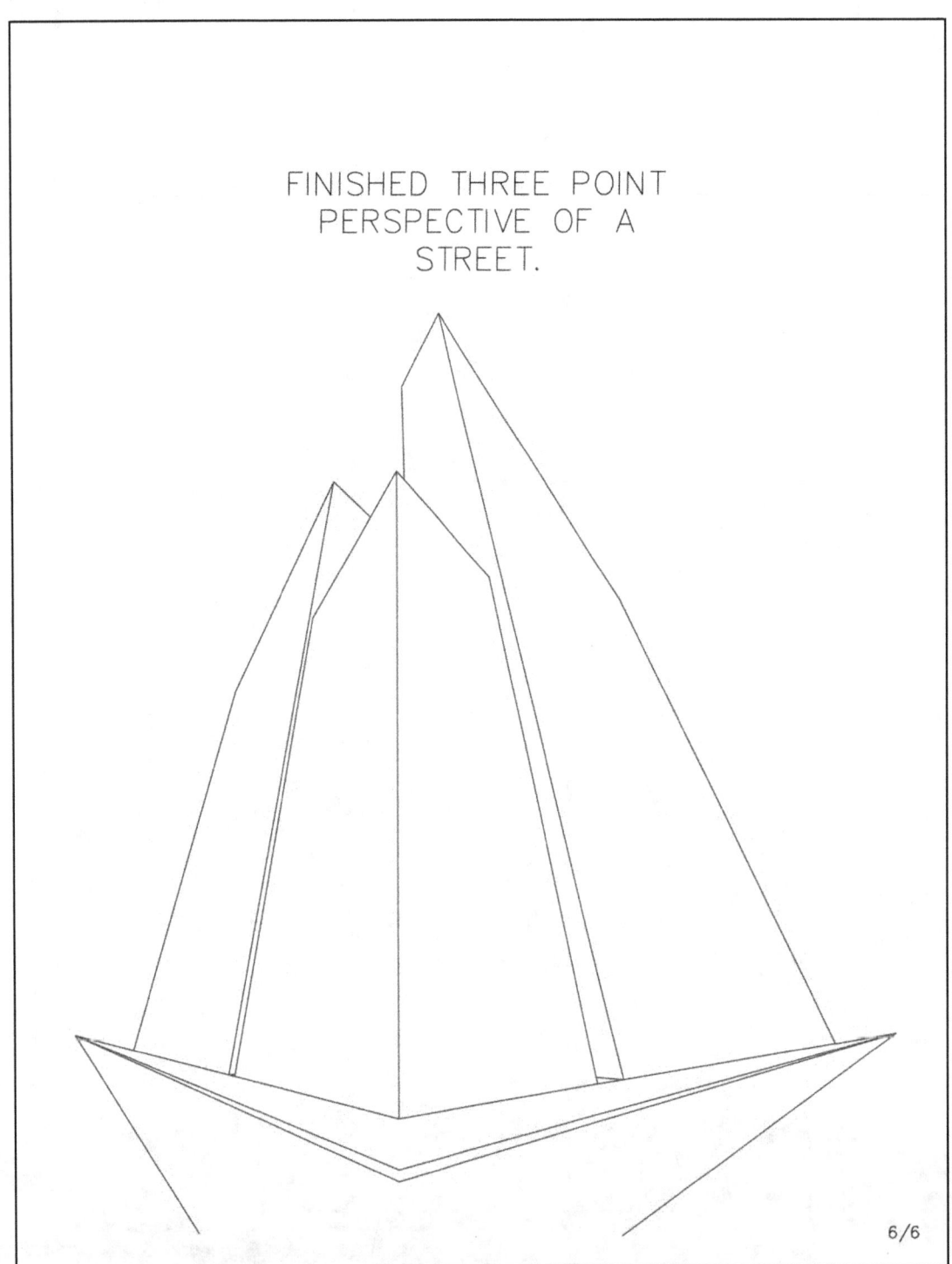

FINISHED THREE POINT
PERSPECTIVE OF A
STREET.

6/6

Example 3-6f. Advanced three point perspective drawing

Practice

Draw a three point perspective drawing of rectangular solids. Follow the steps in Example 3-5. Place them at different locations on the paper such that some are above, below and on the horizon line. For some extra credit and good practice, draw a three point perspective drawing of a street scene similar to Example 3-6.

> **Note:** Often in two and three point perspective drawings the vanishing points are located off the paper which can make layout difficult. If you find your vanishing points are not on the paper, tape your paper to a larger surface on which you can draw the vanishing points. Make sure you have a straightedge long enough to reach your paper from these vanishing points. If that doesn't work you may just have to estimate the vanishing point locations and how they affect the drawing.

Zero Point

There's one more type of perspective drawing, it's the no point or zero point perspective drawing.

Keep in mind, vanishing points work best when there are parallel lines and flat surfaces. A good example of a drawing with no parallel lines is a landscape with no man-made features. These drawings generally have plains and mountains, trees, rivers and maybe animals, but usually don't have many flat surfaces or roads.

It's still useful to understand perspective and how vanishing points work because some of the principles still apply. For example, a tree very close will look bigger than the same tree far away, a river as it meanders will look skinnier in the distance.

Other types of drawings where the principles of vanishing points work but you typically don't need to set them up include still life drawings and portraits.

A still life is a drawing of a group of inanimate objects (things that can't move by themselves). While some of the objects may have flat surfaces, like a book or box, these types of drawings usually have their objects so close to the viewer's eye that the vanishing points would be way off the paper and hard to use. In this case, using good observation skills and understanding how vanishing points work will be easier than actually trying to use vanishing points.

A portrait won't use vanishing points because there are no parallel lines in the face. There is symmetry in the face which can be maintained using vanishing points but again these vanishing points may be so far off the paper they're basically impossible to use. Again, observation of the face and an understanding of perspective is typically enough to draw it correctly.

These types of drawings will be covered in more detail in later volumes. For now understand that perspective is an important tool, knowing how it works and being able to use it will help you lay out your drawings correctly so that when you add tone and shading your drawings will look three dimensional.

Tone and Shading

In addition to perspective, learning to apply correct tone and shading are important skills to develop.

Tone refers to how light or dark the objects in a drawing are. Pencils can only create various shades of gray. Because there are no colors in a pencil drawing, the different shades of gray must represent the color you see. Dark colors require a dark tone, light colors require a lighter tone, and highlights will have the lightest tone or no tone at all.

Shading is used to show the absence of light. When an object is in the path of a light source it blocks the light from traveling further and what is left beyond the object is shadow or, the absence of light. Shadows follow similar rules to perspective drawings, this will be shown later.

Learning to understand shading and use tone is important because in reality, lines don't separate objects. Different colors, shades of color, highlights and shadows are what we actually see. These changes in color and shadow let us know the difference from one object to the next.

The trick in pencil drawing is to take the colors we see and turn them into shades of gray like a black and white picture. Even if making a realistic drawing is not your goal, for instance cartooning or something abstract, it's important to be able to use different tones to separate objects. If you don't use different tones your drawing could end up as a blob of a single shade of gray.

Look at Figures 3-1 and 3-2 below and you can see how different colors must be represented by different tones when using a pencil. You may not be able to tell exactly what color an object is by its tone but you'll be able to tell if it's a light color like yellow or light blue, or a dark color like purple or red.

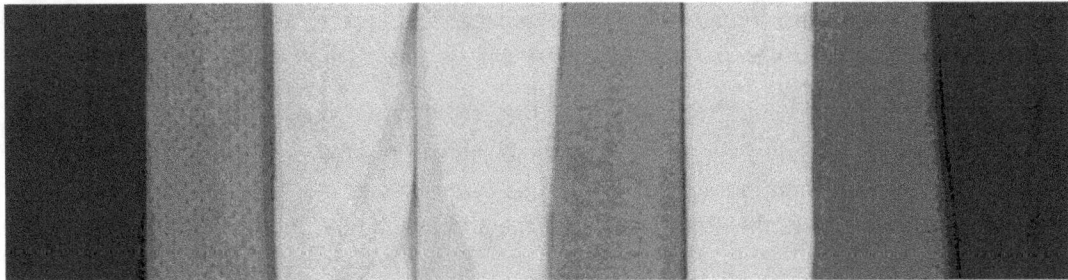

Figure 3-1. Colored fabric in greyscale, from left to right: red, orange, yellow, light green, dark green, light blue, violet, dark blue

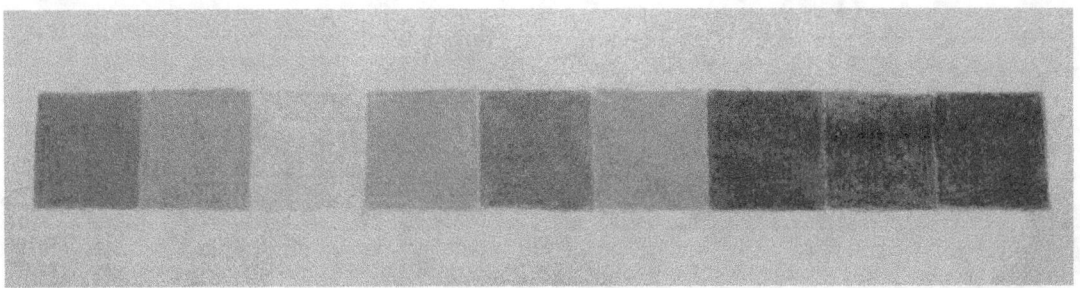

Figure 3-2. Color pencil in greyscale, from left to right: red, orange, yellow, light green, dark green, light blue, indigo blue, violet, purple

Adding Tone

There are some techniques to practice as you develop your ability to add tone and shading. The first technique is to angle the pencil very low to the paper. This is to ensure that as much of the graphite as possible contacts the paper as you move the pencil. Holding the pencil in a loose grip or overhand grip, as discussed in Volume 2, works well for this.

This technique produces a thick soft line and it's a good way to fill in large areas. The more pressure you apply, and/or the more times you draw over the same spot, the darker the tone becomes.

Angling the pencil low will also bring out the texture of the paper. If the paper is rough this technique will give the surface of the object you're drawing a rough look, a smooth paper will give the object a smooth look.

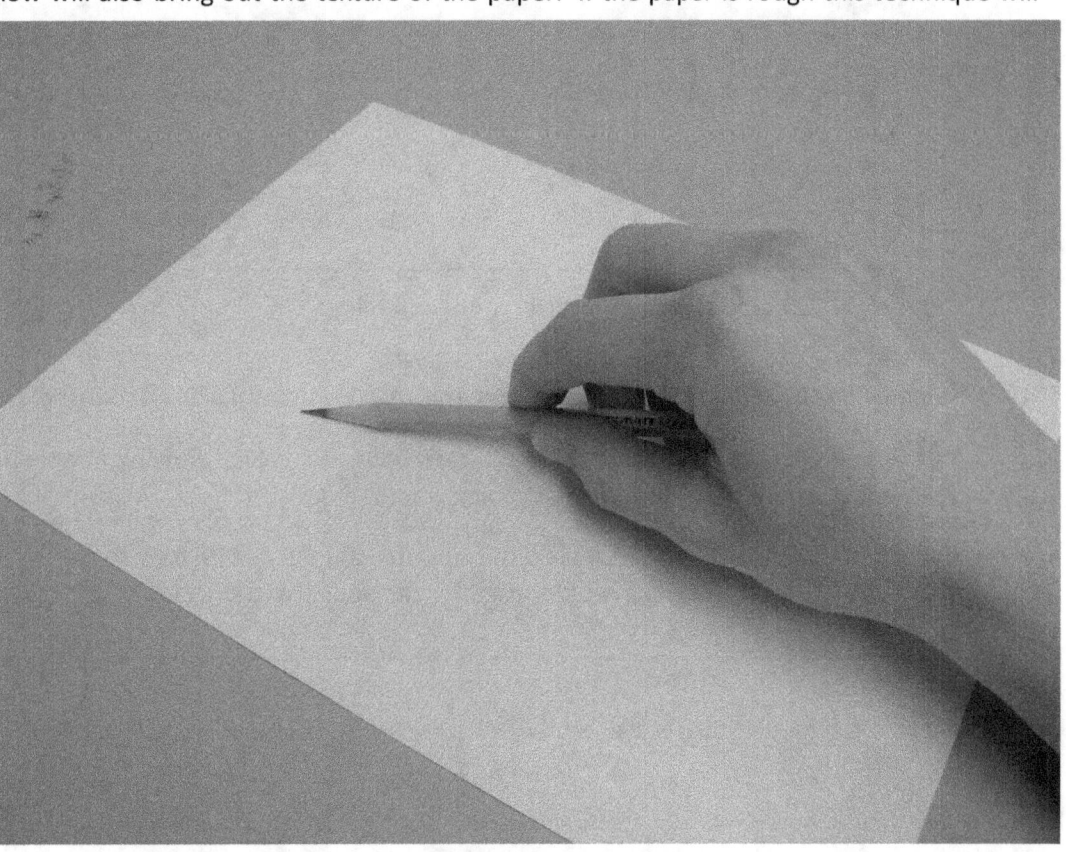

If the tone needs to be very dark the pencil will need to be held more upright and a tighter grip used so that more pressure can be applied without breaking the pencil. Lines made this way will not be as thick so it'll take longer to cover an area but the tone and shadows will be much darker.

Figure 3-3. Overhand grip used for shading

Smudging

Another technique for adding and modifying tone is smudging. Smudging refers to wiping something across the paper to blend the graphite, move it into other areas, and fill small cracks in the paper. The goal is to create more uniform tones and smooth transitions between tones. Smudging can be done with the corner of a folded piece of paper, a piece of cloth, a tissue, and erasers if you don't rub too hard. Your finger can also be used if you don't mind getting a bit messy.

Smudging creates a smoother softer look even if the paper is very rough because it pushes some of the bumps down and evens out the surface of the paper. It also pushes graphite into the tiny cracks in the paper's surface. Smudging can be used to create a smooth transition from a light area to a dark shaded area.

Keep in mind that if you use something harder than the drawing surface to smudge the drawing you may end up scratching it. Scratch marks are very hard to cover up so if you don't want to deal with scratch marks find

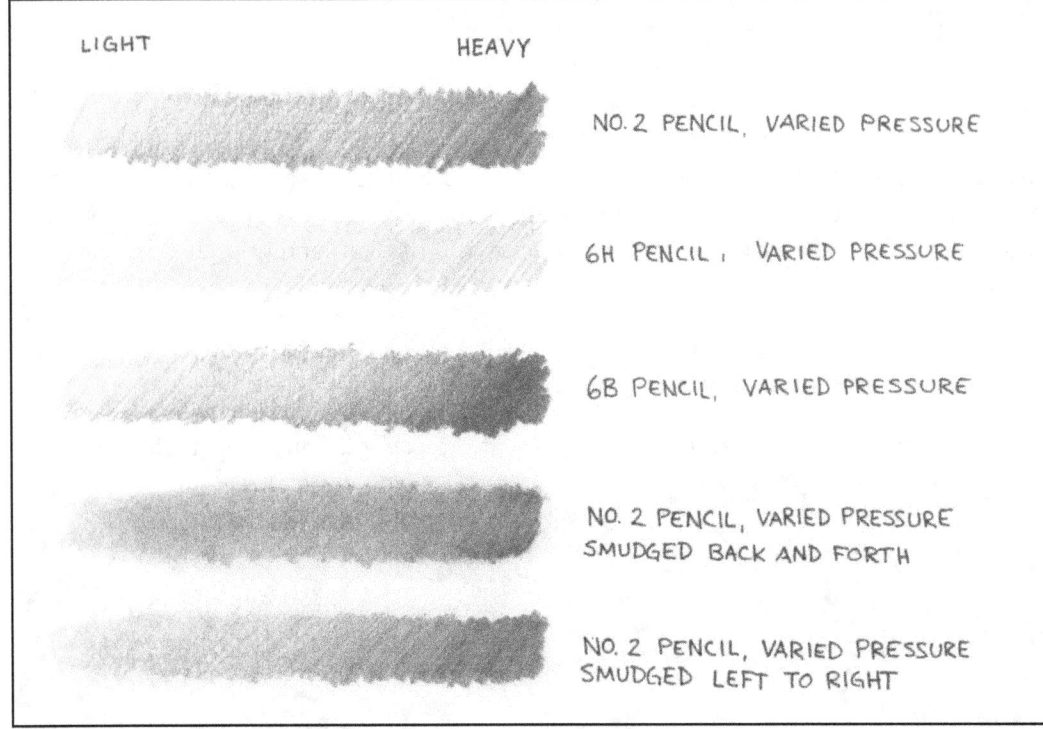

Figure 3-4. Blocks of tone variation and smudging

something softer than the drawing surface to use for smudging. Use a scratch piece of paper to test the material you want to smudge with.

Hatching

Hatching is another technique for adding tone which uses many parallel lines drawn close together. If the lines are drawn straight, the surface of the object will look flat, if curves are used it will look rounded.

Hatching doesn't create as smooth an appearance as regular tone and smudging.

A variation of hatching is crosshatching. Crosshatching involves drawing a second set of parallel lines over the first set but at a different angle. Crosshatching creates a darker tone.

You can add as many sets of parallel lines as you want, all at different angles. The more sets you add the darker the hatch will look. Hatching is often used for cartooning and sketching.

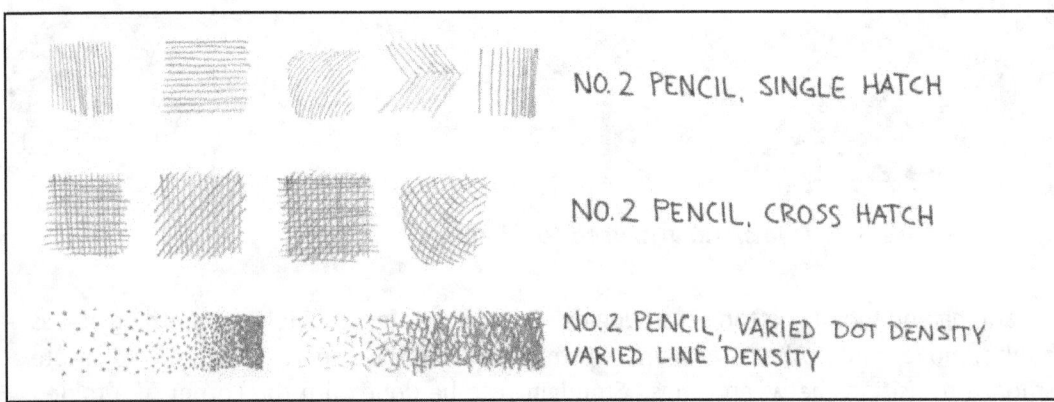

Figure 3-5. Hatching, crosshatching and random hatching

A less uniform type of hatching is random hatching. Basically it's just marks (lines or dots) on the paper in no particular order or direction. You can use it to create tone and texture at the same time.

Practice

On a sheet of paper draw a block of tone by angling your pencil low as you move the pencil back and forth. Start at the top of the paper making blocks of tone using light pressure. Continue making blocks of tone down the paper. Increase the pressure applied to the pencil each time you make a new block of tone. Continue increasing pressure until the graphite starts to crack or break.

On another sheet of paper make three rows of tone across the top. Begin with light pressure and increase pressure as you move across the paper. Below these rows of tone draw three more rows of tone starting with maximum pressure and decreasing the pressure as you move across the page.

Fold a separate piece of paper in half four or five times to make a stiff corner. Use that corner to smudge the rows of varying tone. Try smudging in different ways. Smudge straight across, going the same direction each time; also try smudging back and forth, up and down, and using small circles. Next find a tissue or piece of cloth and smudge the same areas of tone some more. Notice whether the new material smudged better or worse than the piece of paper. If you don't mind getting your finger dirty, try smudging a line of tone with your finger too. Check to see if any of the materials you used to smudge scratched the paper.

On a new sheet of paper practice hatching by drawing sets of vertical parallel lines (lines going up and down). Draw the first set with very little separation between the lines, draw a second and third set of lines the same direction but increase the amount of separation between the lines each time.

Now draw three sets of parallel lines horizontally (side to side), increasing the separation between the lines for each set.

Practice crosshatching by combining the up and down and side to side hatches together. Start by drawing tightly spaced lines and increase the spacing a little for each set. Next, repeat the hatching steps above using curved lines.

Just to see what happens, try smudging the hatching. See if you get the same results you got when you smudged the blocks of tone.

Adding Shadow

As was mentioned before, shading is how the absence or lack of light is shown. Knowing some of the characteristics of light will help you understand how shadows work.

Everything absorbs and/or reflects light, the reflected light is what our eyes see when we look at an object. An object that absorbs all light wavelengths is seen as black, an object that reflects all light wavelengths is seen as white. All other colors are just combinations of reflected light wavelengths.

The three most typical sources of light are the sun, fire, and all the various kinds of light bulbs. Light waves travel in straight lines away from its source, if something gets in the way of the light, it doesn't go any further. The lack of light beyond this point is shadow.

The intensity of light can change across a surface which is how different shades of color are produced. If there is no light, all you are left with is black.

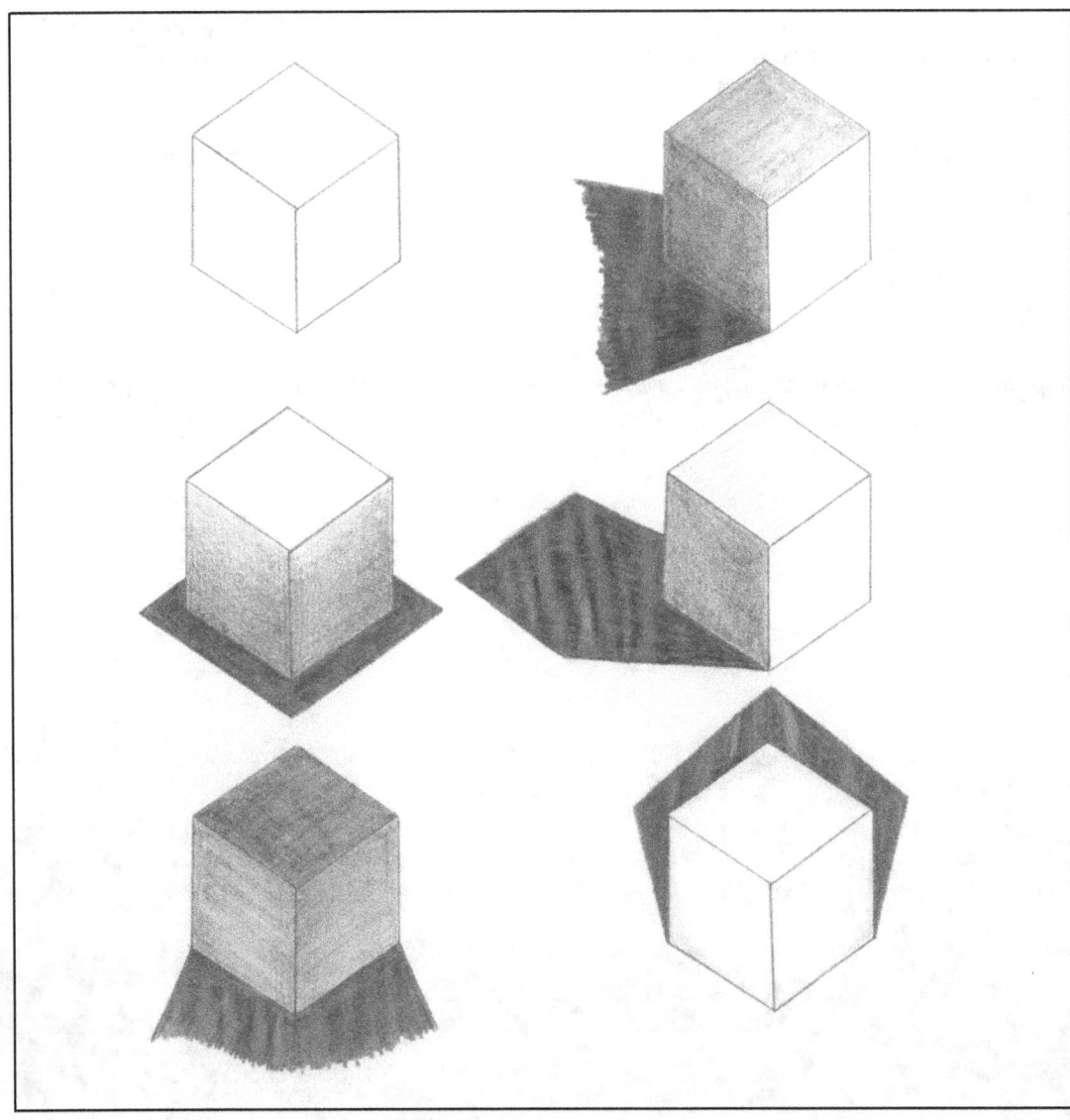

There are two ways light can hit an object, directly or indirectly. How shadows are cast depends on how the light contacts the object. Determining the sources of light and the direction of shadows is something you should keep in mind as you set up any drawing.

Direct lighting is used when there's a dominant light source and the object is the very first thing the light reaches.

Examples of direct light would be taking a flashlight and shining it straight onto something, an object outside on a bright sunny day, car headlights or a lamp close to an object.

Figure 3-6. Direct lighting shadows from a spotlight on a cube

When there's a direct light source any objects in the path of the light will have the side facing the source strongly lit and highlighted; the side opposite the light source will be heavily shaded. A dark, well-defined shadow will be cast away from the light source, the length and shape of the shadow will depend on the height of the light source and what's behind the object.

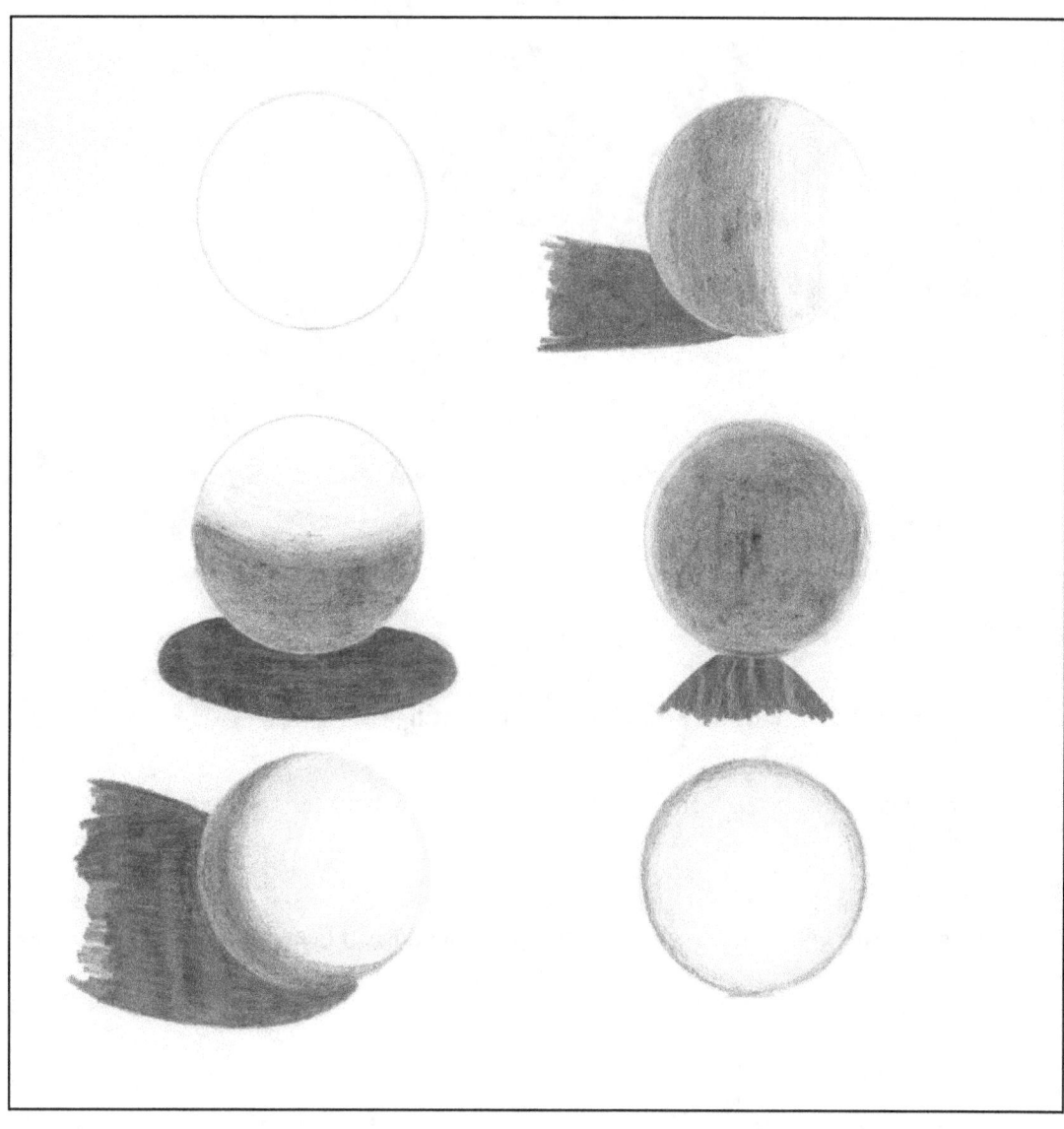

Figure 3-7. Direct lighting shadows from a spotlight on a sphere

Ambient light is a softer more diffused light that hits an object from many different directions. It's often light that is reflected off other surfaces or filtered through something that decreases its intensity.

Situations which create ambient light are when there are multiple lamps or street lights, light reflecting off walls and other objects, or a cloudy day.

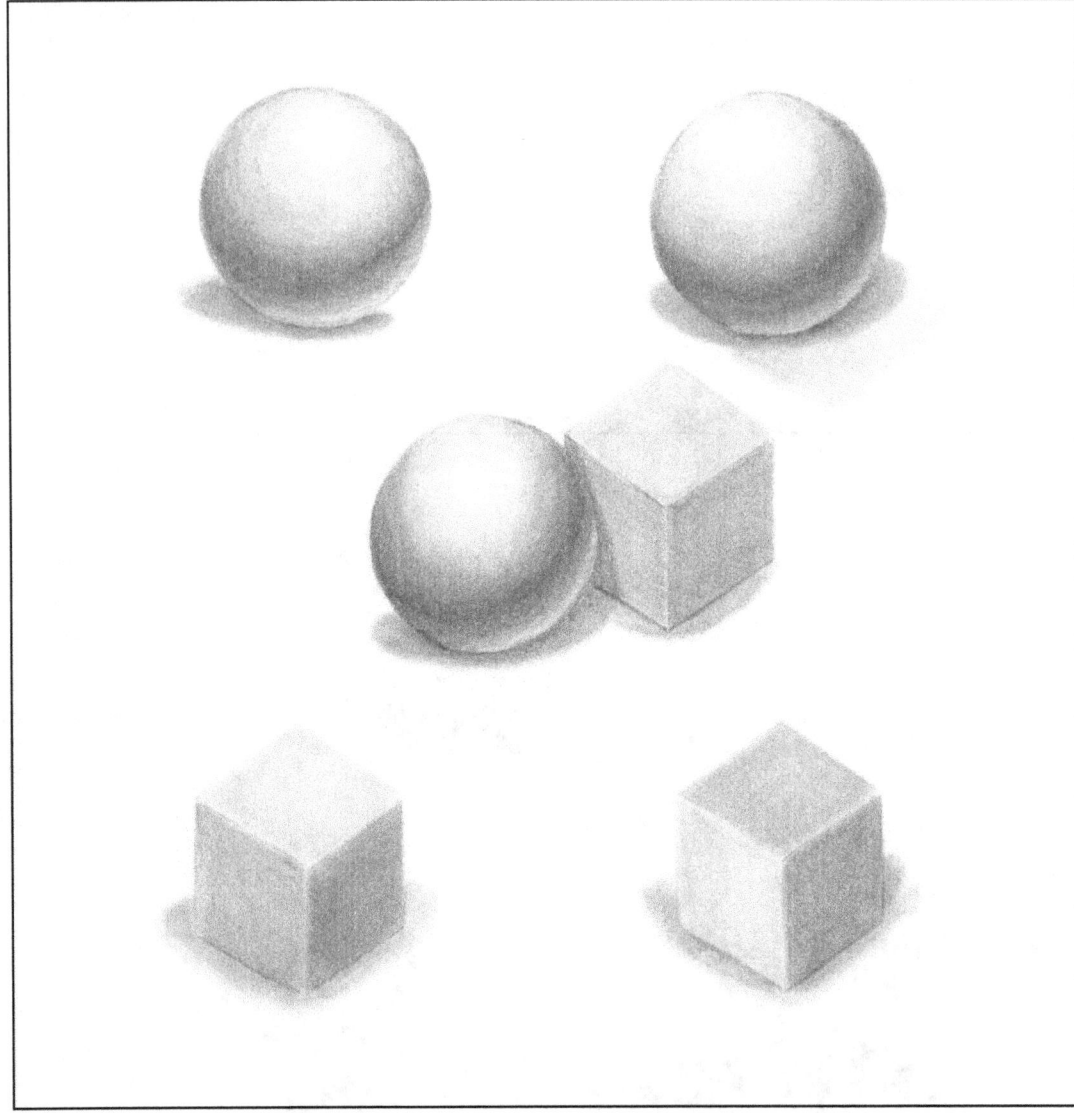

Figure 3-8. Shadows produced by ambient light

Ambient light creates shadows but they're not as dark as the shadows created by direct light. When light hits an object from all directions many of the shadows get canceled out because if you shine light on a shadow it obviously goes away. Typically there will be one or two sources of ambient light that will be stronger than the others so some shadows will remain but they won't be as dark as shadows produced from a direct light source.

The most subtle but important ambient light comes from light reflected off other surfaces. Because light is reflected off other objects it's almost impossible not to have some source of ambient light in any drawing. This source of ambient light creates an effect where the very edge of the object on the shaded side will have a slight highlight.

Look at the spheres in Figures 3-7 and 3-8 and you can see that there's a small highlighted area on the shaded side. This highlight comes from the light reflecting off nearby surfaces.

Constructing a Shadow

Because light travels in straight lines from its source, shadows work by a similar principle to perspective and vanishing points. The steps to make an accurate shadow are as follows:

1. Draw an object, a horizon line and a light source.

2. Draw a vertical line from the center of the light source to the ground/horizon line.

3. Draw lines from the center of the light source to the top of each part of the object, and then extend the lines past the object.

4. Draw lines from the horizon line directly under the light source to the bottom of each part of the object, then extend the lines until they cross the lines from the top of the object.

5. The spot where the top and bottom lines meet is where the shadow will end. Connect the intersection points and fill in the shadow.

Note: This technique is mainly for practice and explanation and should not be relied on. Depending on what the light source is and where it's situated you may not be able to use this technique. This technique also assumes the ground is flat. Sloped or rough ground will distort the shadow.

Look at the following examples to see how this process works. Keep in mind the shadow will only be this perfect if the ground is flat and smooth and the object has flat sides. If the ground was rough or uneven the shadow would be distorted. If the object is round, grids must be drawn on the face of the object and on the ground and the image transferred to the ground using the grid.

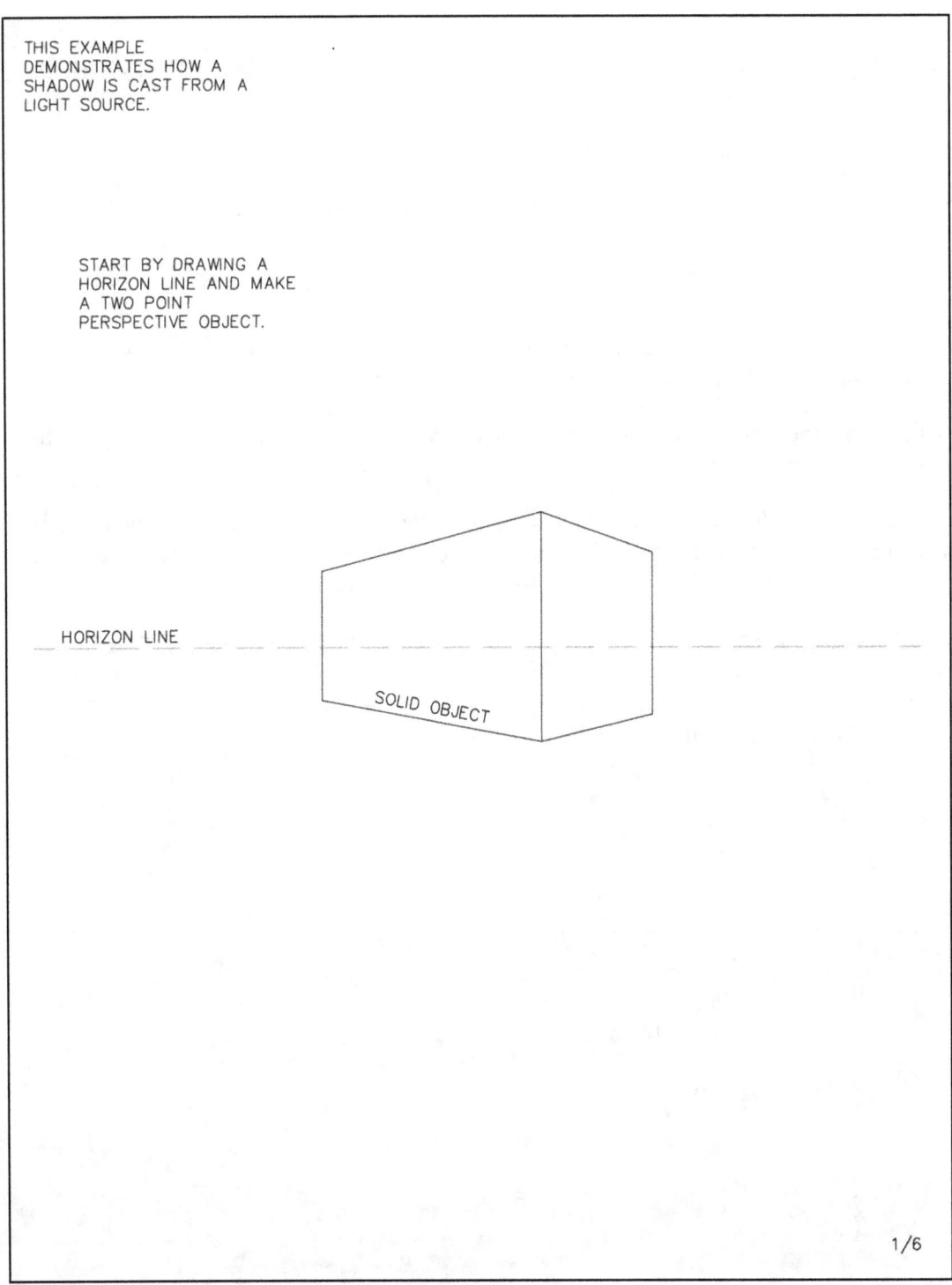

THIS EXAMPLE
DEMONSTRATES HOW A
SHADOW IS CAST FROM A
LIGHT SOURCE.

START BY DRAWING A
HORIZON LINE AND MAKE
A TWO POINT
PERSPECTIVE OBJECT.

HORIZON LINE

SOLID OBJECT

1/6

Example 3-7a. How to construct a shadow

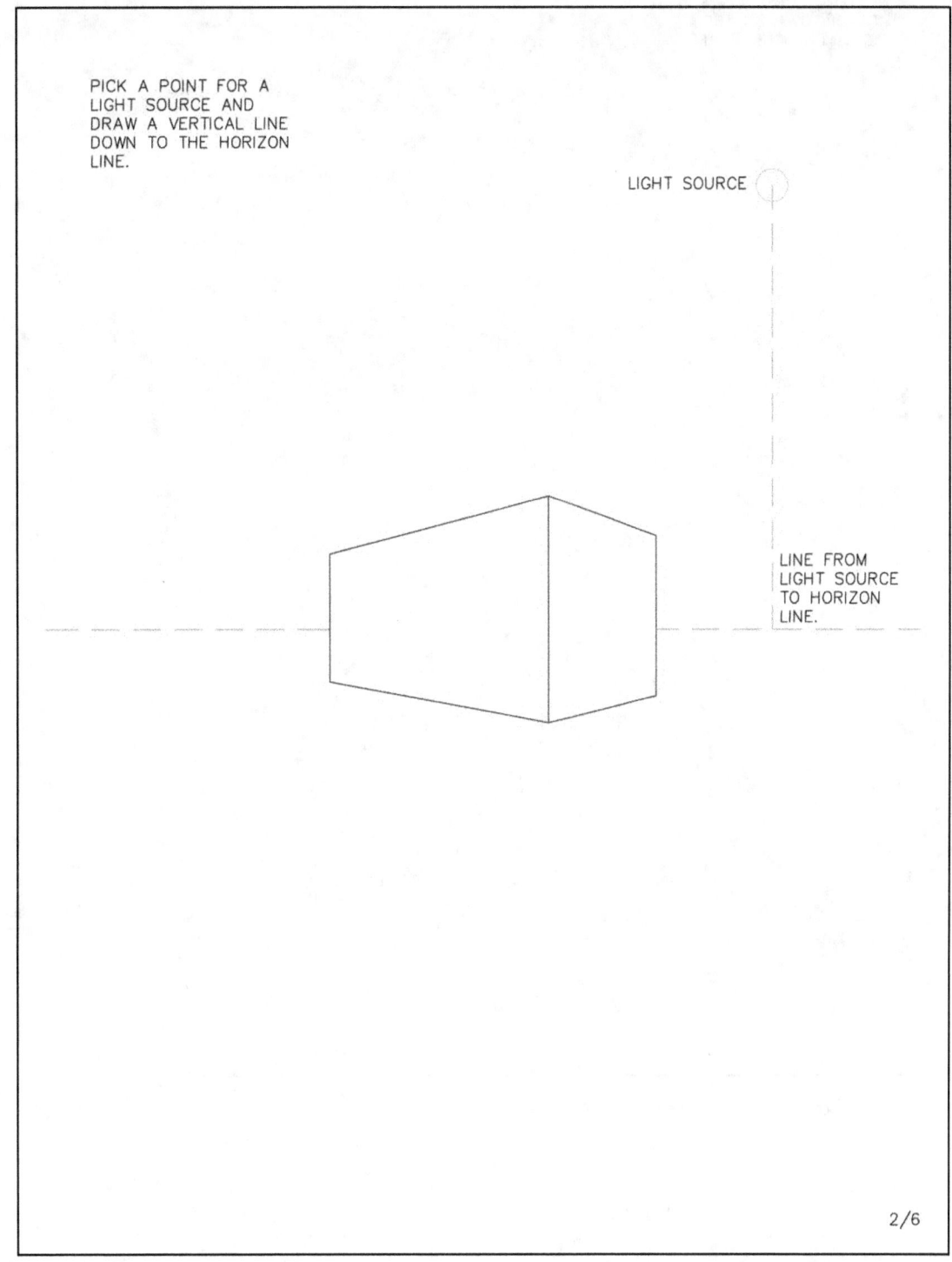

PICK A POINT FOR A
LIGHT SOURCE AND
DRAW A VERTICAL LINE
DOWN TO THE HORIZON
LINE.

LIGHT SOURCE

LINE FROM
LIGHT SOURCE
TO HORIZON
LINE.

2/6

Example 3-7b. How to construct a shadow

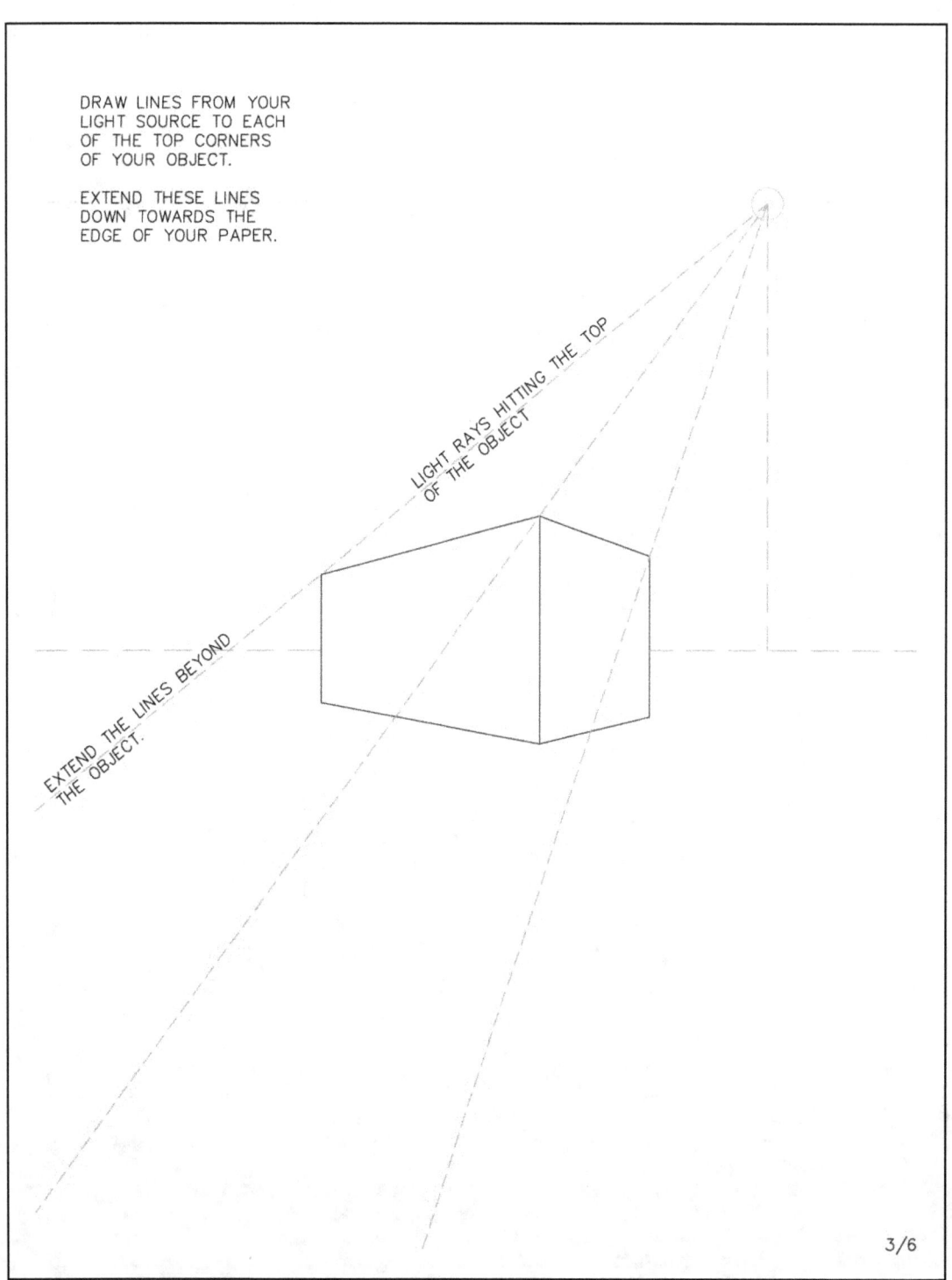

DRAW LINES FROM YOUR
LIGHT SOURCE TO EACH
OF THE TOP CORNERS
OF YOUR OBJECT.

EXTEND THESE LINES
DOWN TOWARDS THE
EDGE OF YOUR PAPER.

LIGHT RAYS HITTING THE TOP
OF THE OBJECT

EXTEND THE LINES BEYOND
THE OBJECT.

3/6

Example 3-7c. How to construct a shadow

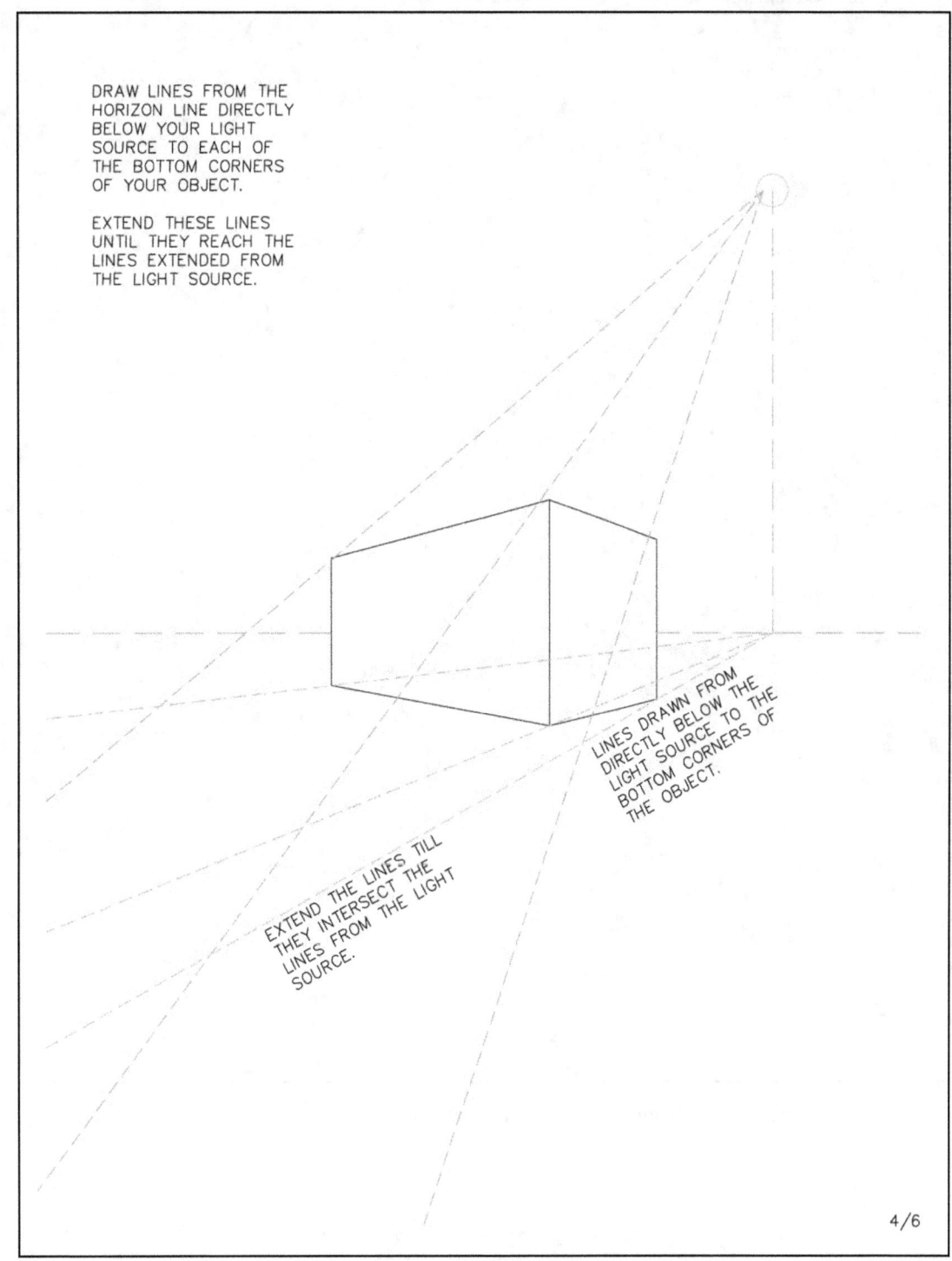

DRAW LINES FROM THE
HORIZON LINE DIRECTLY
BELOW YOUR LIGHT
SOURCE TO EACH OF
THE BOTTOM CORNERS
OF YOUR OBJECT.

EXTEND THESE LINES
UNTIL THEY REACH THE
LINES EXTENDED FROM
THE LIGHT SOURCE.

LINES DRAWN FROM
DIRECTLY BELOW THE
LIGHT SOURCE TO THE
BOTTOM CORNERS OF
THE OBJECT.

EXTEND THE LINES TILL
THEY INTERSECT THE
LINES FROM THE LIGHT
SOURCE.

4/6

Example 3-7d. How to construct a shadow

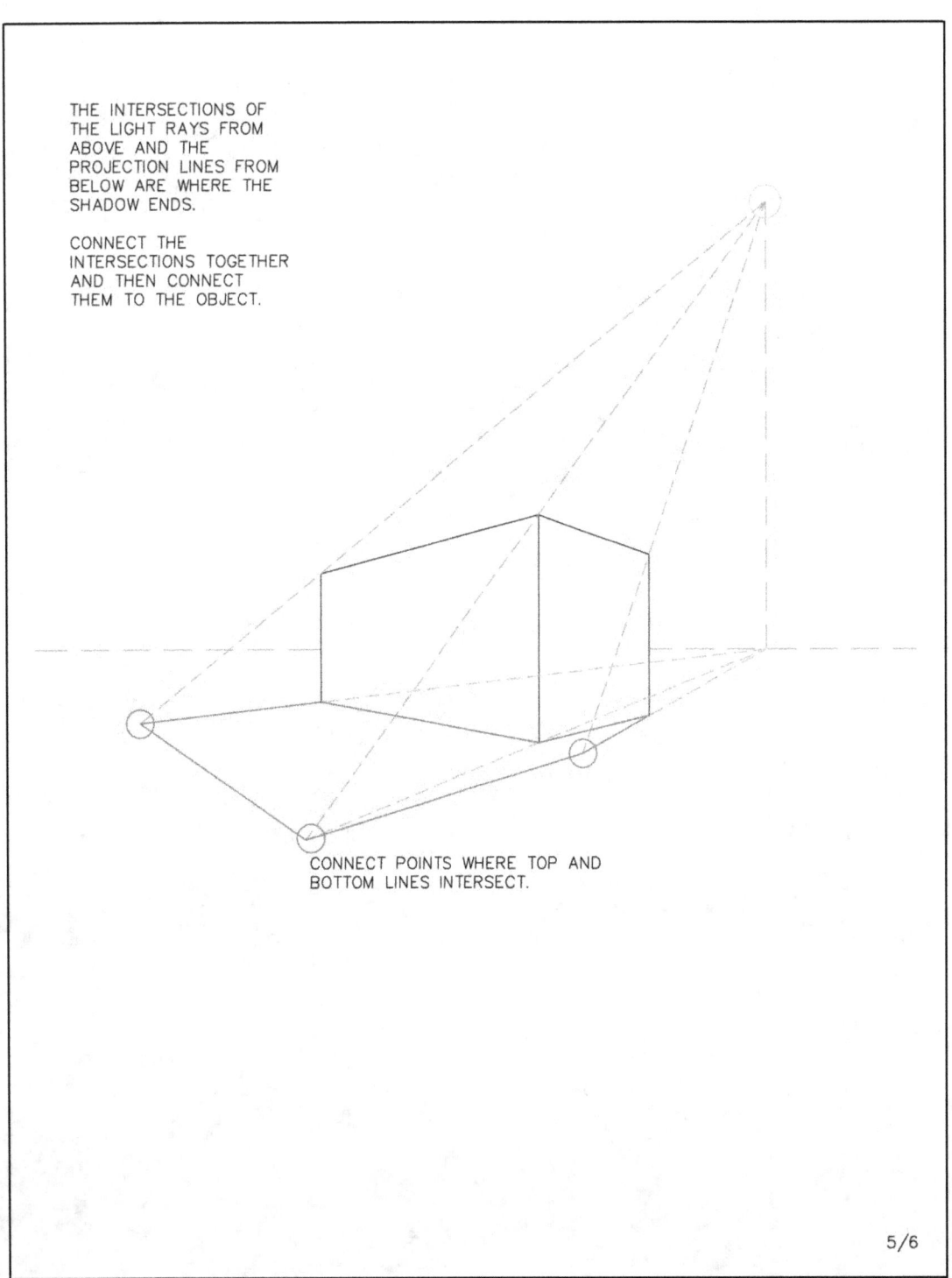

THE INTERSECTIONS OF
THE LIGHT RAYS FROM
ABOVE AND THE
PROJECTION LINES FROM
BELOW ARE WHERE THE
SHADOW ENDS.

CONNECT THE
INTERSECTIONS TOGETHER
AND THEN CONNECT
THEM TO THE OBJECT.

CONNECT POINTS WHERE TOP AND
BOTTOM LINES INTERSECT.

5/6

Example 3-7e. How to construct a shadow

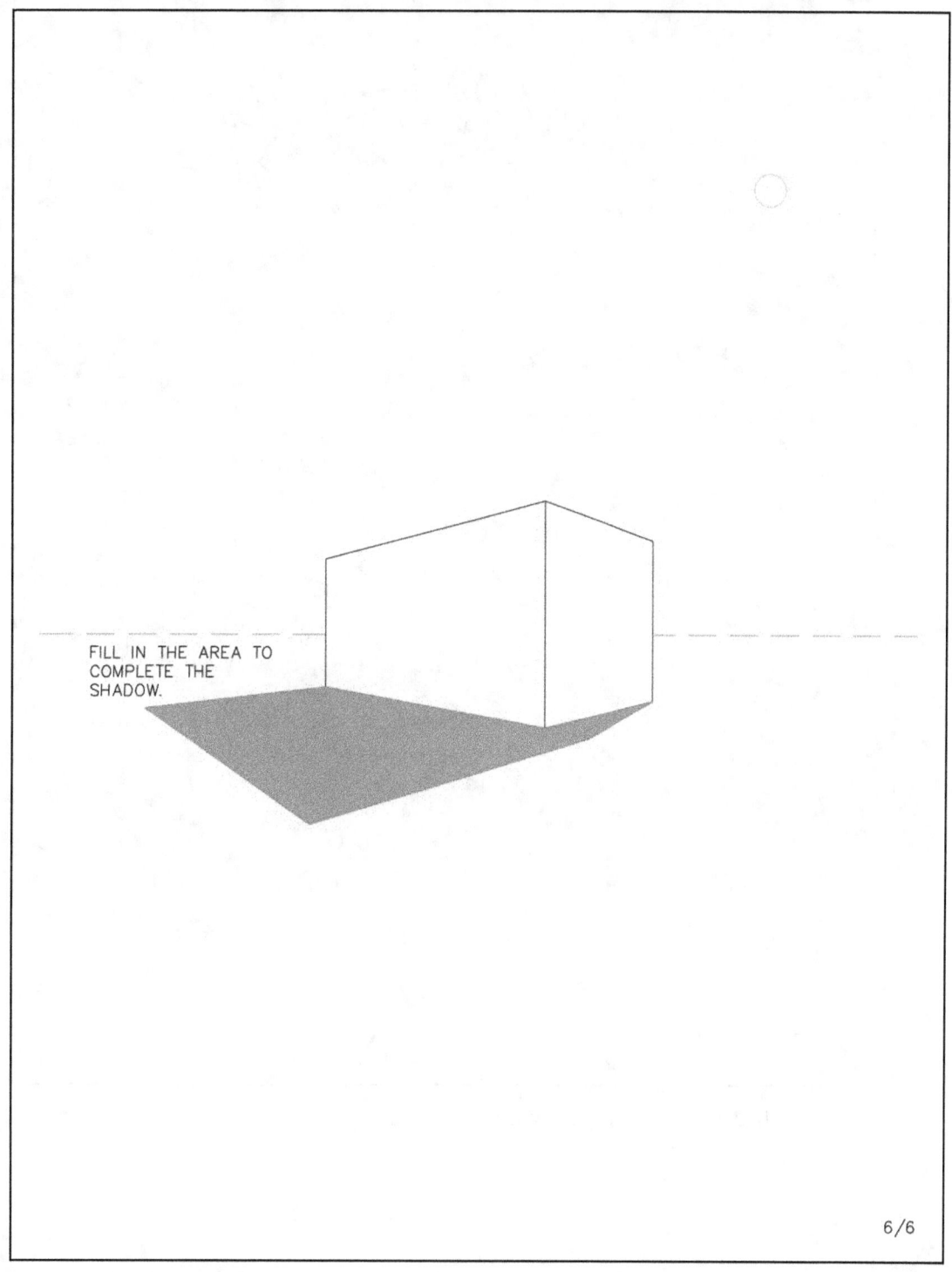

FILL IN THE AREA TO
COMPLETE THE
SHADOW.

Example 3-7f. How to construct a shadow

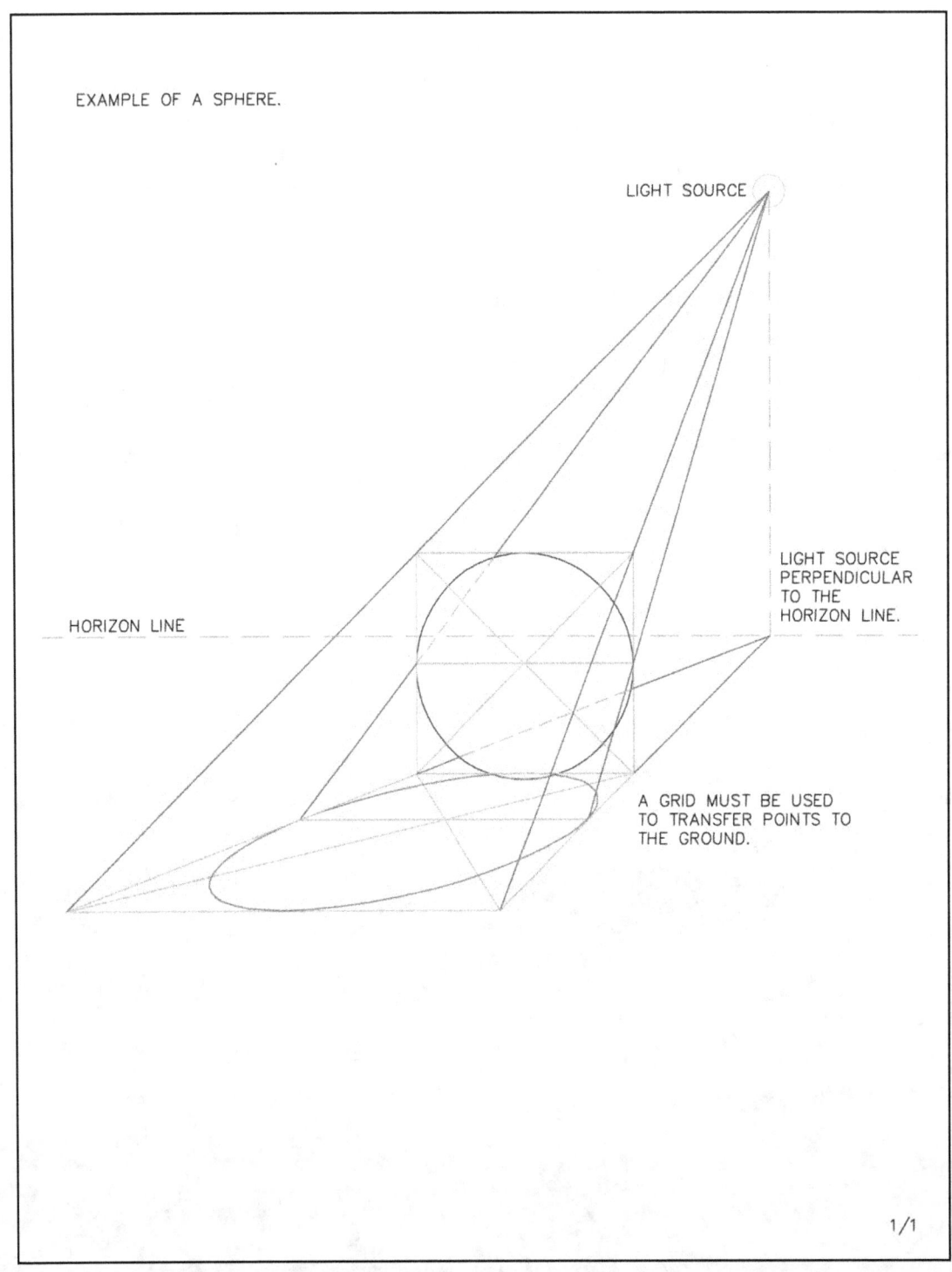

EXAMPLE OF A SPHERE.

LIGHT SOURCE

LIGHT SOURCE
PERPENDICULAR
TO THE
HORIZON LINE.

HORIZON LINE

A GRID MUST BE USED
TO TRANSFER POINTS TO
THE GROUND.

1/1

Example 3-8. Projecting a shadow for a sphere

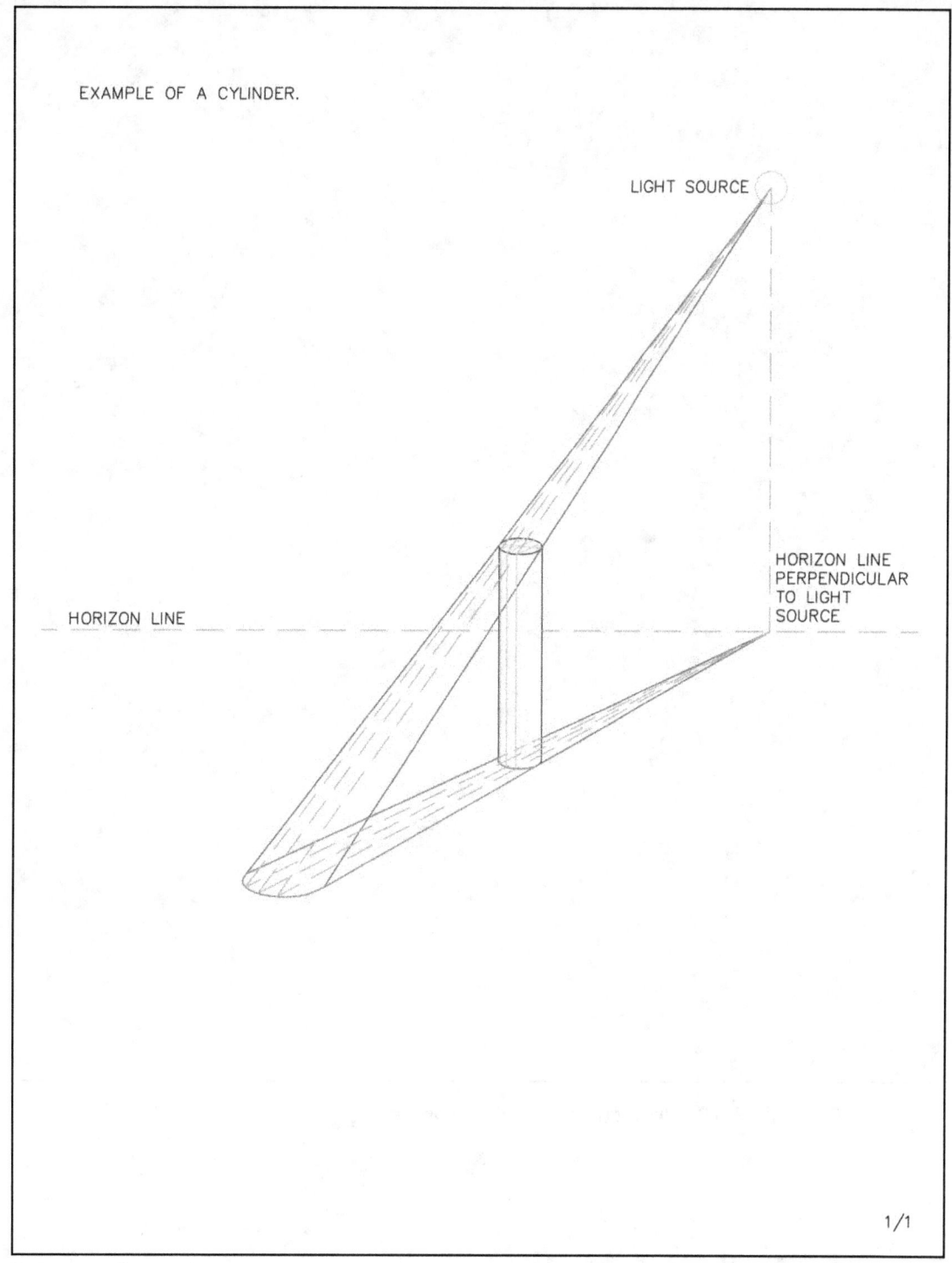

EXAMPLE OF A CYLINDER.

LIGHT SOURCE

HORIZON LINE PERPENDICULAR TO LIGHT SOURCE

HORIZON LINE

1/1

Example 3-9. Projecting a shadow for a cylinder

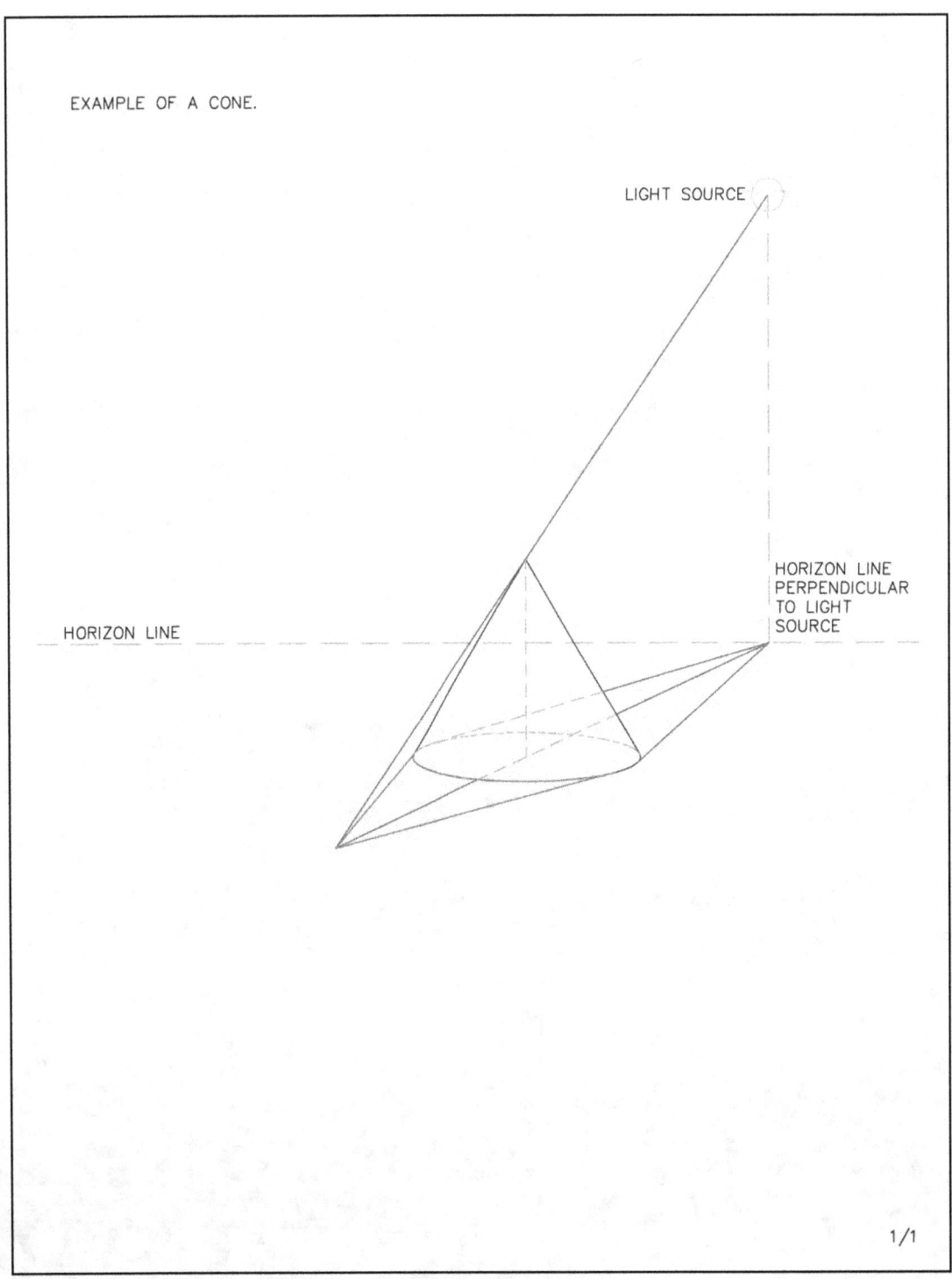

EXAMPLE OF A CONE.

LIGHT SOURCE

HORIZON LINE
PERPENDICULAR
TO LIGHT
SOURCE

HORIZON LINE

1/1

Example 3-10. Projecting a shadow for a cone

All shadows whether from direct or ambient light will follow the rules shown in Examples 3-7 through 3-10. When you're drawing a picture with ambient light sources you need to determine which light sources are the dominant ones in order to know the direction to draw the shadows.

Drawing good shadows takes time and practice. Don't be discouraged if your first attempts aren't perfect, take extra time to look at pictures and observe things around you as you learn to draw shadows. Remember, shadows don't have to perfectly match the object you're drawing, in fact they rarely do. The most important thing at first is to make sure the shadows are drawn in the right direction away from the light source and with the proper tone.

Penumbra

One more thing about shadows (and this is pretty advanced).

There is an effect called **penumbra** that you should be aware of. It occurs because light sources typically have a top and bottom.

When a light source emits light, the rays go straight out in all directions from every part of the light source. That means the light rays from the top of the light source go in all directions and the light rays from the bottom of the light source go in all directions. This causes two different shadows to be made, the shadow where absolutely no light passes the object and the shadow where only the light from the top or bottom of the light source doesn't pass the object.

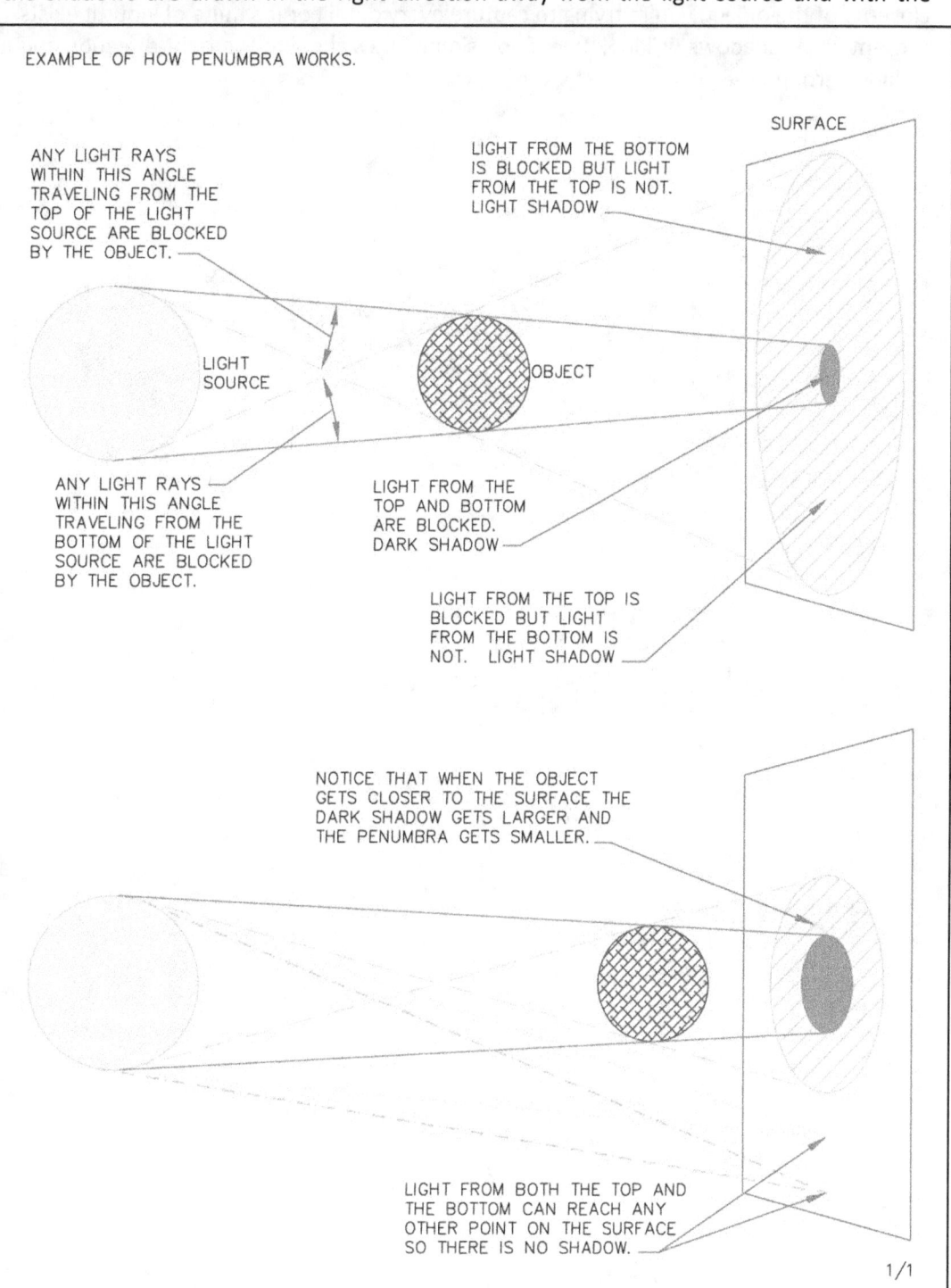

Example 3-11. How penumbra works

97

This concept can sometimes be difficult to understand and it wasn't added to the examples above mainly because the intent of those examples was to teach direction and depth of shadows. Study Example 3-11 to see how penumbra works.

There are two ways to reduce the effect of penumbra. Increase the distance between the light source and the object or decrease the physical size of the light source.

Generally you won't have to worry about penumbra when you're adding shadows unless the drawing is a close-up of the object, you're trying to capture every detail, or it's quite obvious it exists. If you know penumbra is present, most shadows will look fine if you simply draw them in the right direction and make them a little lighter or faded around the edges.

Highlighting

We'll quickly mention highlighting so you know what it is. It will be demonstrated in some of the lessons in later volumes so you'll eventually learn how to use it.

Highlighting is when a part of an object is left white or when some of the tone is erased to show the reflection of light off the surface, it's basically the opposite of making shadows. It's easy to forget to add highlights because you don't use your pencil to make them, but it's a very important step to completing a fully developed drawing.

Almost all objects have highlights and if you don't add them the drawing will look dull and two dimensional even if you did an excellent job shading. Highlights compliment shadows; together they create a fuller look.

Highlights are typically placed on the area of the object closest to the light source and the viewer. They're also found on edges and sharp corners. Don't forget to add them to the shaded edges of objects close to surfaces to show the light reflecting back at them. When highlights are drawn correctly they give the viewer another clue to the shape and size of the object, the texture, and where the light source is.

The types of highlights will vary depending on the surface. Smooth surfaces will have different highlights than rough surfaces and just like anything else it takes observation and practice to get good at applying them.

Practice

This practice will incorporate everything that's been discussed in this volume from 3-D shapes, to tone shading and highlights.

For these exercises you'll need at least six pieces of paper, some sort of small box, a small ball, and at least two light sources (try to find a flashlight if you can). Do these exercises in a fairly dark room (you'll still need enough light to see your paper but you want the shadows to stand out).

Draw three cubes with similar dimensions to the small box you found, and three circles a similar size to the ball you found. Draw one object on each piece of paper using the techniques discussed previously (make two point perspective boxes).

Set your box on a table or floor with nothing around it. Situate it so it looks like the cubes you drew on your paper. Shine your flashlight at one of its sides. Observe the cube for a few minutes.

Two sides should have shadow and one side will be lit. Of the two shaded sides one side will probably look a little darker than the other. Look at the shadow projecting from the box; observe where the shadow connects to the box and which direction it's going. Do you see penumbra? Look at the edges of the box; do you see highlights along the edges?

Fill in one of the cubes you drew to match what you see. Use different amounts of pressure to create different tone. The shadow should be very dark, when drawing it you'll need to apply a lot of pressure to the pencil. The sides of the box and penumbra will not be as dark as the main shadow; don't use as much pressure when adding this tone. The side of the box that's lit may have very little tone unless the box is a dark color. The edges will probably have highlights on them and you may need to use an eraser to add them.

Move the light source to a different location and do this exercise again.

For the third drawing, set the cube next to a wall or in a corner. Shine the flashlight on one side of the cube and situate a lamp on the other side. Draw the tone and shadows you see. There should be more than one shadow. It's likely the shadows won't be as defined as the shadows of the previous two drawings and they probably don't even look like they come from a cube anymore.

Repeat the same process above using the ball.

Conclusion

Congratulations, you have finished Volume 3 of the *Drawing Mentor* series. In this lesson you should have developed proficiency in drawing three dimensional objects by using the techniques of one, two and three point perspective. You have also been taught how to apply tone, shading and highlights to increase the three dimensional effect of a drawing. These are intermediate level skills which you should continually practice and develop. With an understanding of these drawing skills and the skills taught in Volume 2 you are ready to move on to drawing-layout. The next few volumes cover the skills of sketching, why it's important, when to apply it and how to use it. The basic drawing skills and sketching know-how will be invaluable as you go on to full blown drawing projects.

A Brief History of the Pencil and the People Who Shaped it

The pencil that you and I know today developed over hundreds of years. The first mention of a pencil-type writing instrument comes from ancient Rome.

Romans would use a stylus, a thin metal disk made from lead, to make lines on papyrus, an early form of paper. The lead would leave light gray lines to guide scribes as they wrote. The writing instrument they used was like a little paint brush. They called it a pencillus which means "little tail", because that is what it looked like, the name carried over to today's pencils even though they don't look like tails any more.

In the early 1500's the history of writing utensils changed forever when a storm knocked over an old oak tree in Borrowdale England. Local shepherds passing by discovered a smooth slippery, black substance in the tree roots. Thinking it was coal some of the shepherds took it home for fuel but quickly found out it wouldn't burn.

They didn't realize they had discovered one of the greatest and purest deposits of graphite ever found. They did notice that this new substance made very dark marks quite easily. They called it plumbago, which is Latin for "black lead", and began using it to mark their sheep.

Plumbago deposits had been found in other parts of the world but none were as pure or as large as the deposit found in Borrowdale.

The material from other deposits had to be ground into powder so that impurities could be removed. The pure mineral found in the new deposit could easily be sawn into long pieces and used without any further work. Unfortunately for craftsmen, artists and anyone who wanted to write a letter to their mother, the government took over the mine when it was found that plumbago was a great liner for cannon molds. So for a time all the plumbago used for writing had to be smuggled out.

People realized the material had its drawbacks, it was soft, brittle and very messy; so they began looking for ways to fix these problems. Initially they would wrap the plumbago rods in string or use a piece of leather to hold it and give it strength. Adding a wooden case around the plumbago may have been done by several people but there are only a few real claims about who was the first.

Some attribute the first wood case to two Italian brothers, Simonio and Lyndiana Bernacotti. These men were carpenters who found the plumbago useful for marking their work. Initially the brothers would hollow out a juniper stick and insert the plumbago into the hole. Later they determined it was easier to cut the stick in two, carve a groove in one of the sticks, place the plumbago in, and glue the pieces back together (this is basically the same technique used today).

Others claim the wooden case was invented by a joiner who was living in Keswick near the Borrowdale mines, and there are other claims to the invention as well.

It's hard to say who the first person to make a wooden pencil was because it probably wasn't even recorded. The first historical description of a pencil was recorded in 1565 by Konrad Gesner, one of the first modern biologists. He described an object for writing made of wood and a piece of lead, but he believed the lead to be artificial; he called it English Antimony.

The invention of a wooden case around the plumbago was important even if we don't know who actually did it first. The wooden case kept the plumbago from breaking and making a mess on everything it touched; but there were still a couple problems.

The first problem was that all the wooden holding sticks had to be carved by hand and that took a long time. Second, Borrowdale had a monopoly on all the good plumbago. They were the only ones who had it in huge blocks that could be cut into rods; everyone else only had small or impure deposits that needed to be ground into powder to be useful. The majority of pencil history consists in overcoming these two problems.

Nuremburg and the beginning of manufacturing

From its initial conception in the 1500's until the mid to late 1700's the center of pencil manufacture was in Keswick near the Borrowdale mines. The substance was used quite freely at first until it became clear that the supply would soon run out. Because of this, the monarchy forbade export of the material and would actually execute people if they were caught exporting it. With a monopoly on plumbago and the shortage of good material on hand, England began to raise the price of its pencils and the demand for their pencils began to fall.

As the pencil industry started to decline in England it was about to take off in Germany.

The first mention of a pencil maker in Germany is found in a marriage contract dated 1659. "Pencil maker" was written as the occupation of Hannss Baumann who was the father of the groom. Another mention of a pencil maker was in 1662 when a council decreed that Friedrich Staedtler could no longer manufacture pencils.

In 1761 a cabinet maker named Kaspar Faber set up shop in Stein to start making his own brand of simple pencil. The idea at the time was simple, glue square sticks of plumbago into pieces of wood as fast as you can and sell them, ta-da you have a business.

Unfortunately German plumbago was not of the same quality as the English stock and there was a shortage of materials. Rather than solid sticks, they used a mixture of plumbago, sulphur and antimony with binding agents to create sticks that could be used in pencils. These German pencils were very poor quality, in fact some of them weren't pencils at all they were just sticks that had a small plumbago rod inserted a little way into one end.

German pencils came to be known for their poor quality but at the time there was no incentive to make a quality product. Of the roughly 1,800 pencil shops in and around Nuremburg no one had a true brand name to stand behind, and the traders, not the manufacturers determined the prices. This meant that regardless of whether the pencil makers made a good quality pencil or a poor one, they received the same amount of money for it.

Germans continued pencil production despite the bad reputation and over time Germany became a great center for pencil production, in fact many factories are still active today.

As it turned out a discovery happened about this time. It didn't change the course of pencil history but it lets us breathe a sigh of relief today.

When plumbago was first discovered chemistry and science were just beginning and everyone just assumed the material was a type of lead; no one ever took the time to find out exactly what it was. Then in 1779 Karl Wilhelm Scheele, a Swedish chemist, determined that plumbago was not lead at all, he discovered that it was pure carbon. Scheele proposed a new name, graphite, from the Greek word graphein, meaning "to draw/write". It's good to know that the graphite core of a pencil is completely harmless, unlike lead, but by that time people were so used to calling it lead the name just stuck, plus "pencil graphite" just doesn't have the same ring as "pencil lead".

A few years after Mr. Scheele discovered plumbago was actually graphite, another discovery was made which did change the course of pencil history.

In 1794, shortly before the Napoleonic wars, the French were unable to get pencils from England or Germany because good graphite was getting rare and expensive and no one would sell their graphite to the French. The French Bureau of Mines commissioned a chemist, engineer and inventor named Nicholas Jacques Conte to find a good substitute. It only took eight days for Mr. Conte to come up with a solution which he later patented.

Almost simultaneously an Austrian man named Joseph Hardtmuth, an artist, potter and architect for Prince Franz Josef I von Liechtenstein developed the same solution. Some sources date Hardtmuth's discovery around 1792 while others say 1797 so it's hard to tell which one found the answer first but that's not as important as what the invention did for the pencil industry.

What both of these men discovered was a method to make good writing cores without having to have a good source of graphite.

The new method was not only great but it made all other methods for making graphite rods obsolete. They found that if finely powdered graphite was mixed with clay and water into a thick paste, it could be extruded or rolled into rods and fired in a kiln like a clay pot. After firing, the rods would be stable, strong and could still easily write. They also discovered that by changing the amount of graphite or clay, they could vary the hardness of the rods. This gave the manufacturer control over how light or dark a pencil would mark the paper.

This method works so well that it's still used today. Another advantage to this method was that inferior and contaminated graphite could now easily be turned into something of value. Not only did this decrease the price of pencil leads (which was good because by that time the graphite from the Borrowdale mines was very expensive), it also made them more available to ordinary people.

Soon after the Conte process was discovered pencil manufacturers really began to expand on what their fathers and grandfathers had started.

In 1839, Lothar Faber, the great grandson of Kaspar Faber, took over the family pencil company with a determination to make it great.

He started by improving upon the Conte process. He made some technical improvements to the process, standardized it for consistency and incorporated water and later steam powered equipment to mechanize the sawing and planing of wood.

He was also fortunate enough to receive exclusive rights to the graphite from a mine discovered in Siberia by the French explorer and trader Jean Pierre Alibert. This graphite was of a purity and quality which some say surpassed the Borrowdale mines.

Next Faber set out to create standards of lead hardness as well as pencil length and thickness, many of which were adopted by other manufacturers. Within a few years after taking over, A.W. Faber was synonymous with quality. Today A.W. Faber has become Faber-Castel and still strives to make high quality pencils.

In 1848 Joseph Hardtmuth's two sons Karl and Ludwig also took over their father's pencil shop and began to improve it. They relocated the shop to the Ceske Budejovice in present day Czech Republic. Their pencils won many awards for quality.

In 1890 Joseph's grandson Franz introduced a set of pencils in varying degrees of hardness encased in cedar wood and painted in polished yellow. The yellow color was a reference to the orient where some of the finest graphite was to be found. Queen Victoria was so impressed with these pencils she gave them the name Koh-I-Noor after the famous Koh-I-Noor diamond in the Queen's crown jewels.

The Koh-I-Noor Hardtmuth Company continues to make high quality pencils and art supplies and because of them about 75% of all pencils are now painted yellow.

Other Companies that started small in Germany, England and France were also able to increase production and compete in the quickly growing world pencil market.

Pencils are born in America

They say necessity is the mother of invention and she began living in America when the war of 1812 stopped imports from Europe. Up to that time America had not developed a pencil industry. Pencils could easily be bought from other countries, plus, no one in America knew the secrets of the pencil making process, especially how to make a good quality stable core.

It didn't take long before the Americans had developed their own techniques and technology to mass produce pencils.

Many small companies began making pencils but four companies in particular became pencil making giants, Eagle Pencil Co., Eberhard Faber, the American Lead Pencil Co. (General Pencil Company Inc.), and the Joseph Dixon Crucible Co. (Dixon Ticonderoga), none of these were the first but they became the biggest.

The first company to mass-produce pencils was started by William Munroe, a cabinet maker in Concord Massachusetts who saw an opportunity from the lack of imports. After a few months of experimenting he developed a way to make a stable lead and he sold his first pencils in July of 1812.

Unfortunately his pencils were not high quality for two reasons.

First, his graphite was not high quality like the European kind, and second, while he did use a graphite clay mixture for his pencil leads, he did not fire them in a kiln as they did in France and Germany. His method was to simply let the graphite paste air dry in grooves cut into a cedar plank.

As a result his leads were not as strong as the ones produced overseas but they were stable and worked well enough for the time. Once the paste was dry, a second sheet of cedar would be glued on top and pencils were cut from the plank individually. About ten pencils could be cut from one plank but the process was very slow.

Fortunately for Mr. Munroe he hired a young cabinet maker named Ebenezer Wood to help him man the saws that cut the cedar planks. Ebenezer was a creative man and a talented inventor. He was able to develop the technology to mechanize the process so that pencils could be mass produced for market.

It was Ebenezer's inventions that greatly increased pencil production in the United States and according to Wood's contemporary Horace Hosmer he "was an inventor of high order, and his hand and brain largely helped to make Munroe's fortune."

Mr. Wood set up the first circular saw to cut grooves into the cedar planks. His machine could cut six grooves at a time. He also invented a machine to mold and trim the planks as well as a press that could glue 1,728 pencils at a time. He was the inventor of the octagonal and hexagonal pencils (which we still use today).

Ebenezer eventually started his own business. He made pencils but became better known for the quality of his graphite which he ground with a millstone, using the Nashoba Brook as his power source. Initially William Munroe was one of Mr. Wood's customers but by the 1830's he only sold his graphite to the Thoreau Company.

The story of the Thoreau Company starts in 1821 when Charles Dunbar, the brother-in-law of John Thoreau, discovered graphite in Bristol near New Hampshire. Its quality was better than any previously found in the states. He began mining the material and started a pencil business called "Dunbar and Stow" using his newly found graphite.

Attempting to grow his business, Charles invited John to join in 1823. By 1824 the partnership was over, Charles left, and the company acquired the name "John Thoreau & company". John Thoreau was the father of Henry David Thoreau the famous author.

Henry developed his own secret method for making good pencil cores out of powdered graphite using a clay binder and burning the mixture much like the Conte process. This produced a stronger writing core than Munroe's air-drying method. Because the Thoreau business had superior graphite and a superior method of making writing cores they soon came to be known as one of the finest early American pencil makers.

The first of the big four American pencil companies was the Eagle Pencil Company which started in 1856. Heinrich Berolzheimer founded the company in New York shortly after emigrating from Germany where he had also been a pencil maker.

It seems that in 1861 Henry Berolzheimer, who is believed to be Heinrich's son, took over the business and started expanding. They soon started opening offices and factories all over the world. By 1962 they had establishments in London, Mexico, Canada, Colombia and Venezuela.

Eagle made the first eraser-tipped pencil in 1872; they were also the first company to produce a combo pen and pencil which was very innovative for the time. In 1969, Eagle changed its name to Berol Pencil Company which was an Americanized version of the family's last name.

The next of the big four was the American Pencil Company founded by Edward Weissenborn who came to America in 1854. He also learned the art of pencil making in Germany as many of the great pencil makers did, but he did not start his own pencil company until 1864, ten years after he immigrated to America.

His company, based in New Jersey, used pencil leads imported from Germany which were of higher quality than the American made leads.

Weissenborn sold his company in 1885 but the family just couldn't stay away from those pencils. Four years later Edward's son Oscar started making his own pencils from home. After some time he started renting space for the manufacture of his pencils and also set up a machine shop so he could make the necessary machinery for pencil production.

He called his small company "The Pencil Exchange" and it almost went under during World War I when it became impossible to get pencil leads imported from Germany. After some experimentation he was able to develop his own process to make pencil cores. His business finally stabilized in 1923 and became known as General Pencil Co. It continues to expand today, making all varieties of drawing and art supplies.

Eberhard Faber, another immigrant from Germany and part of the famous German pencil making family, came to America and started another branch of his family's huge pencil empire. He was helped in the development of his pencil making machines by Ebenezer Wood (remember him?).

Wood never patented any of his inventions and shared his techniques with anyone who was interested in his work. Faber learned many of Wood's techniques and adapted Wood's machinery to his own business.

In 1861 Faber built one of the first pencil factories in New York and, similar to his family in Germany, started making outstanding pencils. He used the technology developed in America to greatly increase the speed at which he could make his pencils. The superior writing cores he used came from Germany similar to General Pencil Co.

The Joseph Dixon Crucible Company was the first company to start but they did not initially make pencils. Joseph Dixon was an inventor and entrepreneur who in 1847, started a company located in New York to make crucibles which are pots used to melt metal. His company already consumed a lot of graphite in production so he and his wife started using some of the leftovers to make pencils by hand in their home.

Over the years Mr. Dixon invented a wood planing machine that could produce 132 pencils per minute, as well as other machines that greatly increased production speed and pencil quality. Joseph Dixon's pencil company was also one of the first to start using round leads in their pencils.

Up until that time most companies used square leads. The reason for using square leads was that you only had to cut a groove in one of the two pieces of wood; it was easy and saved time. Using a circular lead you must cut a semi-circular groove in two pieces of wood and line them up, this is more difficult, but before Dixon's time, machinery had not been available to accurately mass produce pencils with circular leads.

The advantage of circular leads is that they are easy to sharpen mechanically which is faster, cleaner and safer than using a knife. The company grew quickly, it is estimated that by 1892 Dixon's company manufactured more than 30 million pencils per year. Dixon's pencil company continued and today is known as Dixon Ticonderoga pencil and art supplies.

There it is; a brief look at the development of the pencil. Beyond what is written here there is company expansion, advancement in manufacturing technology, and companies buying each other. It's a very competitive market and each company is still striving to be the best.

Just the Facts

Here is a list of facts about pencils that you may find interesting.

1. Erasers were originally called "rubbers" because they "rubbed out" pencil marks. Coincidentally they were also made from the resin of a rubber tree which just happens to be rubber. In Great Britain, they still call erasers "rubbers" (before the use of erasers people used bread crumbs!).

2. Eraser manufacturers call the eraser on the end of a pencil a "plug".

3. The small band of metal that holds the eraser on the end of the pencil is called a "ferrule".

4. A regular pencil can draw a line 35 miles long, write about 45,000 words and be sharpened 17 times.

5. At first, pencils were not painted so people could see the high quality wood. By the 1890's, many manufacturers were trying to set their pencils apart by painting them and giving them brand names.

6. Early Americans used eastern red cedar for their pencil casings. It was strong, splinter-resistant and grew abundantly in the southeastern United States. By the early 1900's, pencil manufacturers needed more sources of wood. They found that incense cedar from California was better than the red cedar for pencils. Incense cedar is abundant and renewable (which we should support), and has become the wood of choice for most of the pencil manufacturers around the world.

7. An average cedar tree yields approximately 172,000 pencils.

8. Colored pencils are made using a process similar to the regular pencil; the main difference is that a blend of pigment clay and wax is extruded to make up the writing core rather than a graphite/clay mixture.

9. In 1858, Hyman Lipman from Philadelphia was awarded the first patent for attaching an eraser to a pencil.

10. Pencils work even if there is no gravity. Initially they were used on American and Russian space missions, but the flammability of the wood and all the little flecks of floating graphite led to the invention of the pressurized pen.